THE ANALOGY BETWEEN STATES AND INTERNATIONAL ORGANIZATIONS

This book investigates how an analogy between States and international organizations has influenced and supported the development of the law that applies to intergovernmental institutions on the international plane. That is best illustrated by the work of the International Law Commission on the treaties and responsibility of international organizations, where the Commission for the most part extended to organizations rules that had been originally devised for States. Revisiting those codification projects while also looking into other areas, the book reflects on how techniques of legal reasoning can be – and have been – used by international institutions and the legal profession to tackle situations of uncertainty, and discusses the elusive position that international organizations occupy in the international legal system. By cutting across some foundational topics of the discipline, the book makes a substantive contribution to the literature on subjects and sources of international law.

FERNANDO LUSA BORDIN is a Thornely Fellow and Lecturer in Law at Sidney Sussex College and an Affiliated Lecturer at the University of Cambridge. His research focuses on topics of public international law, including law-making, international organizations and the intersection between international law and legal theory. He holds an LLB from the Federal University of Rio Grande do Sul (Brazil), an LLM from New York University, and a PhD from the University of Cambridge. He is a recipient of the Yorke Prize (University of Cambridge), Young Scholar Prize (*International and Comparative Law Quarterly*) and the Diploma of Public International Law (Hague Academy of International Law).

"In this book, Dr Fernando Bordin explores an elusive but fundamental problem: How does general international law apply to international organizations? That leads him to ask, in depth and with great subtlety, the questions what international organizations are from the point of view of international law and how they fit within the international legal system. By analysing the extent to which States and international organizations can be analogised, and how that analogy has served – and can serve – as a basis to extend rules from one category to the other, Dr Bordin provides a theoretically sophisticated and doctrinally informed contribution to our thinking about the sources and subjects of international law."

James Crawford
Judge, International Court of Justice
Emeritus Whewell Professor of International Law, University of Cambridge

CAMBRIDGE STUDIES IN INTERNATIONAL AND COMPARATIVE LAW: 138

Established in 1946, this series produces high quality, reflective and innovative scholarship in the field of public international law. It publishes works on international law that are of a theoretical, historical, cross-disciplinary or doctrinal nature. The series also welcomes books providing insights from private international law, comparative law and transnational studies which inform international legal thought and practice more generally.

The series seeks to publish views from diverse legal traditions and perspectives, and of any geographical origin. In this respect it invites studies offering regional perspectives on core *problématiques* of international law, and in the same vein, it appreciates contrasts and debates between diverging approaches. Accordingly, books offering new or less orthodox perspectives are very much welcome. Works of a generalist character are greatly valued and the series is also open to studies on specific areas, institutions or problems. Translations of the most outstanding works published in other languages are also considered.

After seventy years, Cambridge Studies in International and Comparative Law sets the standard for international legal scholarship and will continue to define the discipline as it evolves in the years to come.

Series Editors
Larissa van den Herik
Professor of Public International Law, Grotius Centre for International Legal Studies, Leiden University
Jean d'Aspremont
Professor of International Law, University of Manchester and Sciences Po Law School

A list of books in the series can be found at the end of this volume.

THE ANALOGY BETWEEN STATES AND INTERNATIONAL ORGANIZATIONS

FERNANDO LUSA BORDIN

University of Cambridge

CAMBRIDGE
UNIVERSITY PRESS

University Printing House, Cambridge CB2 8BS, United Kingdom

One Liberty Plaza, 20th Floor, New York, NY 10006, USA

477 Williamstown Road, Port Melbourne, VIC 3207, Australia

314–321, 3rd Floor, Plot 3, Splendor Forum, Jasola District Centre,
New Delhi – 110025, India

79 Anson Road, #06–04/06, Singapore 079906

Cambridge University Press is part of the University of Cambridge.

It furthers the University's mission by disseminating knowledge in the pursuit of
education, learning, and research at the highest international levels of excellence.

www.cambridge.org
Information on this title: www.cambridge.org/9781107155558
DOI: 10.1017/9781316658963

© Fernando Lusa Bordin 2019

First published 2019

Printed and bound in Great Britain by Clays Ltd, Elcograf S.p.A.

A catalogue record for this publication is available from the British Library.

Library of Congress Cataloging-in-Publication Data
Names: Bordin, Fernando Lusa, 1984– author.
Title: The analogy between states and international organizations /
Fernando Lusa Bordin, University of Cambridge.
Description: Cambridge [UK] ; New York : Cambridge University Press, 2018. |
Series: Cambridge studies in international and comparative law ; 138 | Includes
bibliographical references and index.
Identifiers: LCCN 2018024500 | ISBN 9781107155558 (hardback : alk. paper) |
ISBN 9781316609156 (pbk. : alk. paper)
Subjects: LCSH: International organizations. | International agencies–Law and legislation. |
International agencies–Rules and practice. | International law. | State, The. |
United Nations. International Law Commission.
Classification: LCC KZ4850 .B67 2018 | DDC 341.2–dc23
LC record available at https://lccn.loc.gov/2018024500

ISBN 978-1-107-15555-8 Hardback

To the memory of my grandmother Paulina, who did not
have the chance to go past primary school but used to say that
she would get at least five university degrees in the next life

CONTENTS

vii

FOREWORD

It is difficult to imagine how law could ever function without analogy. Law operates within a conceptual framework that must be at least in part fixed. When that framework evolves, it normally does so by adaptation rather than constant reinvention. It is in order to fix the framework that codifications often begin with a classification of basic concepts. '*All the law which we use concerns persons, things or actions*', in the *Institutes of Gaius*, is an example. Everything the Roman lawyer encountered had to be squeezed into one of these three overarching concepts. Conceptual classifications have consequences: if, for example, in the eyes of the law, animals are 'things' and companies 'persons', it will almost inevitably follow that in regulating them the law will reify the former and anthropomorphise the latter. The analogical application of rules about things to animals (e.g., on liability of owners) in Roman law follows from the conceptual classification under that law. In a legal system based on a different framework – for instance, one where animals were classified as 'persons' and companies as 'things' – the results of the analogical extension of rules would be starkly different.

The analysis of how analogy operates in the law requires, at a minimum, doctrinal and conceptual rigour. In no small measure it also necessitates self-reflective thinking, for analogy within the boundaries of a defined conceptual framework is a habit of the mind for the lawyer – and one that the legal scholar seeking to understand how analogy works needs to interrogate.

The task is even more challenging when the law in question is public international law. There is no codification of basic concepts and categories in international law. Contemporary writing normally eschews the task of conceptual framing and classification of the entire field as a way of systematising it at the outset. Furthermore, international lawyers (or perhaps only the better ones) are also domestic lawyers. They possess a set of concepts embedded in the domestic legal system in which they received their legal education. To complicate things, following the

changes in the world of legal education and practice, a growing number
of lawyers will have more than one domestic legal system of reference,
and therefore more legal concepts and categories to grapple with. Self-
awareness about their provenance is very important. Colleagues who
display little such self-awareness and liberally infuse international law
with concepts typical of their domestic legal system are a cause of regular
irritation for other international lawyers.

But even those of us who strive to maintain a healthy measure of self-
awareness would have to admit, lest we contradict ourselves, that in some
way domestic law influences the way we approach international law.
I suspect, for example, that it is no coincidence that the academic interest
in constitutionalism is mainly an American and German phenomenon,
which has left British international legal academia somewhat lukewarm:
those who operate within a domestic legal system that is constitutionalised, if at all, only in a very idiosyncratic way, may be less attracted to the
idea that international law is or ought to be constitutionalised.

The topic chosen by Dr Bordin for his first major monograph in public
international law is thus replete with complex challenges. As will be clear
from the first pages of this book, shunning complexity does not suit Dr
Bordin's intellectual temperament. In tackling the challenges before him
methodically, Dr Bordin has produced an outstanding piece of legal
scholarship that is a model of rigour and clarity. He begins with a
sophisticated discussion of the role of analogy in legal reasoning, before
proceeding to the key question: how do we justify the analogy between
international organizations and States?

The facile objection to any case for analogy is 'but they are different'.
Of course 'they' are different. If 'they' were identical, there would not be a
problem. Analogical reasoning is premised on difference and similarity.
A case for analogy must begin with a careful analysis of those differences
and similarities, and then advance an argument to justify the analogy and
identify its proper limits. Dr Bordin's argument in support of the analogy
is thorough and thoughtful both conceptually and doctrinally. Those who
disagree will have to do much better than 'but they are different'.

It is in fact Dr Bordin himself who explains the three main counter-
arguments to the analogy to 'further probe' – as he puts it – the case.
A marker of truly great scholarship is how contrary lines of argument are
presented and dealt with. Not only is Dr Bordin keen to do justice to
contrary arguments, he develops them conscientiously before setting out
his balanced and well-reasoned replies. His approach is genuinely dia-
lectical. He engages with the antitheses to the main line of argument that

he set out at the beginning, and then proceeds to qualify and deepen his initial thesis coming, in effect, to a synthesis by the end. The concluding part of the book is where Dr Bordin develops his synthesis by focussing on the limits of the analogy and on what he describes as its normative contestation in various areas.

Before pouring praise on this book, I should have declared a conflict: I supervised the doctoral thesis from which it originates. The thesis focussed on analogy in the work of the International Law Commission on treaties and the responsibility of international organizations. The work of the International Law Commission still features prominently, together with a wide range of other materials, including State practice and judicial decisions, as well as secondary literature from international law and jurisprudence. But the book is broader, more ambitious, and has grown well beyond the excellent doctoral thesis that inspired it. It is, and reads like, a work of mature scholarship.

A lot of what passes for theory in international law today is riddled with shallow postmodernist scepticism that makes it not only inconsequential but also feeble in a doctrinal and jurisprudential sense. Dr Bordin shows that it is possible to take a complex topic and produce a serious work of rigorous legal scholarship that is original, cogently argued, theoretically sophisticated, and thoroughly relevant to the practice and development of the law.

Professor Guglielmo Verdirame
King's College London
20 Essex Street Chambers

ACKNOWLEDGEMENTS

In the journey leading to this book, I was fortunate to have enjoyed the company of wonderful friends and colleagues who engaged with my work and helped make it better. These include: Kenneth Armstrong, Julian Arato, Christiane Ahlborn, Emma Bickerstaffe, Daniel Costelloe, Bart Smit Duijzentkunst, Luíza Leão, Lucas Lixinski, Odette Murray, Jasmine Moussa, Odette Murray, Lorne Neudorf, Sarah Nouwen, Federica Paddeu, Brendan Plant, Surabhi Ranganathan, Cecily Rose, Arie Rosen, Andrew Sanger, Thomaz Santos, Maitê Schmitz, Geraldo Vidigal Neto, Michael Waibel and Rumiana Yotova. I am also much indebted to Professor Guglielmo Verdirame, who served as supervisor for the doctoral thesis from which this book originates, for his trust, guidance, generosity and support; to Professors Jan Klabbers and Roger O'Keefe, who kindly agreed to serve as examiners for the thesis and gave me valuable critique, comment and advice; to Judge James Crawford, who was an early assessor for this work and a source of inspiration throughout; and to Professor Claudia Lima Marques, my mentor at the Federal University of Rio Grande do Sul, for her example and encouragement in the crucial formative stages of my academic trajectory.

I would also like to acknowledge an intellectual debt to two eminent scholars who had a considerable influence on how this project unfolded. The first is Professor José Alvarez, whose seminar on international organizations at New York University was not only an exceptionally stimulating educational experience, but also introduced me to some of the questions that I have set out to examine in this book. The second is Judge Giorgio Gaja, whom I had the honour and privilege of assisting in the sessions in which the International Law Commission concluded the first and second readings of the Articles on the Responsibility of International Organizations for Internationally Wrongful Acts; despite some critical comments on the output of the Commission's work that I feel bound to make as a commentator, I have the greatest respect and admiration for his work as Special Rapporteur, as a scholar and as a judge.

At Cambridge University Press, I owe huge thanks to my editors, Tom Randall and Elizabeth Spicer, for their patience and encouragement.

Finally, I must thank my extraordinary parents, Odolir and Mara, and my brother, Mateus, for their love and unwavering support.

This work could not have been undertaken, let alone completed, without the generous support of the Cambridge Overseas Trust, Sidney Sussex College, and the UK Foundation for International Uniform Law. Funding the research of young academics is a beautiful thing: these institutions have my sincerest appreciation.

The image on the cover is a crop from the mural painting 'Titans', by Lumen Martin Winter, which is on display at the United Nations Headquarters in New York City. The mural depicts the five continents moving the world out of darkness into light, a striking image that not only captures the idea of analogies in the similarly formed yet not identical titans, but is also a metaphor for systemic reasoning pushing international law forward – the optimistic outlook that animates this book. I am indebted to the United Nations and Mr William Grant Winter for giving their permission for the use of the image; the people at the UN Photo Library for their solicitousness and efficiency; and Mr Lucas Welter, Ms Ana Luisa Demoraes Campos and Mr Felipe Rocha dos Santos for their help in brainstorming the cover design.

TABLE OF CASES

International Court of Justice

Permanent Court of International Justice

Court of Justice of the European Union

European Court of Human Rights

International Tribunal for the Law of the Sea

International Criminal Tribunals

World Trade Organization

Arbitral Awards

Domestic Courts

Germany

Italy

Netherlands

Switzerland

United Kingdom

United States

SELECT TABLE OF KEY DOCUMENTS

xx

LIST OF ABBREVIATIONS

AJIL	American Journal of International Law
ARIO	Articles on the Responsibility of International Organizations for Internationally Wrongful Acts
ARS	Articles on the Responsibility of States for Internationally Wrongful Acts
BYIL	British Yearbook of International Law
EJIL	European Journal of International Law
EU	European Union
GYIL	German Yearbook of International Law
HLR	Harvard Law Review
ICJ	International Court of Justice
ICLQ	The International and Comparative Law Quarterly
ILC	International Law Commission
ILO	International Labour Organization
IMF	International Monetary Fund
IO	International Organization
IOLR	International Organizations Law Review
ITC	International Tin Council
PCIJ	Permanent Court of International Justice
RdC	Recueil des Cours de l'Académie de Droit International de la Haye
RGDIP	Revue Générale de Droit International Public
UN	United Nations
UNCLT	Official Records of the UN Conference on the Law of Treaties between States and International Organizations or between International Organizations
UNGA	United Nations General Assembly
UNSC	United Nations Security Council
VCLT 1969	Vienna Convention on the Law of Treaties
VCLT 1986	Vienna Convention on the Law of Treaties between States and International Organizations or between International Organizations
TFEU	Treaty on the Functioning of the European Union
WTO	World Trade Organization
YILC	Yearbook of the International Law Commission

$\backsim$

Introduction

As a legal system evolves, it is usual for it to borrow concepts, principles, methodologies and institutional arrangements from other legal systems. Hersch Lauterpacht's early work has shown that analogies from domestic private law played a distinct part in the formative stages of modern international law.[1] For one, domestic analogies were influential on classical State theory. As States became the legal persons *par excellence* in the emerging international order, their position was assimilated to that of individuals in domestic systems, as reflected in the writings of some of the 'founding fathers' of international law. For Christian Wolff, '[n]ations are regarded as individual free persons living in a state of nature'.[2] Emmerich de Vattel, credited as the scholar who disseminated the view that '[t]he law of the nations is the law of sovereigns',[3] postulated the equality among nations in the following terms:

> '[s]ince men are naturally equal, and a perfect equality prevails in their rights and obligations, as equally proceeding from nature – Nations composed of men, and considered as so many free persons living together in a state of nature, are naturally equal, and inherit from nature the same obligations and rights. Power or weakness does not in this respect produce any difference. A dwarf is as much a man as a giant; a small republic is no less a sovereign state than the most powerful kingdom.[4]

---

[1] H. Lauterpacht, *Private Law Sources and Analogies of International Law* (Archon Books, 1937).
[2] C. Wolff, *The Law of Nations Treated According to a Scientific Method* (Oxford: Clarendon Press, 1934), p. 9, §2.
[3] E. de Vattel, *The Law of Nations* (Indianapolis: Liberty Fund, 2009), p. 85, §11.
[4] Ibid., p. 75, §18. Vattel's conception of nation, similar to Wolff's, is as follows: 'Nations being composed of men naturally free and independent, and who, before the establishment of civil societies, lived together in the state of nature, – nations, or sovereign states, are to be considered as so many free persons living together in the state of nature'; ibid., p. 68, §4.

1

This assumption influenced how various subfields of international law took shape, notably the law of treaties, the law of territory and the law of responsibility, each borrowing rules and structures from contract law, tort law or property law, as the case may be.[5] The view that States are analogous to individuals is nowadays rightly dismissed,[6] with States no longer being viewed as ontological realities but rather as socio-legal constructs established to regulate life within a political community.[7] Yet, many of the system's foundations date back to the time when that view was in vogue. The acceptance of 'general principles of law' recognised by the nations as a source of international law attests to the continuing – albeit restricted – role of domestic law analogies in the identification of international rules.[8]

If the growth and diversification of international law has seen the relevance of domestic law analogies wane, it now invites the drawing of analogies of a different character. As the international legal system becomes more robust through the intensification of multilateral cooperation and treaty-making, the completion of influential codification projects and the accumulation of judgments and awards by international courts and tribunals, the opportunity arises for greater recourse to *systemic* analogies, drawn from existing rules and principles of public international law itself. The emergence of international organizations in the 19th century is a case in point.[9] As intergovernmental institutions

---

[5] Lauterpacht, *Private Law Sources*, pp. 297–303. It should be noted that Lauterpacht's defence of private law analogies was justified not by a facile assimilation of States to individuals, but by the sense that it was 'in the approximation to the analogous general rules of private law that we see embodied the principles of legal justice and of international progress' (at xi).

[6] See, e.g., H. Thirlway, 'Concepts, principles, rules and analogies: international and municipal legal reasoning' (2002) 294 RdC 265 and J. Waldron, 'Are sovereigns entitled to the benefit of the international rule of law?' (2011) 22 EJIL 315.

[7] For an account of this paradigm shift, R. Portmann, *Legal Personality in International Law* (Cambridge: Cambridge University Press, 2010), pp. 139–46. It has been thus suggested that contemporary international law calls for a public law approach rather than private law analogies: B. Kingsbury and M. Donaldson, 'From bilateralism to publicness in international law' in Fastenrath and others (eds.), *From Bilateralism to Community Interest* (Oxford: Oxford University Press, 2011), pp. 83–86.

[8] Art. 38(1)(c), Statute of the International Court of Justice. See L. Siorat, *Le Problème des Lacunes en Droit International: Contribution à l'Étude des Sources du Droit et de la Fonction Judiciaire* (Paris: Librairie Générale de Droit et de Jurisprudence, 1958), pp. 344–45.

[9] When the League of Nations was established in 1919, the difficulty that commentators of the time faced in coming to terms with its legal status is exemplified by Oppenheim's article in the *Revue Générale de Droit international public*, where he concluded that the

began to interact with their members and third parties on the international plane, comparisons with States became inevitable. The question arose of whether, and to what extent, international organizations have rights, obligations and capacities similar to those vested in the State.

More than seventy years have passed since the United Nations was founded, heralding a new era for international institutions, yet there still is a fair amount of doubt regarding what international organizations are and the position that they occupy in the international legal system.[10] Because international law has been traditionally and relentlessly State-centric, a number of concepts and doctrines that were devised by States and for States do not appear to be fully transposable to international organizations.[11] On the one hand, it is commonplace to describe them as 'subjects of international law'. On the other hand, current political and legal discourse often emphasises discontinuities between the two categories of legal subjects. Indeed, at first glance, they appear to have more differences than similarities. While States are self-governing territorial communities, international organizations consist of bureaucracies set up to fulfil tasks of international cooperation. While States are free, within the bounds of international law, to pursue their development and self-realization, international organizations are established to achieve collective goals in diverse forms and fields.

In spite of the differences between States and international organizations, there has been a tendency in practice to extend to international organizations some of the solutions adopted for States. International organizations are party to treaties, maintain external relations with other entities, bring international claims, claim immunities from jurisdiction and can be held liable for internationally wrongful acts. There is no greater example of this tendency of assimilation than the two projects that the UN International Law Commission has completed with a view to identifying the general rules that apply to the treaties and responsibility of international organizations. The project concerning the law treaties, led by Professor Paul Reuter, kept the Commission busy from 1970 to

---

League was a *sui generis* legal person; L. Oppenheim, 'Le caractère essential de la Société des Nations' (1919) 26 RGDIP 234.

[10] J. Klabbers, *An Introduction to International Organizations Law*, 3rd edn (Cambridge: Cambridge University Press, 2015), p. 3.

[11] J. Alvarez, 'Book Review: *International Organisations and Their Exercise of Sovereign Powers* (2007) 101 AJIL 674, 678.

1982 and culminated in the adoption of the 1986 Vienna Convention on the Law of Treaties between States and International Organizations and between International Organizations.[12] The project concerning the law of responsibility was carried out from 2002 to 2011 under the special rapporteurship of Professor Giorgio Gaja, and resulted in a set of Articles on the Responsibility of International Organizations for Internationally Wrongful Acts,[13] which the UN General Assembly took note of and continues to consider periodically.[14] When the Commission carried out these projects, it relied heavily on its previous work on treaties and responsibility of States: the 1969 Vienna Convention on the Law of Treaties and the 2001 Articles on the Responsibility of States for Internationally Wrongful Acts, respectively. It extended most provisions contained in those instruments to international organizations, even in areas where practice and precedent were inexistent or inconclusive. As a result, the 1986 Vienna Convention and the 2011 Articles bear a strong resemblance to the 1969 Vienna Convention and the 2001 Articles. In the case of VCLT 1986, dispute settlement and final clauses aside, only three provisions are at variance with the text of VCLT 1969, while a handful present deviations of minor importance.[15] In contrast, the ARIO showcases greater structural and textual departures from the ARS;[16] still, in the end, meaningful variations with the regime of responsibility envisaged for States were kept to a minimum.

What lies behind this tendency of assimilation? What might be the normative basis for extending to international organizations rules that apply to States? In an oft-cited dictum, the International Court of Justice described international organizations as 'subjects of international law'

---

[12] Vienna Convention on the Law of Treaties between States and International Organizations or between International Organizations, 21 March 1986 (not yet in force), UN/Doc. A/CONF.129/15 (1986) 25 ILM 543.

[13] Articles on the Responsibility of International Organizations, 3 June 2011, YILC 2011/II, part two, p. 40.

[14] Most recently: UNGA Res. 72/122 (2017).

[15] The provisions substantively departing from VCLT 1969 are arts. 6, 7 and 74, the last of them a saving clause. For a general account of these changes, G. Gaja, 'A "new" Vienna Convention on Treaties between States and International Organizations or between International Organizations: a critical commentary' (1988) BYIL 253.

[16] A few provisions from the ARS were omitted, and some new provisions added. Among the omitted provisions are the second sentence of art. 2 ARS and arts. 5, 0, 9 and 10 on attribution of conduct. New provisions include art. 17, art. 40 and the six articles of Part V on 'Responsibility of a State in Connection with the Act of an International Organization'.

which 'as such' would be 'bound by any obligations incumbent upon them under general rules of international law'.[17] The International Criminal Tribunal for Rwanda has similarly held that 'the United Nations, as an international subject, is bound to respect rules of customary international law'.[18] The same position is found in academic commentary; in the words of a leading scholar:

> It can safely be submitted that international organizations are bound by international customary law, either on the ground that all subjects of international law are so bound, or on the ground that the member States were bound by international customary law when they created the organization and thus may be presumed to have created the organization as being so bound, or on the ground that the rules of international customary law are at the same time general principles of law to which international organizations are bound.[19]

But whether it can be 'safely' accepted that international organizations are bound by custom on the grounds offered in the quote is far from self-evident. For one, it cannot be assumed that all categories of international legal subjects are bound by customary international law in the same way, as if possession of 'international legal personality' could somehow have that effect.[20] Likewise, while the intention of member States to bind an organization to custom may be relevant for the relations taking place on the institutional plane, it cannot without more determine the law that

---

[17] *Interpretation of the Agreement of 25 March 1951 between the WHO and Egypt* (Advisory Opinion) [1980] ICJ Rep 73, pp. 89–90. The Court does not explain, however, what is meant by 'general rules of international law'. For a narrow reading, see J. Klabbers, 'Sources of international organizations' law: reflections on accountability' in J. d'Aspremont and S. Besson, *The Oxford Handbook on the Sources of International Law* (Oxford: Oxford University Press, 2017), pp. 993–1000.

[18] *Prosecutor v. Rwamakuba*, Case No. ICTR-98-44C-T, Decision on Appropriate Remedy (2007), para. 48.

[19] H. Schermers, 'The legal bases of international organization action' in R. Dupuy, *A Handbook on International Organizations*, 2nd edn (Dordrecht: Nijhoff, 1998), p. 402. For a similar argument, P. Sands and P. Klein (eds.), *Bowett's Law of International Institutions*, 6th edn (London: Sweet & Maxwell, 2009), pp. 463–64. The assumption that custom applies to IOs is also found in C. F. Amerasinghe, *Principles of the Institutional Law of International Organizations*, 2nd edn (Cambridge: Cambridge University Press, 2005), pp. 386–87. For a more cautious approach, only affirming the applicability of 'secondary rules' to international organizations: Klabbers, 'Sources', pp. 998–99.

[20] For example, only a few international legal regimes concern the rights, obligations and capacities of individuals, despite their progressive acceptance as subjects of international law. For an overview: K. Parlett, *The Individual in the International Legal System* (Cambridge: Cambridge University Press, 2011), in particular pp. 274–77 and 337–39.

applies between the organization and third parties on the international plane. Finally, recourse to the notion of general principles of law is a slippery slope, in that it does not quite explain the basis on which such principles would become binding on intergovernmental institutions.

A more methodologically sound approach to demonstrate that general international law applies to international organizations is to postulate that, following the arrival of organizations upon the scene, the 'rule of recognition' that makes custom and general principles of law a source of international law for States[21] has been widened so that it now covers also the corporate entities that States create.[22] The problem with this line of enquiry is that proving that such a change to the 'rule of recognition' has indeed occurred may be difficult, if not impossible, in the absence of convincing evidence that States have intended it. An alternative approach is to reject the assumption that the customary international law of States applies to international organizations, and require instead that each right, obligation and capacity of organizations on the international plane be established in the usual way, that is, through showing practice and *opinio juris* that independently confirms each of them.[23] The problem with this approach is that it is impractical: as the work of the ILC on treaties and responsibility has revealed, one may be pressed to find practice and precedent concerning international organizations that meets the demanding requirements of the test for custom formulated in the case law of the International Court.[24] The result is uncertainty whenever a question regarding the rules that apply to international organizations on the international plane is asked. If not in custom, where do we find those rules?

In this study, I consider and propose a third approach to address the question of the applicability of general international law to international organizations: the possibility of extending to organizations the rules that

---

[21] See, in this respect, the debate between Kelsen and Hart. While Kelsen postulates the existence of a basic norm establishing 'custom among states as a law-creating fact' (*Pure Theory of Law* [Berkeley: University of California Press, 1967], p. 323), Hart considers this statement a 'useless reduplication of the fact that a set of rules are accepted by states as binding rules' (*The Concept of Law*, 2nd edn [Oxford: Clarendon Press, 1997], p. 236).

[22] A variation of this argument can be found in F. Seyersted, *Common Law of International Organizations* (Nijhoff, Leiden, 2008), p. 57.

[23] This is the view implied, for example, in M. Wood, 'Do international organizations enjoy immunity under customary international law?' (2013) 10 IOLR 287.

[24] E.g., *North Sea Continental Shelf (Federal Republic of Germany/Denmark; Federal Republic of Germany /Netherlands)* [1969] ICJ Rep 33, paras. 74–75.

apply to States by analogy. This approach assumes neither that organizations are *ipso jure* bound by custom nor that custom cannot apply to them unless there is independent proof of practice and *opinio juris*. It rather treats the question as a situation of uncertainty: an extensive gap in the international legal system that emerged together with international organizations. It then ponders how analogical reasoning, a form of systemic reasoning whereby existing rules are extended to novel situations with which they share a relevant similarity, may help in dealing with that situation of uncertainty.[25]

It seems that the idea of an analogy between States and international organizations has been part and parcel of the development of the law that applies to the external relations of international organizations over the past few decades. The intuition that permeates the work of the ILC, relevant judicial decisions and accounts offered by many commentators is that, for all their differences, there is no reason to distinguish between the two categories of international legal subjects when it comes to the application of certain rules of general international law. That intuition, however, has been kept beneath the surface. Underdeveloped and undertheorised, it has caused some eyebrows to raise and attracted a fair share of criticism.[26] Is it plausible to analogise between States and international organizations, given the many differences that exist between self-governing territorial communities and bureaucracies set up to pursue myriad goals of international cooperation? Even if it is, to what extent can that analogy justify extending the rules of States to international organizations?

---

[25] The idea that States and organizations may be analogous for certain purposes has been explored in one form or another in the literature: see e.g., Seyersted, *Common Law*, pp. 396 and 400 and K. Daugirdas, 'How and why international law binds international organizations' (2016) 57 *Harvard International Law Journal* 325, 357–58 (suggesting an analogy between international organizations and 'new states'). But a full investigation of the value, foundations, objections and limits of that analogy is lacking.

[26] See e.g., J. Wouters and J. Odermatt, 'Are all international organizations created equal?' (2012) 9 IOLR 7; V.J. Proulx, 'An uneasy transition? Linkages between the law of State responsibility and the law governing the responsibility of international organizations' in M. Ragazzi, *The Responsibility of International Organizations*; and G. Hafner, 'Is the topic of responsibility of international organizations ripe for codification? Some critical remarks' in U. Fastenrath and others (eds.), *From Bilateralism to Community Interest* (Oxford: Oxford University Press, 2011).

My argument is that because international organizations and States are legally autonomous entities operating on the international plane, reasoning by analogy can provide a general justification for making propositions about the content of the public international law that applies to international organizations. As such, it constitutes a method for filling, on a provisional basis, the gap that arose with the arrival of those organizations upon the international scene.

By reflecting on the role of the analogy between States and international organizations in the shaping of the law of international organizations, this study makes a contribution to the elucidation of two fundamental issues. The first is how techniques of legal reasoning can be – and have been – used by international institutions and the legal profession to tackle uncertainty and advance the law in a legal system where the making and application of the law remains radically decentralised. The second concerns the position that international organizations occupy in that system and the character of the right that States seem to enjoy, under an implicit international rule of incorporation, to establish new subjects of international law possessing separate legal personality. Those are issues that the ILC for the most part overlooked in its work on treaties and responsibility, and deliberately so. But facing them is essential to appraise – and even to apply – provisions contained in instruments such as VCLT 1986 and the ARIO. Whenever courts, arbitral tribunals, governments and international institutions rely on or criticise a rule proposed on the basis of analogy, they must be able to take a stance as to whether or not this rule may be invoked under international law as it now stands. This is not possible without an understanding of the structure, function and value of analogical reasoning in general, and of the assumptions underlying the analogy between States and international organizations in particular.

Terminological Clarifications

A distinction found throughout this book contrasts the 'international plane' with the 'institutional plane'. The phrase 'international plane' refers to the realm of relations between self-governing entities where the rules of public international law apply. The phrase 'institutional plane' refers to the realm constituted and delimited by the international law of international organizations, comprising relations involving organs, members, employees and other entities under constituent instruments and other internal rules. The two phrases thus express the dividing line between the 'total legal order' under which international organizations are established and operate when they relate to the outside world, and the 'partial legal orders' that organizations constitute as personified entities.[27] Though any terminology describing spaces that are intellectual constructs rather than geographical locations is bound to be awkward,[28] the questions addressed in this study – especially the general plausibility of analogising between States and international organizations – attract very different answers depending on whether one looks at organizations from without or from within.[29]

Another phrase that is employed here is 'general international law', in the sense that it has been used in the case law of the International Court of Justice and in the work of the International Law Commission, that is, to describe default rules of general application to be distinguished from special rules (*lex specialis*) that may be agreed or adopted in any given context.[30] I shall often favour that phrase over the related phrase 'customary international law' because it is more inclusive. While 'customary international law' is taken to mean rules deriving from the State practice and *opinio juris* of States, general international law can be used to refer not only to those rules but also to rules deriving from argument by principle and argument by analogy: it does not presuppose a fixed or rigid conception of what constitutes a valid legal proposition under

---

[27] I rely here on the distinction proposed by Kelsen when considering the legal personality of 'juridical persons' under the law: H. Kelsen, *General Theory of Law and State* (Cambridge: Harvard University Press, 1945), pp. 99–100.

[28] As Crawford notes, 'the "international plane" is a construct not a plane': J. Crawford (ed.), *Brownlie's Principles of Public International Law*, 8th edn (Oxford: Oxford University Press, 2012), p. 126. But he is one of many scholars to use the phrase international plane in distinction to other legal realms such as the institutional plane or the 'domestic plane'. The phrase is also found in *Reparation for Injuries Suffered in the Service of the United Nations* (Advisory Opinion) [1951] ICJ Rep 174.

[29] As Klabbers notes, '[w]hat makes the law of international organizations complicated is the fact that it involves three rather different legal relationships': 'the relationship between the organizations and its members states', 'relations between organization and staff, or relations between the various organs of the organization' and 'relations between the organization and the outside world': Klabbers, *An Introduction*, p. 3. Under the distinction adopted here, while relations between the organizations and its members can take place both on the international and institutional planes, relations concerning staff or organs take place on the institutional plane and relations between the organization and the outside world take place on the international plane.

[30] E.g., *Accordance with International Law of the Unilateral Declaration of Independence in Respect of Kosovo* (Advisory Opinion) [2010] ICJ Rep 403; Conclusions of the Work of the Study Group on the Fragmentation of International Law, YILC 2006/II, part two, 179, footnote 976.

international law.[31] Further, 'general international law' also has the advantage of encapsulating the notions of general principles of law recognised by nations and peremptory norms (*jus cogens*).

I shall also use throughout this book terms such as 'corporate entity', 'corporate body' and 'rule of incorporation', which are far more usual in works of domestic company law than in studies of international law. The goal is to emphasise that many of the issues covered here revolve around the use by States of a distinct form of corporate personality, behind which they oftentimes purport to hide.[32] I am not of course proposing to draw analogies between rules of international law and company law, but rather to rely – loosely and for illustrative purposes – on terminology that is helpful for capturing and tackling problems that both systems share.

Finally, the phrase 'rules of the organization' is used interchangeably with 'internal law' or 'internal rules' of international organizations. As defined in VCLT 1986 and the ARIO, the 'rules of the organization' comprise 'the constituent instruments, decisions, resolutions and other acts of the international organization adopted in accordance with those instruments, and established practice of the organization'.[33]

Structure of the Book

The book is divided into three parts.

Part I makes the case for an analogy between States and international organizations. Chapter 1 considers the function and value of analogy in domestic and international legal reasoning, explaining why it is a technique to which the legal profession turns in situations in uncertainty, that is, to fill gaps in the law. Chapter 2 analyses the plausibility of an analogy between States and international organizations, which depends on two conditions being satisfied. First, international law has to admit of international organizations as a general category of legal persons to which a common set of rights, obligations and capacities apply. Second, there must be a relevant similarity between statehood and the status of international organization under international law.

---

[31] See the discussion in Section 1.1.4.

[32] For a study that also finds it illuminating to discuss international organizations as a case of the use of the corporate form, see I. Seidl-Hoheverden, *Corporations in and under International Law* (Cambridge: Grotius, 1987), pp. 69–93.

[33] Art. 2(d) ARIO; see also the slightly different formulation in art. 2(1)(j).

Part II considers objections to the analogy, in the form of principled arguments against assimilation that have been made in the context of, or in reaction to, the ILC's work on treaties and responsibility of international organizations. Chapter 3 discusses how structural differences between States and international organizations affect the possibility of extending rules from one category to the other. Chapter 4 deals with the view that international organizations are 'special subjects' of international law. Under the umbrella of 'speciality' intergovernmental institutions are said to be different from each other and different from States in a number of ways. Does this mean that they ought to be addressed by 'special rules' under general international law? Chapter 5 addresses the view that international organizations, as 'layered subjects' run by their members, are not unitary entities in the same way as States. I examine how this characteristic may affect the application of certain rules of international law to organizations and their members.

Part III investigates the limits of the analogy. Chapter 6 examines the scope of application of rules of general international law, tackling the question of the extent to which those rules can apply in the relations between organizations and their members on the institutional plane. This is where the analogy reaches its breaking point, as organizations and their members can no longer be viewed as self-governing entities operating on the international plane. Chapter 7 discusses the possibility of normative contestation of the analogy, looking into how different worldviews about what international organizations are or ought to be may affect the reception of rules derived by analogy.

PART I

The Case for an Analogy

The case for an analogy between States and international organizations that can bridge the gap between general international law and intergovernmental institutions is built in two steps. First, it is necessary to show that analogical reasoning provides a justification to filling gaps in international law in situations of uncertainty. That is attempted in Chapter 1. Second, the plausibility of analogising between States and international organizations has to be established. That is the task of Chapter 2.

1

Analogy in International Legal Reasoning

Every legal system poses problems of uncertainty, situations of doubt where no existing norm seems to be applicable. This is the realm of the lacunae in the law or, in the words of H.L.A. Hart, the penumbra of legal language.[1] Law's capacity to provide normative guidance is at its most effective when one can state that a certain course of conduct is required by the law and expect this statement to be accepted by the participants in the legal system. But when the facts of life do not fit into the core meaning of a rule, or when a rule is formulated in such a way that this core meaning is left vague or ambiguous, additional legal arguments are required to build the legal proposition along the lines of which the 'hard case' can be cracked.

Reasoning by analogy is widely seen as falling in the category of persuasive arguments that judges rely on in hard cases. As Scott Brewer puts it, an analogy is based on the insight that 'because two (or more) "analogized" items share some characteristics, one may infer that the lesser-known item shares some additional characteristic with the better-known one'.[2] In law, the inference is that because rule α applies to situation β, and because situation β is relevantly similar to situation γ, rule α must also apply to situation γ. It is an assumption shared by the various legal traditions of the world that this type of reasoning provides a justification for extending a rule to factual scenarios that are comparable to those for which the rule was originally envisaged.[3]

As a decentralised legal order comprising neither a legislator nor a system of courts before which all disputes can be brought, international

---

[1] H. L. A. Hart, *The Concept of Law*, 2nd edn (Oxford: Clarendon Press, 1997), pp. 124–136.
[2] S. Brewer, 'Exemplary reasoning: semantics, pragmatics, and the rational force of legal argument by analogy' (1996) 109 HLR 923, 951.
[3] E.g., H. P. Glenn, *Legal Traditions of the World*, 4th edn (Oxford: Oxford University Press, 2010), pp. 75, 187, 115 and 250.

law provides a fertile ground for the drawing of analogies. While a vast number of rights and obligations are established by treaty, the default rules of international law – those applicable to the international community at large – are of a customary character. The upshot of having a system rooted in custom is that identifying customary rules can be a tricky endeavour. The International Court of Justice and its predecessor have articulated the methodology to which the profession resorts for establishing custom. We are told to look for a general or settled practice that is 'carried out in such a way, as to be evidence of a belief that this practice is rendered obligatory by the existence of a rule of law requiring it'.[4] But that test poses considerable epistemological challenges.[5] What counts as State practice? How does one demonstrate the existence of *opinio juris sive necessitates*? How much practice and *opinio juris* is required before one can postulate the existence of a customary rule? It is no easy feat to make sense of the claims, counterclaims, actions and omissions of the more than 190 States that integrate the international community. The end result is that international law suffers from uncertainty to a greater degree than domestic legal systems.[6] When the methodology for custom cannot be convincingly applied, reasoning by analogy is one of the techniques to which the legal profession can turn to tackle the hard case and push the law forward. The analogy between States and international organizations with which this study is concerned is a case in point.

A sophisticated account of the role that analogy may play in the identification and development of international law requires a jurisprudential understanding of legal reasoning. This chapter thus discusses the normative case for analogy, that is, the reasons why it is viewed as an authoritative type of argument in legal discourse, whether domestic or international. It also discusses particularities of the international legal system that could be thought to affect the value of analogy in international legal reasoning, and looks into the use of analogy as a technique for the codification and progressive development of international law, that is, beyond the realm of adjudication.

---

[4] *North Sea Continental Shelf (Federal Republic of Germany/Denmark; Federal Republic of Germany /Netherlands)* [1969] ICJ Rep 33, paras. 74–75.

[5] G. Kammerhofer, 'Uncertainty in the formal sources of international law: customary international law and some of its problems' (2004) 15 EJIL 523, 524–36.

[6] Though not necessarily to a much greater degree than domestic constitutional law: J. Goldsmith and D. Levinson, 'Law for States: international law, constitutional law, public law' (2009) 122 HLR 1791, 1801–22.

1.1   The Normative Case for Analogy in Legal Reasoning

1.1.1   A Jurisprudential Divide

Any assessment of how persuasive analogies are in dealing with situations of uncertainty in the law must start with a fundamental question in legal philosophy: what role do rules and legal reasoning play in legal decision-making? This is a debate reflecting profound disagreements as to the character of law itself.[7] On the one side, there is the view that neither rules nor legal reasoning can account for how judges decide cases. This is typical of the American realist school, characterised by a tradition of rule-scepticism, which, broadly speaking, regards reasoning by principle and reasoning by analogy as artifices that judges employ to cover up decisions made on the basis of extra-legal considerations.[8] In a similar vein, the critical legal studies movement emphasises the problem of the 'indeterminacy' of law, questioning the wisdom of putting too much trust in formal legal techniques.[9] On the other side of the debate are commentators aligning with the positivist school, natural law school or the 'interpretive' approach developed by Ronald Dworkin.[10] Those contend that argument by principle and by analogy provides, if not *the* right answer, justifications for legal decisions that are superior to those deriving from other types of reasoning, such as arguments of policy. Even if extra-legal considerations inevitably influence decisions made in situations of uncertainty, legal reasoning determines the range of acceptable solutions and ensures that hard cases are decided in a way that coheres with the existing rules of the legal system.

---

[7] See Hart, *The Concept of Law*, pp. 136–41. For an account of how the debate plays out in international law, G. Verdirame, '"The divided west": international lawyers in Europe and America' (2007) 18 EJIL 553, 564–67.

[8] A foundational text of which is O. W. Holmes, 'The path of law' (1987) 10 HLR 457, 461. For a particularly scathing analysis of the role of analogy in legal reasoning, R. Posner, *How Judges Think* (Cambridge, MA: Harvard University Press, 2008), pp. 181–91.

[9] For a well-known critical legal studies account of adjudication: D. Kennedy, *A Critique of Adjudication: {fin de siècle}* (Cambridge: Harvard University Press, 1997). In international law: M. Koskenniemi, *From Apology to Utopia: The Structure of International Legal Argument* (Cambridge: Cambridge University Press, 2005), pp. 58–70.

[10] For a positivist perspective: N. MacCormick, *Legal Reasoning and Legal Theory* (Oxford: Clarendon Press, 1978); for a natural law perspective: J. Finnis, *Natural Law and Natural Rights*, 2nd edn (Oxford: Oxford University Press, 2011), pp. 266–73; for the 'interpretive' perspective: R. Dworkin, *Law's Empire* (Cambridge: Harvard University Press, 1986), pp. 225–75.

Evidently, the side one takes in this jurisprudential divide determines one's view on the character, function and value of reasoning by analogy. Solving this debate, which is ultimately tied to opposing world views, is beyond the scope of this book. I propose instead to focus on the perspective that recognises a constructive role for analogy, in the hope that the analysis presented in subsequent chapters will provide a useful starting point for those wishing to consider the analogy between States and international organizations from the opposite point of view.

1.1.2   The Structure of Analogical Reasoning

In order to assess the role of analogy in legal reasoning, it is important to have a clear understanding of the structure of that type of argument. The *Arrest Warrant* case, decided by the International Court of Justice in 2002, provides a helpful illustration. Following an arrest warrant issued by a Belgian judge and circulated by INTERPOL against Abdulaye Yerodia Ndombasi, a Congolese Minister of Foreign Affairs who had been accused of committing crimes against humanity, the Court was asked to decide whether Yerodia enjoyed immunity from jurisdiction under international law.[11] It pointed out that, in the absence of any applicable treaties, the question had to be decided 'on the basis of customary international law'.[12] But instead of discussing State practice and *opinio juris*, the Court based its decision on 'the nature of the functions exercised by a Minister for Foreign Affairs', which includes the 'need to travel internationally to represent the state in its international affairs'.[13] Because 'a Minister for Foreign Affairs ... occupies a position such that, like the Head of State or the Head of Government, he or she is recognized under international law as representative of the State solely by virtue of his or her office',[14] the Court extended the rule applicable to heads of state and heads of government to ministers for foreign affairs. *Arrest Warrant* was thus decided by recourse to analogy.[15]

---

[11] The facts of the case are described in *Arrest Warrant of 11 April 2000 (Democratic Republic of the Congo v. Belgium)* [2002] ICJ Rep 3, paras. 13–21.

[12] Ibid., para. 52.

[13] Ibid., para. 53.

[14] Ibid., para. 53.

[15] Indeed, Judge *ad hoc* Van den Wyngaert criticised the Court for relying on 'a mere analogy with immunities for diplomatic agents and Heads of States' instead of looking into State practice and *opinio juris*: [2002] ICJ Rep 137, paras. 11–23.

Scott Brewer offers an account of the structure of analogical reasoning that can be helpfully used to unpack the reasoning of the Court and show how the analogy was drawn.[16] An analogy is drawn in three steps. The first is *abduction*, defined as 'inference ... from chosen examples to a rule that could resolve the doubt'.[17] Abduction is a concept from the philosophy of science that explains how a discovery is made when a scientist, having observed a given phenomenon, intuitively adopts a working hypothesis that she then sets out to prove or contest through experimentation.[18] In legal reasoning, this can be described as the moment when lawyers 'discover' the relevant similarity between a novel set of facts and those covered by an existing rule, just as when the International Court 'discovered' that the position of minister for foreign affairs was similar to that of heads of state and heads of government.

The second step, *confirmation*, comprises a process of 'reflective adjustment' of the rule inferred by abduction, which Brewer names the 'analogy-warranting rule'. That rule's purpose is to connect the two cases being compared.[19] For example, the analogy-warranting rule in *Arrest Warrant* was that officials recognised under international law as representative of the State by virtue of their office enjoy immunity *ratione personae* before the domestic courts of other States. Once the analogy-warranting rule is formulated, it must be confirmed by 'analogy-warranting rationales' which provide an explanation of and a justification for the proposed comparison.[20] It is at the level of the analogy-warranting rationales that the substantive question is posed of *why* the similarities discovered by abduction are relevant, and the answer must be backed by 'statements of reasons, *motifs*, of a kind that are acceptably justificatory by reference to law'.[21] In *Arrest Warrant*, the analogy-warranting rationale articulated by the Court to explain why ministers for foreign affairs are similar to heads of state and heads of government was the 'nature of the functions

---

[16] Brewer, 'Exemplary reasoning', 951.

[17] Ibid., 925. On abduction in analogical reasoning, see also K. H. Ladeur, 'The analogy between logic and dialogic of law' in P. Nerhot (ed.), *Legal Knowledge and Analogy: Fragments of Legal Epistemology, Hermeneutics and Linguistics* (Dordrecht: Kluwer, 1991), pp. 17–18.

[18] Brewer, 'Exemplary reasoning', 947–48.

[19] Ibid., 968–71.

[20] Ibid., 1021.

[21] N. MacCormick, *Rhetoric and the Rule of Law: A Theory of Legal Reasoning* (Oxford: Oxford University Press, 2005), p. 210. Also: R. Alexy, *A Theory of Legal Argumentation* (Oxford: Oxford University Press, 1989) 283.

exercised by a Minister for Foreign Affairs' as a high-ranking representative of their home State in international relations, which include the 'need to travel internationally'.

The third step of analogical reasoning consists in the *application* of the analogy-warranting rule to the case. That rule serves as the major premise for the syllogism through which the extension of an existing rule to comparable facts is formalised. In *Arrest Warrant*, this would be the Court's conclusion that (i) because officials recognised under international law as representatives of the State by virtue of their office enjoy personal immunity (the major premise), and because ministers for foreign affairs are officials recognised under international law as representatives of the State by virtue of their office (the minor premise), ministers for foreign affairs are entitled to personal immunity under international law.

1.1.3   Systematicity, Formal Justice and the Rule of Law

Brewer's analysis of the structure of analogy makes it clear what the difference is between 'deductive justification' – applying a well-established rule to facts which that rule undeniably covers[22] – and analogical reasoning – extending a rule to a novel situation by claiming that the situation is 'relevantly similar' to that covered by the rule. While deductive reasoning provides a full justification for a legal proposition, the justification provided by analogical reasoning is partial because it relies on an 'abduction' based on the evaluative assessment of a 'relevant similarity'. That being the case, what makes analogy an accepted way to reason about the law in situations of uncertainty?

One can think of various reasons from institutional culture and social psychology, but a philosophical investigation of the matter must consider the relationship between analogy and systemic conceptions of law. When judges postulate that two cases are similar so as to warrant extending a rule from one to the other, they do so on the basis of a conception of the purpose that the rule in question serves within the overall logic of the system.[23] The notion of the legal system has its roots in the

---

[22] On deductive justification, see MacCormick, *Legal Reasoning and Legal Theory*, chapter II.

[23] K. Engisch, *Einführung in das juristische Denken*, 2nd edn (Stuttgart: Kohlhammer, 1959), pp. 292–93.

Enlightenment, and has been given many different interpretations ever since.[24] The once fashionable theory of the 'logical-formal system', according to which the law can provide a solution to any dispute arising from social interaction, inspired the adoption of elaborate civil codes in France, Germany and other jurisdictions in the civil law tradition. Nowadays, with the advantage of studies in linguistic philosophy that expose the limits of language in the creation and application of rules, commentators regard legal systems as open constructs and works in progress, riddled with imperfections and shortcomings. But even if the notion of what a legal system is (or can be) has changed over time, the assumption that law takes the form of a system of norms remains a feature of mainstream scholarship and practice, reflected in the self-perception of jurists.[25]

Jeremy Waldron provides an illuminating contemporary account of that assumption, emphasising that law constitutes a system not only in a formal or institutional sense,[26] but also to the extent that 'systematicity' is an attribute of legal rules and principles. He argues that the accumulation of legislative enactments and judicial decisions over time must reflect, and aspire to, some sort of intelligible systematic organisation.[27] In his words, '[l]egal norms present themselves as fitting together or as aspiring to fit together into a system, each new ruling and each newly issued norm taking its place in an organized body of law which is fathomable by human intelligence'.[28] It is this systematicity that 'helps explain why we think of a body of law as consisting not just of legislation and decisions in particular cases, but also principles whose content reflects powerful themes that run implicitly through the whole body of law and that are reflected in various different ways in explicit norms' – principles that

---

[24] For a historical account: Ladeur, 'The analogy between logic and dialogic of law', pp. 15–31.

[25] K. W. Canaris, *Systemdenken und Systembegriff in der Jurisprudenz: Entwickelt am Beispiel des deutschen Privatrechts* (Berlin: Duncker und Humblot, 1983), p. 15.

[26] As in the conceptions espoused, for example, in Hart, *The Concept of Law*, especially chapters V and VI, and H. Kelsen, *Pure Theory of Law* (Berkeley: University of California Press, 1967), pp. 205–08, which are agnostic not only about the content of the rules, but also about the relationships they may bear to one another.

[27] J. Waldron, 'The concept and the rule of law' (2008–2009) 43 *Georgia Law Review* 1, 34–38.

[28] Ibid., p. 35.

'represent the underlying coherence of [the system's] enacted laws and its formal holdings'.[29]

Systematicity in the law is underpinned by two interrelated concepts. The first is the requirement of formal justice, also referred to as the 'principle of equality', according to which like cases must be treated alike.[30] While the content of rules may be wicked and unjust, a functioning legal system presupposes a degree of impartiality in the application of valid rules lest these become unintelligible and meaningless. This is why formal justice is described as the very 'essence of the idea of law' and as a 'fundamental ethical-juridical requirement'.[31]

The second concept is the political ideal of the rule of law, which provides a normative justification for the view that legal reasoning is a rational enterprise committed to treating like cases alike. The rule of law is of course a controversial notion, for which various formal and substantive conceptions have been proposed.[32] But because systematicity is mainly concerned with the tenets that form the procedural core shared by the great majority of rule of law conceptions, it is not affected by disagreements surrounding the political ideal. Lon Fuller has articulated those basic tenets in the form of eight 'principles of legality', proposing that rules ought to be general; public; non-retroactive; clear; free from contradictions; possible to perform; constant over time; and implemented with congruence by legal officials.[33] It is only when a legal order conforms to a sufficient degree with these principles that it can serve effectively the purposes for which it was enacted and 'respect human dignity' by '[treating] humans as persons capable or planning and plotting their future'.[34]

How does this all help us understand the authoritativeness of analogical argument? Analogy is an acceptable way of reasoning about the

---

[29] Ibid., p. 36. Also: MacCormick, *Rhetoric and the Rule of Law*, pp. 190–93 and Canaris, *Systemdenken und Systembegriff in der Jurisprudenz*, pp. 12–13 and 46.

[30] On the distinction between the formal concept of justice and (competing) conceptions of justice, see J. Rawls, *A Theory of Justice* (Oxford: Oxford University Press, 1999), p. 5.

[31] Canaris, *Systemdenken und Systembegriff in der Jurisprudenz*, p. 16; G. Zaccaria, 'Analogy as legal reasoning: the hermeneutic foundation of the analogical procedure' in Nerhot, *Legal Knowledge and Analogy*, p. 58.

[32] For an overview: B. Tamanaha, *On the Rule of Law: History, Politics, Theory* (Cambridge: Cambridge University Press, 2004), pp. 91–113.

[33] L. Fuller, *The Morality of Law* (New Haven: Yale University Press, 1964), pp. 46–90. Providing a similar account: J. Raz, 'The rule of law and its virtue' in J. Raz, *The Authority of Law* (Oxford: Clarendon Press, 1979), pp. 214–18.

[34] Raz, 'The rule of law and its virtue', pp. 219–26.

content of the law in situations of uncertainty insofar as the solutions that it points to are viewed as expressions of the requirement of formal justice, and thus as those which fit best in the system.[35] When judges extend a rule to a set of facts because it shares the relevant characteristics of the case for which the rule was devised, they do so on the authority that like cases must be treated alike, and as such provide a solution which is 'genuinely derivable from, albeit not dictated by, the existing body of law'.[36] They project, in Waldron's words, 'the existing logic of the law into an area of uncertainty or controversy'.[37] The point is that once one accepts that rules are meaningfully connected to each other so as to fulfil a number of values that the system intelligibly pursues, analogies feature among the acceptable methods to deal with hard cases. They promote values that are essential to the rule of law, for situations of uncertainty are not arbitrarily tackled, but handled in a way that guarantees that the proposed solution is, to the greatest extent possible in the circumstances, subjected to the constraints imposed by the valid rules of the system.

Returning to the example of *Arrest Warrant*, if there were no conclusive State practice and *opinio juris* relating to the personal immunity of ministers for foreign affairs (which was presumably the case), the International Court could justify filling the gap in the way it did on the ground that heads of state and ministers for foreign affairs are like cases that must be treated alike. Ministries for foreign affairs are listed in influential codification instruments as a part of a 'troika', together with heads of state and heads of government, of persons entitled to represent the State in its international relations. If heads of state and heads of government are accorded personal immunity under customary law, extending that rule to ministers for foreign affairs presented itself as the most coherent solution for the situation of uncertainty standing before the Court.

---

[35] E.g., Zaccaria, 'Analogy as legal reasoning', pp. 57–59; Brewer, 'Exemplary reasoning', 1005–006. As Neil MacCormick notes, judges who fail to adhere to formal justice and coherence must be criticised for 'infringing the existing requirements of the system', 'requirements which it is good to have and observe' if one commits to the political ideal of the rule of law: MacCormick, *Legal Reasoning and Legal Theory*, p. 251.

[36] MacCormick, *Rhetoric and the Rule of Law*, p. 203.

[37] Waldron, 'The concept and the rule of law', 37.

1.1.4   Challenging Analogies

The link between analogy and the systematicity of law, the requirement of formal justice and rule of law values explains why well-drawn analogies are viewed as authoritative. But this begs a fundamental question: when is an analogy 'well-drawn'? Formal justice requires us to treat like cases alike, but it does not tell us which cases are like and which are not. There is an element of creation or discovery inherent in the process of positing that a rule should be extended from the standard situation to the novel situation because both share a relevant similarity. Analogies start with an abduction which must be confirmed by analogy-warranting rationales that provide a normative explanation of why the lawyer drawing the analogy has effected 'an acceptable sorting of a range of particular items'.[38] As is the case with all normative arguments, analogy-warranting rationales are open to challenge.

That is not to say, however, that the process of abduction and selection of analogy-warranting rationales is unconstrained. The range of acceptable descriptions of situations as 'like' or 'unlike' is determined by the legal system in question, or, in Zenon Bankowski's words, by its 'legal tradition'.[39] Turning back to *Arrest Warrant*, though the precise contours of the category of persons entitled to represent *ex officio* the State in international relations can be debated,[40] it is clear that it can only encompass a limited number of high-ranking State officials. In a subsequent case, the International Court itself was quick to dismiss the suggestion that a senior prosecuting magistrate and a head of national security could benefit from personal immunity.[41] In short, the 'leap of imagination' inherent in every analogy is 'domesticated within the tradition or discourse and so loses its capacity to surprise, radically to change direction, to transcend'.[42]

Yet, it is important not to lose sight of the fact that analogical reasoning cannot provide a full justification for a legal proposition in the same way that deductive justification can. Ultimately, recourse to

---

[38] Brewer, 'Exemplary reasoning', 962.

[39] Z. Bankowski, 'Analogical reasoning and legal institutions' in Nerhot, *Legal Knowledge and Analogy*, p. 208.

[40] See for example the debate at the International Law Commission: ILC Report 2012, A/68/10, pp. 62–65, paras. 6–12.

[41] *Certain Matters of Mutual Assistance in Criminal Matters (Djibouti v. France)* [2008] ICJ Rep 177, para. 194.

[42] Bankowski, 'Analogical reasoning and legal institutions', p. 212.

analogy can always be tested and contested by an examination of the analogy-warranting rationales. The value of each proposed analogy is contingent and must be accepted on a case-by-case basis in the context of the relevant legal system.

That leads to a more fundamental objection to analogical reasoning, namely that it does not generate 'valid law'. When a judge solves a hard case by drawing an analogy, is she interpreting the law or making new law? Is analogy, to borrow Victorio Villa's terminology, a 'productive argument' or an 'interpretive argument'?[43] It is not uncommon for analogy to be described as a productive argument, that is, an argument entailing law creation, as opposed to an argument related to the ordinary application of a norm.

The way one characterises reasoning by analogy depends on one's conception of what law is. In modern analytical legal philosophy, we find on the one end of the spectrum H.L.A. Hart's positivist theory, and on the other Dworkin's interpretive theory. For Hart, in hard cases falling within the penumbra of legal language, the judge does not decide hard cases by applying the law, but rather by exercising judicial discretion.[44] The judge's 'conclusion, even though it may not be arbitrary or irrational, is in effect a choice'.[45] For Dworkin, as an 'interpretive practice' law does not derive exclusively 'from some set of factual criteria for law every competent lawyer accepts'. Rather, law is compounded by those prescriptions that, in any given case, best fit with existing legal practice (that is, legislation, precedent, etc.) and that are best justified in the sense that they offer 'the best constructive interpretation of the political structure and legal doctrine of [the] community'.[46] Thus, if the judge resorts to analogy in a hard case both to make her decision fit with existing legal practice and present it in the best light from the standpoint of political morality, she will be deciding that case in accordance with the law. No arbitrary line between deductive justification and systemic reasoning ought to be drawn.

Whatever side one takes in this debate, to dismiss analogy by affirming without more that law-appliers are 'making new law' fails to make sense of the reasons why analogy is the source of acceptable legal arguments.

---

[43] V. Villa, 'Legal analogy between interpretive arguments and productive arguments' in Nerhot, *Legal Knowledge and Analogy.*

[44] Hart, *The Concept of Law*, pp. 124–36.

[45] Ibid., p. 127.

[46] Dworkin, *Law's Empire*, pp. 254–58 and 260–63.

Positivists concede that even if we are speaking of 'new law', that new law is 'being made with support from the existing body of law, because fully coherent with it and hence already inside its present frame of reference',[47] or 'in accordance with principles of underpinning reasons recognized as already having a footing in the existing law'.[48] According to Villa, legal reasoning should be understood as a spectrum encompassing, at one end, logical and quasi-logical legal arguments, and, at the other, legal arguments pertaining to fields in which 'positive law' is lacking.[49] Instead of trying to define categorically where analogy stands in this spectrum, it may be a better strategy to focus on its systemic qualities and limitations in the context of actual hard cases.

A final caveat concerns the morality of the justification that analogies provide. That reasoning by analogy is underpinned by central tenets of the political ideal of the rule of law does not mean that the solutions to which it points will be morally tenable or worth upholding. If a rule is wicked, then extending it to a novel situation will produce a legally justifiable but morally unsound result. Returning to *Arrest Warrant*, one might question, for example, whether the rule of personal immunity that applies to high-ranking State officials withstands moral scrutiny, especially in situations when enforcing it means sheltering individuals from prosecution for heinous crimes.[50] The moral quality of justifications provided by analogies thus mirrors the moral qualities of the legal system in which those analogies fit. It should be noted, in this connection, that for those who adhere to substantive conceptions of the rule of law, the political ideal demands more than compliance with procedural tenets of clarity, consistency and coherence.[51] Values such as equality before the law and the protection of individual rights are sometimes added to the 'rule of law package', and rules derived by analogy may well fall short of those.

1.2   Analogy in International Legal Reasoning

That the use of analogy is a feature of international legal reasoning is borne out by the practice of international courts of tribunals, as

---

[47] McCormick, *Rhetoric and the Rule of Law*, p. 204.
[48] Hart, *The Concept of Law*, p. 274.
[49] Villa, 'Legal analogy', pp. 180–81.
[50] See e.g., the dissenting opinion of Judge Al-Khasawneh: [2000] ICJ Rep 95.
[51] E.g., T. Bingham, *The Rule of Law* (Penguin Books, 2011).

exemplified by the *Arrest Warrant* case. Other examples in the case law of the International Court include the analogy between complicity in genocide and aid and assistance in the commission of an internationally wrongful act which the Court drew in *Bosnian Genocide* to determine whether Serbia was internationally responsible for complicity in the genocide committed in Srebenica in 1995,[52] and the application of rules of the law of treaties to declarations made under Article 36(2) of the ICJ Statute to accept the compulsory jurisdiction of the Court.[53] Recourse to analogy is by no means unique to the jurisprudence of the International Court. Though a comprehensive survey is yet to be carried out, analogies can be found in the case law of institutions as diverse as the International Tribunal for the Law of the Sea[54] and investment arbitral tribunals.[55]

But are the postulates underpinning systemic reasoning in domestic law – systematicity, formal justice, the rule of law – freely transferrable to international law? Jurisprudential accounts of legal reasoning take for granted certain attributes found in *centralised* legal systems, in particular the existence of courts with compulsory jurisdiction. Though none of the particularities of the international legal order puts into question its commitment to treat like cases alike, one must consider the degree to which those particularities may affect the role, function and limits of systemic reasoning. It might be suggested, on the one hand, that international law does not constitute a legal system in the same way as domestic law, or that there is no such thing as an 'international rule of law'. On the other hand, international law deploys systemic reasoning in forms that are seldom discussed in the domestic context, such as in the codification and progressive development of the law. The case for the use of analogy in international law thus requires further elaboration.

---

[52] *Application of the Convention on the Prevention and Punishment of the Crime of Genocide (Bosnia and Herzegovina v. Serbia and Montenegro)* [2007] ICJ Rep 43, paras. 419–20.

[53] *Military and Paramilitary Activities in and against Nicaragua (Nicaragua v. United States of America)* (Preliminary Objections) [1984] ICJ Rep 392, para. 63; *Land and Maritime Boundary between Cameroon and Nigeria* (Preliminary Objections) [1998] ICJ Rep 275, para. 30; and *Fisheries Jurisdiction (Spain v. Canada)* (Preliminary Objections) [1998] ICJ Rep 432, para. 46.

[54] E.g., *Responsibilities and Obligations of States Sponsoring Persons and Entities with respect to Activities in the Area* (Advisory Opinion, Seabed Chamber) [2011] ITLOS Rep 10, para. 60 (stating that the Vienna Convention may 'by analogy, provide guidance' for the interpretation of instruments adopted by the parties under the UNCLOS).

[55] See A. Roberts, 'Clash of paradigms: actors and analogies shaping the investment treaty system' 107 AJIL 45.

1.2.1   The Systematicity of International Law

While Hans Kelsen described international law as a 'primitive legal system',[56] H.L.A. Hart went as far as to argue that international law did not constitute a legal system because it lacked a proper 'rule of recognition'.[57] But great though the shortcomings of international law-making processes may be, neither Kelsen nor Hart have suggested that the rules of international law do not 'present themselves as fitting together or as aspiring to fit together into a system'.[58] Quite the contrary, Hart posited an 'analogy of content and function' between international law and domestic law, observing that there were a 'range of principles, concepts, and methods which are common to both municipal and international law, and makes the lawyers' technique freely transferable from the one to the other'.[59]

In international legal scholarship, the most prominent recent debate on the systematicity of international law was prompted by the phenomena of the fragmentation of international law and the proliferation of international courts and tribunals.[60] The increase in number of legal regimes and institutions in the past few decades, marked by a tendency towards specialisation, has generated the fear that international law may no longer – if it ever did – form a coherent system.[61] But the mainstream position that the international legal profession has taken on this matter is clear. As the International Law Commission stated in the first paragraph of its Conclusions on the Fragmentation of International Law, '[i]nternational law is a legal system'. While recognising that, in times of fragmentation,

---

[56] Kelsen, *Pure Theory of Law*, p. 323.

[57] A contention that has given rise to a lively debate: S. Besson, 'Theorizing the sources of international law' in S. Besson and J. Tasioulas (eds.), *The Philosophy of International Law* (Oxford: Oxford University Press, Oxford 2010), pp. 180–81; A. Paulus, 'The international legal system as a constitution' in J. Dunoff and J. Trachtman (eds.), *Ruling the World? Constitutionalism, International Law, and Global Governance* (Cambridge: Cambridge University Press, 2009), p. 74; D. Lefkowitz, '(Dis)solving the chronological paradox in customary international law: a Hartian approach' (2008) 21 *Canadian Journal of Law and Jurisprudence* 129, 146.

[58] To use Waldron's phrase: Waldron, 'The concept and the rule of law', 33.

[59] Hart, *The Concept of Law*, p. 237.

[60] On fragmentation, see e.g., the several contributions compiled in (1999) 31 *NYU Journal of International Law and Politics* and B. Simma and D. Pulkowski, 'Of planets and the universe: self-contained regimes in international law' (2006) 17 EJIL 483.

[61] See e.g., B. Kingsbury, 'The International Legal Order' in P. Cane and M. Tushnet (eds.), *Oxford Handbook of Legal Studies* (Oxford: Oxford University Press, 2003), pp. 280–81.

international law may lack institutional coherence, the Commission emphasised that it is not a 'random collection' of norms.[62] It rather possesses an overall systematicity.[63]

The Commission likewise accepted that legal reasoning is as relevant for international law as it is in the domestic context. It described '[l]egal interpretation' and 'legal reasoning' as building systemic relationships between rules and principles by envisaging them as parts of some human effort or purpose.[64] This is reflected in legal techniques that solve conflicts of norms (the maxims *lex specialis derogat legi generali* and *lex posterior derogat legi priori*) and ensure the systemic interpretation of interconnected norms (the principles of 'harmonization' and 'systemic integration', the latter found in Article 31(3)(c) VCLT 1969).[65] The systemic view espoused by the Commission is particularly evident in its treatment of the so-called 'self-contained regimes'. It is understood that even highly specialised treaty regimes remain embedded in the general law, which retains a 'gap-filling' function to be fulfilled whenever the 'special law' is silent or fails.[66]

The intuitions fleshed out in the Commission's Conclusions and accompanying report are also found in the practice of judicial and arbitral institutions. To give a well-known example, in the *Interpretation of the Agreement* advisory opinion, the International Court stated that 'a rule of international law, whether customary or conventional, does not operate in a vacuum' but rather 'in relation to facts and in the context of a wider framework of legal rules of which it forms only a part'.[67] In his separate opinion at the reparations phase in the *Diallo* case, Judge Greenwood similarly observed that '[i]nternational law is not a series of fragmented specialist and self-contained bodies of law,

---

[62] As Crawford stresses, international law is 'made up of conventional and customary rules' that, through 'the basic constructs of personality, sources, treaties, interpretation and responsibility', 'interact, interlink, reinforce each other and sufficiently cohere'; J. Crawford, 'Chance, order, change: the course of international law' (2013) 365 RdC 13, 146.

[63] Conclusions of the Work of the Study Group on the Fragmentation of International Law, YILC 2006/II, part two, para. 1.

[64] M. Koskenniemi (Rapporteur), 'Report of the Study Group of the ILC: Fragmentation of International Law', A/CN.4/L.682 (2006), para. 35.

[65] Conclusions of the Study Group, YILC 2006/II, part two, paras. 5–30.

[66] Ibid., e.g., paras. 15–16.

[67] *Interpretation of the Agreement of 25 March 1951 between the WHO and Egypt* (Advisory Opinion) [1980] ICJ Rep 73, para 10.

each of which functions in isolation from the others' but rather 'a single, unified system of law'.[68]

Accepting and promoting international law's systematicity is part and parcel of the political ideal of an 'international rule of law'. In recent times, this phrase has become a prominent feature in international political discourse. That legality is a goal to be promoted in the international sphere is affirmed by several resolutions and declarations adopted under the auspices of the United Nations, with the General Assembly declaring its 'solemn commitment to an international order based on the rule of law and international law' and reiterating the need for 'universal adherence' to the international rule of law.[69] It is nevertheless true, as Sir Arthur Watts pointed out, that the rule of law in international affairs has been more frequently invoked than properly understood.[70] It has been invoked to convey the necessity of obeying international law; as an argument for expanding the scope of international regimes; and as a yardstick to criticise the behaviour of States and the activities of international institutions. As is the case with studies focusing on domestic law, authors and institutions have espoused various competing substantive conceptions of what the political ideal entails at the international level.[71] But the question posed here – whether viewing international law as a system and embracing systemic reasoning as a methodology to tackle uncertainty finds normative justification in the notion of an international rule of law – is much narrower, and takes us back to that procedural core that is shared by most rule of law conceptions. The answer is straightforward enough: if international law is to be understood as a rational, purposeful enterprise, then the systemic techniques that compose the toolkit of the domestic lawyer should be also employed by the international lawyer. Mastering and deploying reasoning by principle and reasoning by analogy is, if anything, even more necessary with respect to international law, given its coherence

---

[68] *Ahmadou Sadio Diallo (Republic of Guinea v. Democratic Republic of the Congo)* (Compensation) [2012] ICJ Rep 391, para. 8.

[69] See most recently UNGA Res. 70/118 (2017). Also: UNGA Res. 2625(XXV) (1970) and UNGA Res. 55/2 (2000).

[70] A. Watts, 'The international rule of law' (1993) 36 GYIL 15.

[71] E.g., see Watts, 'The International Rule of Law'; S. Beaulac, 'An inquiry into the international rule of law' (2007), EUI Max Weber Programme Series, Working Paper No. 2007/14 <http://cadmus.eui.eu/handle/1814/6957> accessed 11 February 2018; and R. McCorquodale, 'Defining the international rule of law: defying gravity?' (2016) 65 ICLQ 277.

deficit and institutional decentralisation. In this connection, it is telling that academic commentary on the identification of customary international law often discusses analogy and other modes of systemic reasoning as 'methods' for establishing custom without distinguishing them sharply from the well-accepted inductive methodology based on State practice and *opinio juris*.[72]

1.2.2 Completeness of the System and the Lotus Closure Rule

It should thus be evident that analogy can be as valuable a technique for the justification of legal propositions in international law as is the case in the domestic context. But two additional features of international law that may potentially bear on its systematicity and the suitability of systemic reasoning must be briefly noted.

The first feature concerns the question of the completeness of the international legal system, and of whether findings that the law does not provide a solution for a dispute (*non liquet*) are admissible. While Hersch Lauterpacht has shown that this is an issue that also arises under municipal law,[73] there are at least two reasons why it is more problematic at the international level than at the domestic level. First, domestic legal systems invariably contain rules of adjudication conferring upon courts the competence to decide all disputes submitted to them, so that the discussion on the possibility of *non liquet* is of little consequence.[74] Legal theorists spend much time discussing how courts ought to decide hard cases, but rarely (if ever) question their institutional competence to do so. Second, as a decentralised system, international law is more prone to gaps and situations of uncertainty than domestic legal orders.[75] This has

---

[72] See e.g., P. Tomka, 'Custom and the International Court of Justice' (2013), 12 *The Law and Practice of International Courts and Tribunals* 195, 202 and 215; S. Talmon, 'Determining customary international law: the ICJ's methodology between induction, deduction and assertion' (2015) 26 EJIL 417, 423–27.

[73] H. Lauterpacht, *The Function of Law in the International Community* (Oxford: Clarendon Press, 1933), pp. 70–71.

[74] *Non liquet* is sometimes expressly prohibited, as in art. 4 of the French Civil Code, which provides that '[a] judge who refuses to give judgment on the pretext of legislation being silent, obscure or insufficient, may be prosecuted for being guilty of a denial of justice'. Code Civil Français (1804), translation available at <www.legifrance.gouv.fr/content/download/1950/13681/.../Code_22.pdf> accessed 11 Feb 2018.

[75] L. Siorat, *Le Problème des Lacunes en Droit International: Contribution à l'Étude des Sources du Droit et de la Fonction Judiciaire* (Paris: Librairie Générale de Droit et de Jurisprudence, 1958), pp. 9–11; H. Lauterpacht, 'Some observations on the prohibition of

led Julius Stone to argue that the question of *non liquet* must not be regarded as a 'mere incident of judicial procedure' but rather as a 'reflection of the undeveloped state of legislative organs in the international legal order'.[76] He contended that there was no obligation upon international judges to render a judgment when the law is inexistent or unclear.[77] Would the character and institutional features of international law militate in favour of leaving gaps alone instead of filling them by recourse to systemic reasoning?

Contemporary discussions on *non liquet* invariably turn to the International Court's inability to 'conclude definitively', in *Legality of the Threat and Use of Nuclear Weapons*, 'whether the threat or use of nuclear weapons would be lawful or unlawful in an extreme circumstance of self-defence, in which the very survival of a State would be at stake'.[78] This is the only example of *non liquet* that one finds in international judicial practice. It is debatable, however, whether the Court's hesitation did in fact constitute a *non liquet*. For one, the decision was made in advisory proceedings relating to a question asked in the abstract. Moreover, the Court's conclusion does not seem to match the conflicting, but comparatively straightforward, views that individual judges on the bench espoused on the legal limitations on nuclear weapons.[79] In other words, the *non liquet* was more an agreement to disagree within a deeply

---

"*non liquet*" and the completeness of the law' in E. Lauterpacht (ed.), *International Law* (Cambridge: Cambridge University Press 1970–2004), p. 220.

[76] J. Stone, '*Non-liquet* and the function of law in the international community' (1959) 35 BYIL 124, 131.

[77] Ibid., 138–9 and 149–53. This view is shared by D. Bodansky, '*Non liquet* and the incompleteness of international law' in B. Charzournes and P. Sands (eds.), *International law, the International Court of Justice and Nuclear Weapons* (Cambridge: Cambridge University Press, 1999), pp. 167–70.

[78] *Legality of the Threat or Use of Nuclear Weapons* (Advisory Opinion) [1996] ICJ Rep 247, para. 105(2)(E).

[79] The only judge that seemed to share the opinion reflected in the text was President Bedjaoui. Most of the other judges seemed to be either of the opinion that an extreme situation of self-defence would justify the use of nuclear weapons contrary to international humanitarian law (e.g., Guillaume, Ferrari-Bravo, Fleischenhauer and Schwebel) or otherwise (e.g., Koroma and Weeramantry). For the position that the Court did *not* pronounce a *non liquet*, but was instead unable to decide given the facts at its disposal, S. Neff, 'In search of clarity: *non liquet* and international law' in K. Homi and M. Bohlander (eds.), *International Law and Power: Perspectives on Legal Order and Justice* (Leiden: Nijhoff, 2009), pp. 76–79.

divided Court than a reasoned recognition of the indeterminacy of the existing law.[80]

There is thus nothing in the *Nuclear Weapons* advisory opinion that suggests that *non liquet* should be favoured over techniques of legal reasoning in tackling hard cases in international law. Rather, the international legal profession adheres to the regulative idea that international law constitutes a legal system that is relatively complete and sufficiently determinate in the sense that it is able to provide solutions to situations of uncertainty. It may contain lacunae and areas in which the existing law will be difficult to ascertain, but it provides a number of accepted methods for dealing with those. The mainstream position remains that:

> every international situation is capable of being determined *as a matter of law*, either by the application of specific legal rules where they already exist, or by the application of legal rules derived, by the use of known legal techniques, from other legal rules or principles.[81]

The second feature of international law that may bear upon recourse to systemic reasoning is the closure rule articulated by the Permanent Court of International Justice in the *Lotus* case.[82] Most domestic systems comprise closure rules that determine what happens when the law is silent on a certain matter. Typical of liberal domestic systems is the rule according to which individuals are free to act unless otherwise prescribed by the law[83] and, as a corollary, that governmental entities can only exercise public power when the law so authorises. In international law, the Permanent Court's judgment in *Lotus* remains the *locus classicus* for the proposition that, absent legal prohibitions, States are free to act. When the French vessel *The SS Lotus* collided with the Turkish vessel *Boz-Kourt*, Turkey took custody of the first officer of the *Lotus* and tried him for manslaughter. Proceedings were then instituted before the Permanent Court, which was asked to rule on whether Turkey's exercise of

---

[80] For a sophisticated discussion of the *Nuclear Weapons* case, which sees in it greater implications than the present study: G. Hernández, *The International Court of Justice and the Judicial Function* (Oxford: Oxford University Press, 2014), pp. 266–76.

[81] A. Watts and R. Jennings (eds.), *Oppenheim's International Law*, 9th edn (Harlow: Longman, 1992), pp. 12–13. See also H. Lauterpacht, 'Some observations', pp. 221–22.

[82] I borrow the term 'closure rule' from J. Raz, 'Legal reasons, sources and gaps' in Raz, *The Authority of Law*, p. 77.

[83] As expressed as early as in the French Declaration of the Rights of Man and of the Citizen, art. 4, 'the exercise of the natural rights of every man has no bounds other than those that ensure to the other members of society the enjoyment of these same rights. These bounds may be determined only by Law'.

criminal jurisdiction had been in accordance with international law. In giving an affirmative answer, the Court stated that '[r]estrictions upon the independence of States cannot . . . be presumed'.[84] This statement has since been construed as signifying that, in international law, whatever is not prohibited is permitted.[85]

The so-called 'Lotus principle' occasionally features in legal argument and the decisions of international courts and tribunals. In Nicaragua and Nuclear Weapons, the starting point taken by the International Court was that 'the illegality of the use of certain weapons as such does not result from an absence of authorization but, on the contrary, is formulated in terms of prohibition'.[86] Likewise, in Kosovo the Court found the declaration of independence with respect to Kosovo to be in accordance with international law in that it was not prohibited by customary rules and the relevant lex specialis.[87] While the Court refrained from citing Lotus in those judgments, the application of the closure rule is implicit in its reasoning. And fairly so, one might add – despite the criticism levelled against the Lotus principle, which some view as a relic from a bygone era of international law, its basic proposition is largely unproblematic as a default position, and does not constitute a negation of international law. It is a feature of a decentralised system having independent States as its primary subjects that those States retain a margin of freedom to pursue their interests so long as that freedom is not restricted by rules deriving from existing law-making processes.[88]

---

[84] The Case of the S.S. 'Lotus' (France/Turkey) [1927] PCIJ, Series A No. 10, p. 18.

[85] O. Spiermann, 'Lotus and the double structure of international legal argument' in Charzournes and Sands, International Law, the ICJ and Nuclear Weapons, p. 141.

[86] Legality of the Threat or Use of Nuclear Weapons, para. 52; Military and Para-Military Activities in and against Nicaragua (Nicaragua v. USA) (Merits) [1986] ICJ Rep 135, para. 269.

[87] Accordance with International Law of the Unilateral Declaration of Independence in Respect of Kosovo (Advisory Opinion) [2010] ICJ Rep 403, para. 79. The Lotus case was invoked by a large number of participants in the proceedings, and was also the object of the criticism of some judges. See, in particular, Judge Simma's Declaration [2010] ICJ Rep 478, paras. 2–3.

[88] Even Lauterpacht, a fierce critic of the application of the residual principle, recognised that the reasoning whereby the 'silence [of the law] in a particular case must be regarded as having a decisive and negative influence on the claim before the Court . . . may frequently be correct': Lauterpacht, The Function of Law, p. 86. See also H. Kelsen, Principles of International Law (New York: Holt, 1967), pp. 438–40 and G. Kammerhofer, 'Gaps, the "Nuclear Weapons" advisory opinion and the structure of international legal argument between theory and practice' (2009) 80 BYIL 333.

That does not mean, of course, that the *Lotus* principle can fill all the gaps in international law. As Ole Spiermann cautions, it is a mistake to read into *Lotus* a sweeping presumption of State freedom in cases in which the law is unclear or conflicted. Rather, *Lotus* expresses a residual principle according to which freedom of action ensues from the *absence* of prohibitive rules.[89] Whether the law is silent can only be ascertained by a thorough identification of existing rules and principles, of which the deployment of the techniques of legal reasoning – including argument by analogy – is an integral part. Under international law, recourse is also admitted to general principles of law as envisaged in Article 38(1)(c) of the ICJ Statute, which Lauterpacht thought made 'available without limitation the resources of substantive law embodied in the legal experience of civilized mankind'.[90] Ultimately, freedom of action will only be the solution for a situation of uncertainty when that is allowed by the system. The law of international organizations is a case in point. Does the absence of general practice and *opinio juris* specifically confirming a right to immunity for organizations and their officials entail that a third State may subject them to the jurisdiction of its courts if it so pleases? Freedom of action in a case like this does not present itself as an acceptable solution, and recourse to systemic reasoning is to be favoured over the blunt application of the closure rule.[91]

1.3 Analogy in the Codification and Progressive Development of International Law

1.3.1 Systemic Codification by Analogy

The international legal system does not comprise a legislature empowered to enact binding rules of general application for the international community at large. The closest to a legislature that it has are the diplomatic conferences of States that adopt conventions laying down rules aspiring to universal acceptance.[92] The quintessential mechanism

---

[89] Spiermann, '*Lotus* and the double structure', pp. 137–48.
[90] H. Lauterpacht, 'Some Observations', pp. 221–22.
[91] See the discussion in 7.1.1.
[92] Much has been said about the exercise of 'legislative powers' by the UN Security Council: e.g., S. Talmon, 'The Security Council as world legislature' (2005) 99 AJIL 175. While the Council has the power to make decisions that are binding upon UN members under Article 25 of the Charter, it is better described as an 'executive organ' whose occasional use of resolutions of a quasi-legislative character gives rise to constitutional questions.

whereby conventions of this kind are drafted and adopted is set out by Article 13 of the Charter of the United Nations, which entrusts to the UN General Assembly the task of initiating studies and making recommendations for 'the purpose of ... promoting international co-operation in the political field and encouraging the progressive development of international law and its codification'. To pursue this goal, in 1947 the General Assembly established the International Law Commission. In the past seventy years, the Commission has formulated several of the most important texts that articulate rules of public international law, many of which were submitted to diplomatic conferences for adoption in treaty form.

Under its Statute, the Commission is empowered to pursue the 'progressive development of international law' by tackling 'subjects which have not yet been regulated', or its 'codification' by engaging in the 'more precise formulation and systematization of rules of international law in fields where there already has been extensive State practice, precedent and doctrine'.[93] Sets of draft articles, reports and studies are gestated over years of debates, in which proposals made by Special Rapporteurs are discussed in plenary and sent to drafting committees.[94] The procedure followed by the ILC also features a continuous dialogue with States and other relevant stakeholders, not only through the Commission's reporting annually to the Sixth Committee of the General Assembly, but also through its inviting additional comments on a regular basis.[95] In surveying the State practice, the judicial and arbitral precedent and the work of commentators on which it bases its projects and proposals, the Commission inevitably faces situations of uncertainty – even more so than is the case with international tribunals, because, instead of settling disputes, one of the Commission's key missions is to offer systematizations of entire subfields of international law.

It should come as no surprise, therefore, that in carrying out its mandate the Commission often turns to techniques of legal reasoning, including analogy. For example, analogies from the law of treaties have informed the drafting of several provisions in the Articles on State

---

[93] Art. 15, Statute of the International Commission (UNGA Res. 174 (II), Nov 1947).

[94] On the working methods of the Commission, see generally I. Sinclair, *The International Law Commission* (Cambridge Grotius Publications, 1987), pp. 32–44.

[95] See in general F. Berman, 'The ILC within the UN's legal framework: its relationship with the Sixth Committee' (2007) 49 GYIL. On balance, Berman sees this relationship as a 'healthy one' (at 125).

Responsibility. Those include the rule in Article 49(3) ARS, according to which '[c]ountermeasures shall, as far as possible, be taken in such a way as to permit the resumption of performance of the obligations in question', which was modelled upon Article 72(2) VCLT, providing that the parties to a suspended treaty must 'refrain from acts tending to obstruct the resumption' of that treaty.[96] Likewise, the ILC relied on Article 60 VCLT in drafting Article 42 ARS, which defines the 'injured State' entitled to invoke responsibility. The cases in which the parties to a treaty 'are entitled to respond individually and in their own right to a material breach by terminating or suspending it' are relevantly similar, the Commission thought, to those in which a State can invoke another's responsibility on the grounds that it has suffered an injury.[97] And then there is the striking example with which this book is concerned: the Commission's work on international organizations, where rules that had been developed for States were extended to international organizations on the assumption that there was no reason to distinguish between the two categories of international legal subjects. In contrast with the topical uses of analogy which one finds in the codification of the law of State responsibility, in the field of international organizations analogy seems to have been employed less as a technique to fill the occasional gap than as a general method.

The use of analogy in the codification and progressive development of international law takes legal reasoning out of its 'natural habitat', the realm of adjudication. Is it a technique that an entity such as the ILC can legitimately deploy? This question invites reflection on the mandate of the Commission and on how it has evolved over time. Many codification instruments have become central to international legal discourse, not because they resulted in widely ratified treaties, but because they have come to be perceived as authoritative restatements of customary international law.[98] While the process of translating customary rules into words necessarily involves an element of creation, as those entrusted with the task must make choices as to how to present materials that are

---

[96] YILC 2001/II, part two, p. 131, para. 3.

[97] Commentary to art. 42, YILC 2001/II, part two, p. 131, paras. 4–5. The Commission noted, of course, the differences in scope and purpose of the two provisions. In particular, while art. 60 only applies where there is a 'material' breach of a treaty, the rule in art. 42 can apply whenever an international obligation is breached.

[98] This point is further developed in F. Bordin, 'Reflections of customary international law: the authority of codification conventions and ILC draft articles in international law' (2014) 63 ICLQ 535.

far from unequivocal, the vocabulary of 'codification' and 'progressive development' is commonly employed by the legal profession to distinguish between provisions in a non-binding codification instrument which are regarded as well established and those which are not. If the provision is said to fall on the codification side of the spectrum, the elements of progressive development that it may contain are regarded as negligible, the provision is applied as reflecting existing law, and – over time – it may become impossible to distinguish what has been restated from what has been created. Conversely, if a provision is considered as falling on the progressive development side of the spectrum, it is assumed that it cannot exercise any authority unless it is adopted in treaty form, in which case only States expressing their consent will be bound.

Because it does not possess legislative powers, the Commission rarely, if ever, takes on topics with an overt character of progressive development as defined in its Statute.[99] It appears to be aware that, being an expert body composed of jurists, it must refrain from proposing rules reflecting idiosyncratic political sensibilities or from re-imagining the structure of the international legal system.[100] As a member of the Commission once noted, the Commission's 'job is "lawyers' law", not "politicians' law"', that is, 'to understand the logic of the existing rules and to develop them in the framework of this logic, not to change the underlying logic.' It is no coincidence that the Commission's most celebrated codification efforts – in particular VCLT 1969 and the ARS – capture this ethos. By capitalising on its expertise and focusing on producing reasonably thorough restatements of the law as it stands, the Commission has managed to make long-lasting contributions to the consolidation and development of international law.[101]

[99] J. Dugard, 'How effective is the International Law Commission in the development of international law? A critique of the ILC on the occasion of its fiftieth anniversary' (1998) 23 *South African Journal of International Law* 33, 41.

[100] S. Murphy, 'Codification, progressive development, or scholarly analysis? The art of packaging the ILC's work product' in M. Ragazzi (ed.), *The Responsibility of International Organizations: Essays in Memory of Sir Ian Brownlie* (Leiden: Nijhoff, 2013), p. 40 (arguing that 'the Commission's authority and legacy will ultimately turn on whether States and other relevant actors view the Commission as adhering to its statutory role, or perceive it as aggregating to itself the role of legislator').

[101] A. Pellet, 'Responding to new needs through codification and progressive development' in V. Gowlland-Debbas, *Multilateral Treaty-Making: The Current Status of Challenges to and Reforms Needed in the International Legislative Process* (The Hague: Nijhoff, 1998), p. 16.

Given this institutional reality, analogical reasoning allows the Commission to build a bridge between existing rules and novel situations in a way that falls squarely within its mandate. As such, it constitutes an ingenious method for the *systemic codification* of the law, as existing norms are projected onto situations of uncertainty in the way that best allows the international legal system to pursue coherently the goals set out by those norms. Crucially, the justification provided by analogical reasoning to legal propositions in situations of uncertainty can boost the output of the work of the Commission, in particular in cases where codification instruments never become formally binding, either because they are adopted as treaties that do not enter into force (as is the case with VCLT 1986) or because they are left in the form of non-binding sets of draft articles (as is the case with the ARIO).

The extent to which provisions derived by analogy can be compared to provisions induced on the basis of a survey of State practice and *opinio juris* depends on the answer one gives to the larger question of whether analogy is a 'productive argument' (creating new law) or an 'interpretive argument' (elucidating existing law).[102] What is clear, nonetheless, is that systemic reasoning can claim a degree of authority surpassing that of rules drafted in an exercise in progressive development as traditionally understood. Even when analogical reasoning is described as 'extending' or 'developing' the law, that 'extension' or 'development' takes place within the bounds of the legal system, grounded on the requirement that like cases must be treated alike.[103] To put it another way, if reliance on analogical reasoning leads to progressive development of the law, that is progressive development in the spirit of the codification ideal.

1.3.2   Analogy as a Method in the Projects on Treaties and Responsibility of IOs

If analogy is indeed a valuable technique for the codification and progressive development of the law, it is somewhat puzzling that a methodological discussion of the technique is lacking in the two projects in which recourse to it would appear to be most salient: the set of articles eventually adopted as the 1986 Vienna Convention and the Articles on the Responsibility of International Organizations.

---

[102] Section 1.1.4.
[103] The German term for the operation is *Rechtsfortbildung*: K. Larenz and C. W. Canaris, *Methodenlehre der Rechtswissenschaft*, 3rd edn (Berlin: Springer, 1996), pp. 187–90.

The ILC's deference to the 1969 Vienna Convention in the project on treaties[104] was partly explained by the practical concern of ensuring that the outcome of the work of the Commission could be applied harmoniously alongside VCLT 1969.[105] Pursuant to Article 3(c) VCLT 1969, the Convention applies as between States even if other subjects of international law are party to the treaty in question. In the Commission's opinion, that would preclude 'any marked discrepancy between the rules applicable respectively to treaties between States and to treaties to which international organizations are parties'.[106] But Special Rapporteur Reuter also provided a more substantive justification for the Commission's approach: the 'general principle of consensualism, which constitutes the basis of any treaty commitment and entails the legal equality of the parties'.[107] According to Reuter:

> since the Vienna Convention [is] based on the principle of consensus, international organizations in general should, with very rare exceptions, be assimilated to States ... [T]he same rules [hold] good for treaties between States only, between international organizations only, and between States and international organizations.[108]

Invoking the 'principle of consensualism' that applies to States does not explain, however, why consensualism must be extended to international organizations, that is, why international organizations are analogous to States for the purpose of concluding treaties. Yet, recourse to that principle suggests that the Commission purported to anchor its methodology in some form of systemic reasoning. It should be noted, in this connection, that the argumentative burden placed on the Commission was eased by the fact that practice at the time showed that international organizations concluded agreements relying on rules and procedures that did not differ from those codified in VCLT 1969. That the 1969 Convention should serve as a starting point for the project was thus a position

---

[104] Special Rapporteur Paul Reuter has gone as far as to refer to VCLT 1969 as a 'miraculous instrument' in the debates in the ILC: YILC 1973/I, p. 209, para. 10.

[105] A notable exception being Rosenne: YILC 1971/I, p. 202, para. 17 (noting that it would not be 'appropriate to take the articles of [VCLT 1969] as the starting point, for that would imply a mechanical approach and overlook the nature of things ... because of the material difference in the nature of the consent of an international organization in comparison with the consent of a State to be bound by a treaty').

[106] YILC 1971/II, part two, p. 188, para. 12.

[107] YILC 1981/I, pp. 45–46, para. 5.

[108] YILC 1978/I, p. 185, para. 25.

that members of the Commission and other stakeholders were prepared to accept.

In contrast, although the Commission extended most rules found in the ARS to international organizations, it made an effort to distance itself from systemic reasoning, and from the analogical method in particular. While the Commission did allude to the 'quality' of its previous work on State responsibility and the need to keep 'some coherence' in the law of international responsibility,[109] it sought to downplay the relevance of the ARS for the project, observing that VCLT 1969 was a codification convention (which presumably meant that it enjoyed greater authority than a non-binding set of articles) and that 'the issues that [were] specific to the responsibility of international organizations [were] more numerous than with regard to treaties'.[110] The Commission thus rejected the notion that there was a presumption of similarity between the law of State responsibility and the law of responsibility of international organizations:

> While the [ARIO] are in many respects similar to the articles on State responsibility, they represent an autonomous text. Each issue has been considered from the specific perspective of the responsibility of international organizations ... When in the study of the responsibility of international organizations the conclusion is reached than an identical or similar solution to the one expressed in the articles on State responsibility should apply with respect to international organizations, this is based on appropriate reasons and not on a general presumption that the same principles apply.[111]

But a presumption of similarity is precisely what the Commission followed in reality. Instead of offering 'appropriate reasons', the commentary to the ARIO largely justifies extending rules from the ARS on the ground that there would be 'little' or 'no' reason to distinguish between States and international organizations with respect to the rule or issue concerned.[112] This is a fallacy: logically, the absence of a reason

---

[109] YILC 2002/II, part two, p. 94, para. 474. The Commission thus referred to the ARS as a 'source of inspiration'.

[110] Ibid. Here the Commission was attempting to affirm the autonomy of the project by distancing itself from the criticism that the exercise culminating in VCLT 1986 had been unnecessary given the great resemblance that it bears to VCLT 1969.

[111] General commentary, YILC 2011/II, part two, p. 46, para. 4.

[112] See YILC 2011/II, part two, commentaries to art. 3 (p. 52, para. 1); art. 11 (p. 64); art. 12 (p. 65); art. 13 (p. 65); chapter IV of Part II (p. 65, para. 1); art. 14 (p. 66, para. 1); art. 15 (p. 67, para. 1); chapter V of Part I (p. 70, para. 2); art. 23 (p. 73, para. 2); art. 24 (p. 74,

to differentiate cannot constitute a reason to assimilate, unless a presumption in favour of assimilation exists, such as that which a well-drawn analogy could provide. On occasion, the commentary suggests that rules in the ARS contain principles of general application,[113] or that the applicability of certain rules should not depend on the 'nature' of the subject concerned,[114] but those are points that the Commission did not pursue further. In fairness, Special Rapporteur Gaja, in his Second Report, pointed to the need for 'coherency in the Commission's work', which would require that changes to the rules adopted for States needed to 'find justification in differences concerning the relevant practice or objective distinctions in nature' between the two categories of legal subjects.[115] Some members of the Commission similarly viewed the rules on State responsibility as expression of 'general principles of international law' that would apply to international organizations.[116] But these underdeveloped hints at systemic reasoning stand in contradiction with the Commission's avowed position not to follow a general presumption that States and international organizations are analogous.

Ultimately, the Commission made the following disclaimer in the General Commentary to the ARIO:

> The fact that several of the present draft articles are based on limited practice moves the border between codification and progressive development in the direction of the latter. It may occur that a provision in the articles on State responsibility could be regarded as representing codification, while the corresponding provision on the responsibility of international organizations is more in the nature of progressive development. In other words, the provisions of the present draft articles do not

---

para. 2); art. 26 (p. 75, para. 3); art. 27 (p. 76, para. 3); art. 28 (p. 76); art. 29 (p. 76, para. 4); art. 35 (p. 79, para. 2); art. 39 (p. 81, para. 1); art. 44 (p. 138, para. 1); art. 49 (p. 89, para. 6); art. 51 (p. 92, para. 1); art. 58 (p. 97, para. 3); and art. 59 (p. 98, para. 3).

[113] YILC 2011/II, part two, commentaries to art. 4 (p. 81, para. 1) and to chapter III of Part Two (p. 63, para. 3).

[114] YILC 2011/II, part two, commentaries to art. 14 (p. 66, para. 1) (stating that responsibility for aiding and assisting 'does not depend on the nature and character of the entities concerned') and to art. 55 (p. 95, para. 1) (affirming that the conditions for the taking of countermeasures are not 'related to the nature of the targeted entity'). In one case – that of attribution of conduct acknowledged and adopted by an IO as its own – replicating the corresponding rule in the ARS was justified by reference to the absence of policy reasons militating against that: see commentary to art. 9, p. 62, para. 5).

[115] Gaja (Second Report), YILC 2004/II, part one, p. 4, para. 5.

[116] Nolte, A.CN.4./SR.3081 (2011), p. 9; Pellet, A.CN.4./SR.3082 (2011), p. 4 (referring to 'one unequivocal notion of responsibility in international law'); Vázquez-Bermúdez, ibid., p. 10.

necessarily yet have the same authority as the corresponding provisions
on State responsibility.[117]

It is regrettable that instead of offering a more robust justification for
relying on the ARS the Commission decided to throw away the cham-
pagne with the cork, accepting without more the criticism that the ARIO
is backed up by limited practice.[118] If, as argued, analogical reasoning
provides a technique for the systemic codification of international law,
and if the analogy between States and international organizations is
sound, the ARIO can claim much greater authority than the General
Commentary suggests. As things are, the ARIO runs the risk of being
unfairly discarded as mere 'progressive development', thus having its
potential to contribute to the elucidation of the law of international
organizations diminished.

1.3.3   The Ripeness Objection

There are a number of reasons that may explain the ILC's reluctance to
embrace analogical reasoning as a method in its projects on treaties and
responsibility. An ostensible reliance on analogy could have slowed
down – and even undermined – the project by inviting greater methodological and substantive scrutiny. For an expert commission managing the
expectations of States, international organizations and members of the
legal profession, playing to shared intuitions such as the practical need to
keep the ARS and the ARIO in line with each other may look like a more
effective strategy to get the job done than presenting an elaborate theoretical framework that could have failed to resonate and attract
acceptance.

Whether such strategic reasons are defensible is a matter for debate,
but a more substantive objection to the use of analogical reasoning in

---

[117] General commentary, YILC 2011/II, part two, pp. 46–47, para. 5.

[118] E.g., Xue, YILC 2004/I, p. 87, para. 11; Economides, YILC 2006/I, pp. 75–76, para. 22;
Rodríguez Cedeño, ibid., p. 76, para. 24. A number of IOs commenting on the articles
suggested that because of the lack of 'actual practice', provisions of the ARIO should be
viewed as exercises in progressive development. See e.g., IMF, A/CN.4/637 (2011), p. 10;
OECD, ibid., p. 13; World Bank, ibid., p. 14. The ILO suggested that '[i]f the idea is that
the draft articles codify existing customary law, they would need to rely on both general
practice and *opinio juris*', but it was 'difficult to detect any general practice' and 'the
views of international organizations reflect not only the lack of *opinio juris* but rather a
clear opposition to the existence of any customary law in the field except for a very
narrow set of norms'; ibid., p. 15.

codification and progressive development needs to be addressed here. If analogy is used as a general method rather than to fill the odd gap, this is because practice and precedent on the topic being codified are relatively limited. It could then be argued that that topic is not ripe for codification, in which case it should not have been taken on by the codifying entity in the first place.

The ILC Statute provides little guidance on this matter. Article 18 simply directs the Commission to 'survey the whole field of international law with a view to selecting topics for codification'. In its first decades, the Commission relied on surveys of international law prepared by the UN Secretariat,[119] but as the list of 'classical topics' became shorter, a Working Group was established to discuss the Commission's long-term programme of work. This Working Group has identified the following criteria for selecting a topic:

> (a) The topic should reflect the needs of States in respect to the progressive development and codification of international law;
> (b) The topic should be sufficiently advanced in stage in terms of State practice to permit progressive development and codification;
> (c) The topic is concrete and feasible for progressive development and codification.[120]

In 2000, on the recommendation of a syllabus drafted by Alain Pellet, the Working Group suggested adding the topic of responsibility of international organizations to the Commission's long-term programme of work. Pellet pointed to the 'sufficiently advanced in stage in terms of State practice, which is not well known, but now quite abundant'.[121] However, some commentators have since disagreed with this assessment, arguing that the topic did not fulfil the criteria for codification, and expressing scepticism as to the feasibility and relevance of the ARIO as drafted by the Commission.[122]

---

[119] Notably the survey prepared by Sir Hersch Lauterpacht: United Nations, *Survey of international law in relation to the work of codification of the International Law Commission, Memorandum submitted by the Secretary-General*, A/CN.4/1/Rev.1 (1949).

[120] YILC 1997/II, part two, p. 72, para. 238.

[121] YILC 2002/II, part two, p. 136.

[122] J. Wouters and J. Odermatt, 'Are all international organizations created equal?' (2012) 9 IOLR 7, 8–11; and V.J. Proulx, 'An uneasy transition? Linkages between the law of State responsibility and the law governing the responsibility of international organizations' in Ragazzi, *The Responsibility of International Organizations*, p. 114. Likewise, Hafner argued that 'the scarce practice on the responsibility of IOs, upon closer scrutiny, remains inconclusive and overly general so that the requirement of concreteness must be

Indeed, one might ask, should the Commission have waited for clearer patterns in practice to emerge before embarking on the task of codifying and progressively developing the law governing the responsibility of international organizations? This is a normative question involving a judgement as to the appropriateness and desirability of a codification of the subject matter at stake. The question can be posed at two levels. At the theoretical level, the decision whether or not to embark on a codification project depends on the view one takes as to the value of codified law. While codifications contribute to reducing uncertainty in the law, they can forestall its development in desirable directions.[123] At the practical level, the decision depends on the perceived usefulness of pursuing the codification of the topic in question. Two factors would appear to be relevant in guiding an institution such as the ILC in reaching a decision.

First, there is the position of the main stakeholders, in particular States: whether it is in their interest to have a project carried out at any particular point in time. In the case of the codification on the law of treaties of international organizations, the ripeness objection was not raised because there was wide consensus on the desirability of considering the topic in the immediate aftermath of the 1968–1969 Vienna Conference on the Law of Treaties. The ILC had previously considered including international organizations in the scope of the text ultimately adopted in the form of VCLT 1969,[124] but decided against this on the assumption that 'special characteristics' of international organizations, which merited further study, might affect the applicability of the general

denied': G. Hafner, 'Is the topic of responsibility of international organizations ripe for codification? Some critical remarks' in U. Fastenrath and others (eds.), *From Bilateralism to Community Interest* (Oxford: Oxford University Press, 2011), p. 704. But it should be noted that underlying all these criticisms is a scepticism as to the plausibility of the analogy between States and IOs: none of these commentators elaborate much on the use of analogy as a methodology for codification.

[123] E.g., S. Villalpando, 'Codification light: a new trend in the codification of international law at the United Nations' (2013) VIII *Brazilian Yearbook of International Law* 117, 126–27. Also, Proulx, 'An uneasy transition?', 115 (remarking that 'codification initiatives may impede genuine and forward-looking, policy-driven advances in the realm of the responsibility of international organizations').

[124] Indeed, all of the Special Rapporteurs appointed by the Commission had suggested at one stage or another that this be done: C. Brölmann, *The Institutional Veil in Public International Law: International Organizations and the Law of Treaties* (Oxford: Hart, 2005), pp. 144–65.

rules of the law of treaties to them.[125] For similar reasons, an amendment proposed at the 1968–1969 Vienna Conference to enlarge the scope of VCLT 1969 to include agreements concluded between States and 'other subjects of international law' was withdrawn.[126] But States taking part in the Conference adopted a resolution recognising the 'the importance of the question of treaties concluded between States and international organizations or between two or more international organizations' and recommending that the UNGA refer the topic to the ILC.[127] In contrast, it has been suggested that 'there never seemed to be a strong desire from states themselves' for the topic of responsibility of international organizations to be taken up by the ILC.[128] But neither has there been any serious objection on the part of States to the Commission's endeavour.[129] On the contrary, the Commission secured from the UNGA an express endorsement to begin work on the topic.[130]

Second, as the Working Group established to discuss the ILC's long-term programme of work has noted, 'the Commission should not restrict itself to traditional topics, but could also consider those that reflect new developments in international law and pressing concerns of the international community as a whole'.[131] In the case of responsibility of international organizations, the normative concern militating in favour of codification and progressive development is the need to promote the accountability of international organizations for breaches of international law. Special Rapporteur Gaja argued that it was 'necessary to have a system in place, a set of general rules, even though practice might not be extensive', and described the elaboration of such rules as 'a vital step in

---

[125] Commentary to art. 1, YILC 1966/II, part two, p. 187, para. 2.

[126] See an account of the debate at the Vienna Conference in Brölmann, *The Institutional Veil*, pp. 168–73.

[127] Resolution relating to Article 1 of the Vienna Convention on the Law of Treaties, UNCLT 1968–69 (Documents of the Conference), p. 285.

[128] Wouters and Odermatt, 'Are all international organizations created equal?', 19.

[129] See the topical summary of the debates in the Sixth Committee from 2003 to 2012. At the beginning of debate on the topic, '[t]he view was expressed that the topic of the responsibility of international organizations was largely a reflection of the development of international law and the work undertaken by the Commission was an absolute necessity for that development'; A/CN.4/537 (2003), p. 6, para. 6. Towards the end, '[t]he importance of the adoption of a set of rules on the topic as an element of the rule of law at the international level was emphasized, and the method applied by the Commission, taking into account comments made on earlier versions of the draft, was welcomed': A/CN.4/620/Add.1 (2009), p. 2, para. 1.

[130] UNGA Res. 56/82 (2002) ('requesting' the ILC to begin work on the topic).

[131] YILC 1997/II, part two, p. 72, para. 238.

the development of the international legal order'.[132] A related consideration is whether practice on the topic being assessed is likely to build up in the foreseeable future. In the case of international organizations, where third-party dispute settlement remains rare,[133] would it have been worth it for the Commission to sit and wait for practice that was probably not forthcoming instead of attempting to catalyse such practice? If, as Special Rapporteur Gaja noted, '[t]he very existence of the current articles [has] furthered the development of practice relating to the responsibility of international organizations',[134] the project may already be regarded as a success from a normative point of view.

Therefore, while the ripeness objection can provide a reason not to embark on codification projects when practice is still incipient, it can be defeated when the project is in the interest of the relevant stakeholders and when there are strong normative reasons militating in favour of carrying it out. If, as in the case of the ARIO, systemic reasoning provides a general method for dealing with the uncertainty resulting from lack of practice, the project will have a considerable potential to contribute to the consolidation and development of the law.

1.4 Concluding Remarks

Analogical reasoning belongs to the category of arguments that justify decisions in 'hard cases', when the law is unclear or when novel factual circumstances arise which are not yet directly regulated by existing law. An analogy is persuasive when it is seen as an externalization of the requirement to treat like cases alike, and this perception is deeply connected with our adherence to prevailing conceptions of the rule of law that require us to approach and apply law as if it constituted a purposeful system. This is also true for international law, which constitutes a system in the sense that, for all its institutional and normative peculiarities, it shares with municipal law the attribute of systematicity.

It is thus not surprising that analogical reasoning should feature not only in international adjudication, but also in the codification and progressive development of international law. Analogical reasoning is a technique that fits well within the mandate of entities such as the ILC

---

[132] Gaja, A.CN.4/SR.3080 (2011) 5–6.
[133] General commentary, YILC 2011/II, part two, p. 46, para. 5.
[134] A.CN.4/SR.3080 (2011) 6.

because it provides a systemic method for dealing with uncertainty in international practice and precedent.

Systemic thinking, however, has important limits and its authoritativeness cannot be measured in the abstract. Rather, it has to be demonstrated on a case-by-case basis through a convincing explanation of why a situation is 'relevantly similar' to another. International law and domestic law do not differ in this respect. But for the international lawyer, who operates in a system with no centralised decision-making authorities, the stakes are often higher.

2

The Foundations of the Analogy between States and International Organizations

As evidenced by international adjudication and codification projects, analogical reasoning is a technique to which the legal profession can turn – and has indeed turned – to make propositions about the content of international law in situations of uncertainty. Because analogies are particularised exercises based on a judgement of 'relevant similarity' between the situation covered by a norm and the situation to which that norm will be extended, the relevance of analogical reasoning in any given case depends on the plausibility of the proposed analogy in the context of the legal tradition where it is drawn. Therefore, to appraise the relevance of the analogy between States and international organizations in the development of the law of international organization, it is necessary to consider how convincing that analogy is in contemporary international law. This entails investigating in what sense States and international organizations may be considered as 'relevantly similar', and addressing arguments militating against assimilation.

This chapter begins the work by looking into the theoretical foundations of the analogy between States and international organizations *qua* subjects of international law. For the analogy to be plausible, two conditions must be satisfied. First, international law has to admit of international organizations as a general category of entities to which a common set of rights, obligations and capacities can apply, as is the case with States. This requires seeing them as international legal subjects proper – as opposed to mere treaty transactions between their member States – and identifying the unifying principle that brings a wide range of existing institutions within the same category. Second, there must be attributes that all the entities falling under that general category share and which can be persuasively compared with attributes shared by the category formed by States. In other words, the attributes of the status of international organizations under international law must be relevantly similar to the attributes of statehood in a way that justifies extending rules from one category to the other.

In discussing these theoretical assumptions in the light of relevant practice and precedent, the chapter revisits debates that have taken place within the International Law Commission with respect to the definition, legal personality and capacities of international organizations, as those provide an illustration of the evolution in thinking on the status of international organizations under international law. The aim is to offer a fresh perspective on the elusive position that these institutions occupy in the international legal system. While many commentators limit themselves to registering the controversy surrounding the status of international organizations, one cannot investigate the applicability of general international law to them without taking a position on the 'existential question' of what they are from a legal point of view. Doing that is all the more important at a time when international organizations are increasingly active in the making and breaking of international law.

2.1   International Organizations as a Category of International Legal Subjects

From the perspective of general international law, States are viewed as forming a category of sovereign entities enjoying equal rights, obligations and capacities.[1] While they may present striking differences in size, resources and political power – one has only to compare China with Vanuatu to press the point – sovereignty operates as a unifying principle that, by conferring legal equality upon territorial communities under government, lays the foundations of the international legal system as we know it.[2] Evidently, the legal position of no two individual States will be identical in practice, insofar as each will have contracted myriad international obligations limiting or enhancing the rights and duties to which it was entitled under general international law. But because the capacity to be bound by international agreements is viewed as an attribute of sovereignty,[3] the specific obligations to which States consent do not alter the original position as a matter of principle.[4]

---

[1] E.g., art. 2(1) UN Charter.

[2] On sovereignty as a structural principle, B. Kingsbury, 'Sovereignty and inequality' (1998) 9 EJIL 599. See also J. Crawford, 'Sovereignty as a legal value' in J. Crawford and M. Koskenniemi (eds.), Cambridge Companion of International Law (Cambridge: Cambridge, 2012), pp. 117–19.

[3] The SS Wimbledon, PCIJ Ser. A No. 1 (1923), p. 25.

[4] The series of cases in which the German Constitutional Court stressed the constitutional limits of integration attests to this proposition: 'the powers [to transfer competences to the

The position of international organizations in general international law is much less well defined. To begin with, no principle equivalent to that of sovereign equality has been articulated for international organizations.[5] While States proclaim their equality before the law,[6] it does not appear to be in their interest to confer formally any similar status to international organizations. As a consequence, it is a motif in academic work and political discourse that international organizations are not only different from States, but also 'fundamentally unequal' inter se. In the words of Paul Reuter:

> An intergovernmental organization ... is based on a treaty between States; each intergovernmental organization is shaped individually by the will of its founders, and subsequently of its members. This is one of the points on which the clearest distinction can be made between States and international organizations. States can *all*, without any exception, perform the same legal acts: *a sovereign equality* prevails among them. Organizations are, on the contrary, fundamentally unequal: the structure and powers of each organization are entirely dominated by its constituent instrument, which itself has been drawn up essentially with a view to serving functions which vary from one organization to another.[7]

Reuter's reference to the dominating influence of constituent instruments points to an important factor: whether one accepts the existence of a unifying principle that brings international organizations under the same category depends on the view one takes as to the status of their 'internal law'. One of the reasons why the view that each international organization is unique is widespread is that constituent instruments and other institutional rules are 'visible' to the international lawyer in a way that the domestic law of States is not.[8] When one looks into the legal position of States in international law, the content of domestic law is seldom taken into consideration, even though domestic law often imposes crucial

EU] are granted under the condition that the sovereign statehood of a constitutional state is maintained on the basis of an integration programme according to the principle of conferral and respecting the Member States' constitutional identity ... ': BVerfG, Judgment of the Second Senate of 30 June 2009 [2009] 2 BvE 2/08, paras. 226 and 228.

[5] G. Verdirame, *The UN and Human Rights: Who Guards the Guardians?* (Cambridge: Cambridge University Press, 2011), pp. 65–66.

[6] E.g., UNGA Res. 2625/XXV (1970), the 'Friendly Relations Declaration', adopted without a vote.

[7] Reuter (Third Report), YILC 1974/II, part one, p. 146, para. 5.

[8] Or, to quote Brölmann, 'transparent': C. Brölmann, *The Institutional Veil in Public International Law: International Organizations and the Law of Treaties* (Oxford: Hart, 2005), pp. 29–33.

limitations on their capacity to act in their international relations.[9] In contrast, the activities of international organizations on the international plane tend to be assessed with regard to the powers and capacities with which they were entrusted. And it is when one looks into that 'internal law' that differences become most apparent: 'open organizations' aspiring to universal membership are contrasted with 'closed organizations' of a regional character; organizations performing political functions are distinguished from organizations dealing with technical questions; organizations possessing extensive (sometimes 'supranational') powers seem different from those which mostly serve as forums for States to debate topics on the international agenda.[10]

But does this mean that international organizations are indeed unequal in the eyes of general international law? While the theme of inequality recurs, the legal profession appears to share the intuition that international organizations do form a category of 'subjects of international law' to which some common rules and principles apply.[11] I suggest that these conflicting views of international organizations as fundamentally different and yet belonging to a single category arise from a tension between two competing explanations of the position that international organizations occupy in the international legal system. Those will be referred to here as the 'treaty conception' – according to which international organizations are no more than treaty transactions between States – and the 'subject conception' – according to which international organizations are legal persons under a rule of general international law. The present analysis rethinks and reorients two recurring debates in the field. The first revolves around the question of whether international organizations have 'objective personality', in the sense that they enjoy a legal existence that has to be acknowledged by

---

[9] See F. Seyersted, *Common Law of International Organizations* (Leiden: Nijhoff, 2008), p. 49 and J. Klabbers, *An Introduction to International Institutional Law*, 2nd edn (Cambridge: Cambridge University Press, 2009), p. 42.

[10] See in general M. Virally, 'Definition and classification of international organizations: a legal approach' in G. Abi-Saab (ed.), *The Concept of International Organization* (Paris: Unesco, 1981), pp. 56–64 and H. Schermers and N. Blokker, *International Institutional Law: Unity within Diversity*, 5th edn (Leiden: Nijhoff, 2011), pp. 50–59.

[11] P. Sands and P. Klein (eds.), *Bowett's Law of International Institutions*, 6th edn (London: Sweet & Maxwell, 2009), p. 16 (but insisting that '[e]ach organization is unique', at 23). Klabbers notes that the leading textbooks synthetizing the rules of different IOs into general headings appear to intuit that 'there is something holding the discipline together', although '[w]hat that something is … remains to be spelled out': J. Klabbers, 'The Paradox of international institutional law' (2008) 5 IOLR 151, 164.

third parties. The second concerns the source of their separate personality, that is, whether legal personality originates directly, as a matter of treaty law, from the will of the members, or whether it is bestowed upon the organization by a rule of general international law that is triggered when the members set up the organization.[12]

2.1.1   Two Conceptions of the Status of International Organizations

Given that international organizations are typically created by international agreements concluded by their members, their legal status under international law can be explained by reference to the law of treaties. If international organizations are conceived as treaty transactions, whether an organization constitutes an entity with separate legal personality depends solely on the intention of the members, and, crucially, its existence as a body corporate will not affect the position of third parties under the *pacta tertiis nec nocent nec prosunt* principle. This cardinal principle of the law of treaties, as expressed in Article 34 of VCLT 1969, prescribes that '[a] treaty does not create either obligations or rights for a third State without its consent'. International organizations cannot thus be said to enjoy 'objective personality': were this the case, the treaties concluded to establish them would affect the position of third States.[13] That said, an international organization would be capable of

---

[12] This is a debate, as Klabbers would put it, between the 'will theory' and the 'objective theory' of international legal personality: J. Klabbers, 'Presumptive personality: the European Union in international law' in M. Koskenniemi (ed.), *International Law Aspects of the European Union* (The Hague: Kluwer, 1998), pp. 234–38; 240–42. See also Schermers and Blokker, *International Institutional Law*, pp. 988–90.

[13] Authors ascribing to this position include: H. J. Hahn, 'Euratom: The Conception of an International Personality' (1958) 71 HLR 1001, 1048–50; I. Seidl-Hoheverden, *Corporations in and under International Law* (Cambridge: Grotius, 1987), pp. 86–88; K. Schmalenbach, 'International organizations or institutions, general aspects' (2006) *Max-Planck Encyclopedia of Public International Law*, paras. 23–25; and M. Mendelson, 'The definition of "international organization" in the international law commission's current project on the responsibility of international organizations' in M. Ragazzi (ed.), *International Responsibility Today* (Leiden: Martinus Nijhoff, 2005), pp. 384–89. Some authors, on the basis of the *Reparation* advisory opinion, distinguish between universal and regional organizations: G. Hafner, 'Is the topic of responsibility of international organizations ripe for codification? some critical remarks' in Fastenrath and others (eds.), *From Bilateralism to Community Interest* (Oxford: Oxford University Press, 2011), pp. 707–12; and Schermers and Blokker, *International Institutional Law*, 990–91. See also, though less unequivocally, H. Mosler, 'Réflexions sur la personnalité juridique en droit international public' in Baugniet (ed.), *Mélanges Offerts à Henri Rolin*

maintaining relations with third parties whenever accorded *recognition*, in which case the treaty that it embodies would become a 'reality' for the third parties choosing to interact with it.[14]

In the alternative, international organizations can be conceptualised as forming a category of legal persons under general international law to which certain rights, duties and capacities accrue. This 'subject conception' can be formulated in two propositions. First, the emergence of international organizations has brought about a structural change to the international legal system, which now comprises a right for States (and perhaps other entities) to establish corporate bodies under general international law with certain *erga omnes* effects.[15] International law thus contains, as is common in domestic legal systems, a rule of incorporation for international organizations.[16] It follows that the legal personality of international organizations is 'objective' in the sense that no formal recognition on the part of third parties is necessary for an organization to participate in international relations.

Second, the internal law of an international organization is analytically separate from international law, and cannot be taken to govern the relations between the organization and third parties. While the fact that international organizations are established by treaty means that their internal law is international in origin, the treaty performs a constitutional role by laying down a discrete legal system governing the relations between international organizations and their members on the institutional plane.[17] As Hans Kelsen has explained, the constituent rules of a

(Paris: Pedone, 1964), pp. 249–50 and C. Chinkin, *Third Parties in International Law* (Oxford: Oxford University Press, 1993), pp. 89–90.

[14] See the works cited in footnote 13. In the words of Seidl-Hohenveldern, '[a]lthough a third State will generally be able to disregard the establishment of an organization as *res inter alios acta* it cannot do so if it recognizes the legal personality of the organization concerned': Seidl-Hohenveldern, *Corporations*, p. 90.

[15] E.g., Seyersted, *Common Law*, p. 386: '[o]nce an organization or a State has been established, no matter how, it is *ipso facto* a general subject of international law'. See also the works referred in the footnotes to Section 2.1.1.2.

[16] Rosalyn Higgins favours a domestic law analogy in the following terms: 'There exist throughout the world associations and bodies that a claimant is not called upon to "recognise" ... The fact that international organizations are established by treaty rather than by, e.g., articles of association, does not change the position and introduces no relevant element of *res inter alios acta*': R. Higgins, 'Preliminary exposé' (1995) 66-I *Annuaire de l'Institut de droit international* 276.

[17] C. Ahlborn, 'The rules of international organizations and the law of international responsibility' (2012) 8 IOLR 397, 413. In the words of the ICJ, constituent instruments are 'treaties of a particular type' that 'create new subjects of law endowed with a certain

juridical person always constitute a 'partial legal order' which is to a certain extent separate from – albeit in a relationship with – the 'total legal order' under which that juridical person is established.[18]

2.1.1.1 The Two Conceptions in the Work of the ILC

Both the 'treaty conception' and the 'subject conception' offer relatively plausible theoretical explanations of the status of international organization under international law, and have been espoused by commentators and practitioners at different points in time. The debates at the ILC in the projects on the law of international organizations provide an illuminating example of the evolution in thinking on this issue. While the Commission made a conscious effort to stay clear of controversies relating to the status of international organizations,[19] it could not have embarked on the codification of the law of treaties and the law of responsibility without adopting a working hypothesis about what those organizations are. That was particularly so when the Commission tackled questions relating to their capacity to make treaties and to be held internationally responsible.

The capacity of international organizations to conclude treaties was possibly the most controversial conceptual question arising in the ILC's work on the law of treaties in the 1970s. Article 6 VCLT 1969 provides that '[e]very State possesses capacity to conclude treaties'. In considering whether that rule should be extended to international organizations, the question arose of whether the treaty-making capacity of an international organization stemmed from general international law (which would be in line with the 'subject conception') or from its internal law (which would be in line with the 'treaty conception'). The Commission was divided between those advocating the adoption of a provision affirming the 'inherent right' of international organizations to conclude treaties, those suggesting that any such capacity would fall short of an 'inherent right',

---

autonomy, to which the parties entrust the task of realizing common goals': *Legality of the Use of Nuclear Weapons in Armed Conflict* (Advisory Opinion) [1996] ICJ Rep 66, para 19.

[18] H. Kelsen, *General Theory of Law and State* (Cambridge: Harvard University Press, 1945), pp. 99–100. Kelsen further explains that '[t]he relation between the total legal order constituting the State, the so-called law of the State or national legal order, and the juristic person of a corporation is the relation between two legal orders, a total and a partial legal order, between the law of the State and the by-laws of the corporation' (at 100). This is further discussed in Chapter 6.2.1.

[19] As the commentary to art. 2 stated, 'the main purpose of the present draft is to regulate, not the status of international organizations, but the regime of treaties to which one or more international organizations are parties': YILC 1982/II, part two, p. 20, para. 21.

and those wishing the Commission to refrain from taking a position on the matter.[20] The Commission settled for a compromise solution. It drafted a provision, later adopted as Article 6 VCLT 1986, that prescribes that '[t]he capacity of an international organization to conclude treaties is governed by the relevant rules of that organization', but clarified in the commentary that this formulation 'should in no way be regarded as having the purpose or effect of deciding the question of the status of international organizations in international law'.[21]

The record suggests that this Salomonic approach, rather than an accurate synthesis of the opinions voiced during the debate, was a result of the Special Rapporteur's influence. Paul Reuter himself had proposed an alternative draft according to which '[t]he extent of the capacity of international organizations to conclude treaties, a capacity acknowledged in principle by international law, is determined by the relevant rules of each organization'.[22] Several members expressed their support for the alternative draft and for recognising, one way or another, a general capacity to conclude treaties under international law.[23] While explaining that he would 'personally' favour the alternative formulation, Reuter thought that it was his role as Special Rapporteur to push for the original draft because it 'respected simultaneously the will of States, which satisfied those who considered that will the only source of international law, the social reality, which satisfied those who emphasized that aspect of the problem, and the autonomy of international organizations, which feared restriction of their creative power'.[24]

---

[20] Reuter, YILC 1973/I, p. 209, paras. 13–15. Reuter himself was at first opposed to the idea of dealing with the question of legal capacity, but changed his mind in the light of the lively debate that the issue prompted within the Commission. Ibid., para. 16.

[21] Commentary to art. 6, YILC 1982/II, part two, p. 24, para. 2.

[22] Reuter (Third Report), YILC 1974/II, part one, p. 150, para. 20.

[23] See the support expressed by Tammes, YILC 1974/I, p. 136, para. 56; Hambro, ibid., p. 145, para. 4; Ramangasoavina, ibid., p. 146, para 14; El-Erian, ibid., p. 148, para. 33, and the interventions of Sette-Câmara, YILC 1974/I, p. 202, para. 38; Martínez-Moreno, ibid., p. 143, para. 9; Ushakov, ibid. p. 135, para. 39; and Calle y Calle, ibid. p. 137, para. 58. Members disagreeing with the proposition include Yasseen, ibid., p. 147, para. 21 and Bilge, ibid., p. 148, para. 45.

[24] YILC 1974/I, p. 164, para. 70. Curiously, the four Special Rapporteurs on the law of treaties between States would have been prepared to go further than Reuter as regards the treaty-making capacity of IOs. James Brierly proposed a provision according to which '[a]ll States and international organizations have capacity to make treaties, but the capacity of some States or organizations to enter into certain treaties may be limited': Brierly (First Report), YILC 1950/II, p. 230. Hersch Lauterpacht likewise suggested that treaty-making capacity was '[u]ndoubtedly, the consequence of [IOs'] international

The Special Rapporteur's measured but contradictory position reflected his own ambivalence as to the legal status of international organizations under international law. In an apparent nod to the 'subject conception', Reuter conceded the existence of 'a general rule of public international law which would be permissive in character and would make this particular effect of constituent instruments [i.e., treaty-making] possible'.[25] He also said that 'it followed clearly from the draft articles that an international organization could be a subject of international law, which almost necessarily implied that it participated in conventional acts'.[26] But he was hesitant to accept that such a 'general rule of international law' had effected a 'radical – and to some extent a structural – change in the international community'.[27] Rather, he reverted to the 'treaty conception' by positing that 'the general principle of public international law which authorizes the attribution of capacity to international organizations is well known: it is the principle *pacta sunt servanda*', for '[t]he capacity of international organizations to conclude treaties (like all their other capacities) is merely the result of the creative power of treaties embodied in the constituent instrument'.[28] Reuter likewise contended that 'the existence of [an international organization] with respect to third States [would] depend on its recognition by them and is thus also derived from the rule *pacta sunt servanda*'.[29] For him, the acknowledgment of a priori capacity to conclude treaties

personality', while noting that, 'personality [not being] coterminous, in kind and extent, with that of States', there appeared to be a 'general limitation' to what was required by the purposes and functions of IOs: Lauterpacht (First Report), YILC 1953/II, p. 141. On his part, Gerald Fitzmaurice suggested defining a treaty as an 'international agreement ... made between entities both or all of which are subjects of international law possessed of international personality and treaty-making capacity', and adding a provision making the draft 'applicable, *mutatis mutandis*, to international organizations': Fitzmaurice (First Report), YILC 1956/II, p. 107. Finally, Humphrey Waldock, perhaps a bit more ambiguously, proposed to include 'other subjects of international law invested with such capacity by treaty or by custom' (YILC 1962/II 35, Art. 3, *chapeau*), with the specification that '[i]nternational capacity to become a party to treaties is also possessed by international organizations ... and to the extent that, such treaty-making capacity is expressly created, or necessarily implied, in the instrument or instruments prescribing the constitution and functions of the organization and entity in question' (ibid., p. 36).
[25] Reuter (Third Report), YILC 1974/II, part one, p. 150, para. 20.
[26] YILC 1974/I, p. 164, para. 68.
[27] Reuter (Third Report), YILC 1974/II, part one, p. 150, para. 20.
[28] Ibid., para. 21.
[29] Reuter (Second Report), YILC 1973/II, p. 82, para. 41.

would not prejudge 'questions relating to the *recognition* of that capacity by other subjects of international law'.[30]

It thus seems that it was the 'treaty conception' that carried the day in the ILC of the 1970s. Neither the Commission nor its Special Rapporteur was ready to conceive international organizations as more than treaty transactions between States, body corporates originating from the *pacta sunt servanda* principle, which, in the absence of recognition, existed only vis-à-vis their members.

The codification of the law of responsibility of international organizations followed a different path. When the issue arose, the Commission's approach to the status of international organization under international law was consistent with the 'subject conception'. Signs of a shift from the 'treaty conception' to the 'subject conception' were already discernible a decade earlier, when the *Institut de Droit international* adopted a resolution on 'The Legal Consequences for Member States of the Non-fulfilment by International Organizations of their Obligations toward Third Parties'.[31] At the *Institut*, Rapporteur Rosalyn Higgins observed that 'the objective existence of an organization on the international plane is not simply a matter of widely shared participation in the founding treaty (as in the case of the UN), but of an objective reality'.[32] Higgins proposed to characterise international legal personality as 'opposable to third parties', and 'not dependent upon any recognition by them'.[33] Though this proposal generated little discussion, two members came in defence of the 'treaty conception': Jean Salmon, who thought it necessary for third States to recognise the international organization lest there be a breach of the *res inter alios acta* principle,[34] and Ibrahim Shihata, who doubted that 'any two States have the power to confer an international legal personality which is opposable to all States as a matter of international law'.[35] It seems that those objections were effective, for the draft considered by the *Institut* in its session of 1995 in Lisbon no longer included a paragraph on objective personality.

---

[30] Reuter (Third Report), YILC 1974/II, part one, p. 150, para. 23. See also Quentin-Baxter, YILC 1974/I, p. 149, para. 48. Contra: Sette-Câmara, YILC 1973/I, p. 202, para. 38. Other than that, there was no specific discussion of the issue of objective personality in the debates within the Commission or at the 1986 Vienna Conference.

[31] See (1995) 66-I *Annuaire de l'Institut de droit international*, pp. 444–53.

[32] Ibid., p. 276 (Preliminary Exposé)

[33] Ibid., p. 465 (Draft Resolution of October 1994).

[34] Ibid., pp. 342–43.

[35] Ibid., p. 445.

The justification offered by the Rapporteur was that 'there had been divergent practice on whether it is necessary at the domestic level for a State to be a party to an international organization, or to declare expressly that it was not, before a third party might be able to bring claims'.[36] But even if the *Institut* did not formally endorse Higgins' original proposal, its treatment of the subject suggests that the view of international organizations as subjects of general international law was gaining traction. A decade later, at the ILC, Special Rapporteur Giorgio Gaja maintained that the 'characterization of an organization as a subject of international law ... appears as a question of fact', and that while 'the view has been expressed that an organization's personality exists with regard to non-member States only if they have recognized it, this assumption cannot be regarded as a logical necessity'.[37] This position was readily accepted.[38] The commentary to the ARIO thus states that 'it would not be necessary to enquire whether the legal personality of an organization has been recognized by an injured State before considering whether the organization may be held internationally responsible according to the present articles.'[39]

2.1.1.2 Weighing the Conceptions

The shift in approach that one sees in the work of the ILC is also reflected in academic commentary. Early authors tended to favour the 'treaty conception', while more contemporary scholarship, with a few exceptions,[40] has embraced the notion of international organizations as subjects of international law which, among other attributes, enjoy objective legal personality.[41]

---

[36] See (1995) 66-II *Annuaire de l'Institut de droit international*, p. 253.

[37] YILC 2003/II, p. 111, para. 19.

[38] Maurice Kamto was the only member who appeared to reserve his position by speaking of the 'functional international personality' of IOs 'regardless of whether that personality was "objective"': YILC 2003/I, p. 23, para. 5. Expressly favouring objective personality: Pellet, YILC 2003/I, p. 9, para. 17; Ojo, YILC 2007/I, p. 169, para. 64; and Vasciannie, YILC 2007/I, p. 137, paras. 6–7.

[39] Commentary to art. 2 ARIO, YILC 2011/II, part two, p. 50, para. 9.

[40] E.g., Haffner, 'Is the topic of responsibility'; Schmalenbach, 'International organizations or institutions'; and Mendelson, 'The definition of "international organization"'.

[41] It is arguably becoming an influential 'textbook position': J. Crawford (ed.), *Brownlie's Principles of Public International Law*, 8th edn (Oxford: Oxford University Press, 2012), p. 171 ('there are good reasons for applying [objective legal personality] to *all* international organizations, and in practice this has occurred'); D. Akande, 'International organizations' in M. Evans (ed.), *International Law*, 4th edn (Oxford: Oxford University Press, 2014), p. 255; and P. Daillier, M. Forteau and A. Pellet, *Droit International Public*,

It is understandable that, faced with a new phenomenon, lawyers are at first inclined to make it fit within existing categories and structures.[42] The law of treaties was a natural starting point for international lawyers of the 1950s and 1960s to adopt in trying to make sense of the arrival of international organizations on the scene. What is attractive about the 'treaty conception' is that it does not require us to postulate that the basic structure of the State-centric international legal system changed with the creation of international organizations. It is also largely compatible with the various actions that international organizations and members take on the institutional plane: States are entitled to regulate their relations with one another by treaty as they please, including by establishing corporate bodies to which they entrust certain goals and accord certain rights, duties and capacities.

The tasks that are given to international organizations, however, oftentimes require organizations to take action outside the institutional framework, that is, to maintain relations with third parties – and, occasionally, their own members – on the international plane. It is here that the 'treaty conception' begins to falter. For one, employing the notion of recognition to explain how a treaty which would otherwise be *res inter alios acta* may become relevant for third States does not sit comfortably with the framework of the law of treaties as codified in VCLT 1969. According to Article 35 VCLT 1969, a treaty may only impose obligations on a third State if this result is intended by the parties and the third State expressly accepts that obligation in writing. Likewise, pursuant to Article 36 a treaty confers rights on a third State if, the parties having also intended this result, 'the third State assents thereto', the difference being that such an assent 'shall be presumed so long as the contrary is not indicated'. Would recognition imply that States 'accept' or 'assent to' the internal law of the organization as embodied in its constituent treaties?

8th edn (Paris: LGDJ, 2009), p. 661. Also, C. F. Amerasinghe, *Principles of the Institutional Law of International Organizations,* 2nd edn (Cambridge: Cambridge University Press, 2005) 91 and – albeit taking a more tentative approach – J. Alvarez, *International Organizations as Law-Makers* (Oxford: Oxford University Press, 2005), p. 139.

[42] That when they do not skirt the new issue altogether. In fact, writers spent decades avoiding the issue of the status of intergovernmental organizations: it was only after World War II that a more concerted effort to engage with the issue could be observed, leading to the emergence of the 'law of international organizations' as a discipline. See the historical survey and argument in G. F. Sinclair, 'Towards a postcolonial genealogy of international organizations law' (2018) 31 *Leiden Journal of International Law* (forthcoming).

Would it somehow render general international law, in particular customary rules, applicable to the relations between the third State and the organization?

Those are difficulties that arise when one attempts to import into the law of treaties a concept that belongs to the law relating to the subjects of international law.[43] In this respect, international law has not always been clear even with regard to States, as evidenced by the debate between the 'declaratory' and 'constitutive' schools of recognition of statehood. Nowadays, there is broad agreement, at least at the level of international legal discourse, that recognition of statehood is declaratory of a pre-existing legal position.[44] However, given the emphasis on State consent by which the international legal system was and remains still characterised, the 'declaratory theory' was not always the dominant position: 'constitutive theories' subordinating the creation of States to recognition by other States were once mainstream. A fundamental problem with the constitutive theories is their relativism, that is, the proposition that States can only exist in a relative way, to the extent that they are recognised by one another.[45] As Crawford suggests, this position is untenable, for '[i]f individual States were free to determine the legal status or consequences of particular situations and to do so definitively, international law would be reduced to a form of imperfect communications, a system for registering the assent or dissent of individual States without any prospect of resolution'.[46] The theoretical debate on the recognition of States suggests

---

[43] As Seyersted puts it, those who deny objective legal personality stretch 'the concept of implied recognition beyond what has hitherto been assumed in respect of States . . . ' and are forced to resort to 'new and wider concepts, such as "acquiescence," "acknowledgment" or "implied consent"', which nonetheless remain 'too restrictive, or imply fictions or both': Seyersted, *Common Law*, p. 390.

[44] E.g., Arbitration Commission Opinion No. 10 (4 July 1992) 92 ILR 206, para 4; Crawford, *Brownlie's Principles of Public International Law*, pp. 144–46. For a nuanced endorsement of the constitutive doctrine: J. Dugard, 'The secession of states and their recognition in the wake' (2013) 375 RdC 9, 36–72.

[45] J. Crawford, *The Creation of States in International Law*, 2nd edn (Oxford: Oxford University Press, 2006), pp. 21–22.

[46] Ibid., p. 20. Also, S Talmon, 'The Constitutive versus the Declaratory Theory of Recognition: *Tertium non Datur?* (2004) 75 BYIL 101, 102–03. Interestingly, Kelsen did not find this notion troubling. To him, '[s]ince we have to acknowledge the relativity of time and space – the general conditions of natural existence – relativity of legal existence is no longer paradoxical': H. Kelsen, 'Recognition in international law: theoretical observations' (1941) 35 AJIL 605, 609. This is premised on a radical view of international law as a decentralised system, which 'does not institute special organs authorized to establish in a legal procedure the existence of concrete facts as determined by the law in order that the

that there is something odd about the idea of 'relative subjects' of a legal order. Because treaties constitute 'parallel universes' of sorts, it is possible to conceptualise international organizations as legal subjects only existing within the confines of their constituent instruments. But whenever organizations start to interact with the outside world, explaining how each 'parallel universe' expands and contracts on an *ad hoc* basis becomes increasingly complex.

Those challenges are avoided once one adopts the subject conception, but this solution presents a challenge of its own: that of postulating a structural rule of general international law admitting international organizations to membership in the international community, that is, an *international rule of incorporation*. As Paul Reuter said, accepting that international organizations can be subjects of international law in accordance with 'a general rule of international law . . . implies a radical – and to some extent a structural – change in the international community'.[47] But how does one prove such a structural change? One possible route is to rely on the inductive method for establishing customary international law, that is, State practice and *opinio juris*. Finn Seyersted has argued that the existence of international organizations as general subjects of international law possessing a more or less defined set of rights, duties and capacities – which he refers to as the 'common law of international organizations' – is rooted in customary international law.[48] But he is at a loss to point to actual instances of practice, let alone *opinio juris*, that would meet the threshold for the establishment of an international rule of incorporation.[49] It is indeed difficult to show practice supporting a 'structural norm' at that level of abstraction and

consequences also prescribed by the law may be attached to these facts', and rather 'leaves these functions to the interested parties' (at 607). Taken to its last consequences, this position would condemn international law to the fate of a profoundly dysfunctional system, as noted by Crawford. The prevailing view is that, despite the absence of centralised dispute settlement processes, legal questions arising under international law can be 'objectively' assessed; for a recent statement of this notion, see Guideline 3.3.3 of the ILC's Guide to Practice on Reservations, stating that '[a]cceptance of an impermissible reservation by a contracting State or by a contracting organization shall not affect the impermissibility of the reservation': ILC Report 2011, A/66/10, p. 38.
[47] Reuter (Third Report), YILC 1974/II, part one, p. 150, para. 20.
[48] Seyersted, *Common Law*, p. 57: 'the international capacities and personality of IGOs, like those of States, have been established as a general principle of international law through the practice of IGOs generally. And this practice certainly is consistent and extensive enough to constitute customary international law.'
[49] J. Klabbers, 'On Seyersted and his *Common Law of International Organizations*' (2008) 5 IOLR 381, 382 and 387–88.

sophistication: the best one can do is perhaps point to the absence of recent instances in which a non-member State has refused 'to acknowledge the personality of an organization on the ground that it was not a member State and had not given the organization specific recognition'.[50] Whether this practice is accompanied by the legal conviction required to constitute a customary rule of incorporation is difficult to ascertain, especially if one follows the strict approach adopted by the Permanent Court of International Justice in *Lotus* and by the International Court of Justice in *North Sea Continental Shelf*.[51]

That does not mean, however, that the 'subject conception' may not offer a better *rationalisation* of existing practice than the 'treaty conception'. For one, the 'subject conception' not only explains the relations that international organizations maintain with third parties without the need of (or resort to) recognition, but also the participation of regional organizations such as the European Union in multilateral treaties (notably, the 1982 United Nations Convention on the Law of the Sea[52] and the 1994 Agreement Establishing the World Trade Organization[53]), as well as the fact that a great number of intergovernmental organizations are given observer status at the United Nations.[54] It is, moreover,

---

[50] C. F. Amerasinghe, 'International legal personality revisited' (1995) 47 *Austrian Journal of Public and International Law* 123, 141. The only known instance of a State challenging the legal existence of an international organization is that of the Soviet Union vis-à-vis the European Communities, expressed in the former's reluctance to interact with the latter. See H. M. Blix, 'Contemporary aspects of recognition' (1970) 120 RdC 587, 621, who did not think that the Soviet Union's conduct meant that it did not 'consider [the EEC] as a subject of international law'. This position has, in any event, been abandoned in the 1990s.

[51] In *Lotus*, the PCIJ stated that the alleged lack of examples of prosecution the crew of foreign ships could at best 'show that States had often, in practice, abstained from instituting criminal proceedings, and not that they recognized themselves as being obliged to do so; for only if such abstention were based on their being conscious of having a duty to abstain would it be possible to speak of an international custom'; *The Case of the S. S. 'Lotus' (France/Turkey)* [1927] PCIJ, Series A No. 10, p. 28. See also *North Sea Continental Shelf (Federal Republic of Germany/Denmark; Federal Republic of Germany /Netherlands)* [1969] ICJ Rep 3, paras. 77–78.

[52] Art. 305(f) UNCLOS allows for the participation of international organizations subject to the conditions laid down in Annex IX.

[53] Art. XI(1), 1994 Agreement Establishing the World Trade Organization. Art. XII(1) envisages the accession of other 'separate customs [territories] possessing full autonomy in the conduct of its external commercial relations'.

[54] A list of observing international organizations, including the African Union and the European Union, is available at <www.un.org/en/sections/member-states/intergovern mental-organizations/index.html> accessed 27 January 2018.

reflected in the case law of international tribunals, at least to a degree. In fact, the 'treaty conception' suffered a severe blow when the International Court, in *Reparation for Injuries*, put forth the view that the United Nations possessed objective legal personality. Considering whether the United Nations could bring a claim against a State that was not a member of the organization, the Court stated the following:

> On this point, the Court's opinion is that fifty States, representing the vast majority of the members of the international community, had the power, in conformity with international law, to bring into being an entity possessing objective international personality, and not merely personality recognized by them alone, together with capacity to bring international claims.[55]

This ground-breaking *dictum*, it must be conceded, is an exercise in obscurantist reasoning which raises more questions than it answers. First, from where does the 'power' to establish an 'entity possessing objective international legal personality' stem? The Court added the phrase 'in conformity with international law', which would suggest that it was referring to a *right* under customary international law in line with the 'subject conception', but refrained from elaborating on the issue. Second, in referring to 'fifty States, representing the vast majority of the members of the international community', did the Court envisage a numeric threshold for the creation of entities with objective personality? Is this a 'power' that has to be exercised by the 'vast majority' of the international community? If so, how many States does it take to create an international organization with objective legal personality?

Unsurprisingly, the *Reparation* case has given rise to different interpretations. Some commentators, leaning towards the 'treaty conception', suggested that the advisory opinion establishes a distinction between organizations of universal membership – which can possess objective personality – and regional organizations – which cannot.[56] But because the Court did not make such a distinction in a principled manner, no persuasive *a contrario* reading of the opinion can be proposed to deny that international organizations falling short of universality may possess

---

[55] *Reparation for Injuries Suffered in the Service of the United Nations* (Advisory Opinion) [1951] ICJ Rep 174, 185.

[56] Schermers and Blokker, *International Institutional Law*, pp. 990–91; Hafner, 'Is the topic of responsibility', 707. Others have gone as far as claiming that underlying the *dictum* was a finding that third States had tacitly recognised the legal personality of the UN, which is hardly reconcilable with the text of the opinion: Hahn, 'Euratom', 1049.

objective legal personality.[57] While reading the advisory opinion as direct authority for the proposition that *all* international organizations possess objective legal personality is similarly problematic, the idea that States have the power, 'in conformity with international law', to set up corporate bodies to act collectively on the international plane is at the core of the Court's reasoning, and it seems to have been in this spirit that subsequent practice and precedent have evolved.[58] In *Interpretation of the Agreement*, the Court described international organizations as 'subjects of international law and, as such ... bound by any obligations incumbent upon them under general rules of international law, under their constitutions or under international agreements to which they are parties'.[59] In *Nuclear Weapons (WHO Request)*, the Court again referred to international organizations as 'subjects of international law' and to their constituent instruments as treaties creating 'new subjects of law endowed with a certain autonomy'.[60]

The codification of the law of treaties and the law of responsibility concerning international organizations, culminating in instruments purporting to extend rules originally envisaged for States to *all* organizations, is itself another step in the direction of embracing the proposition that international organizations constitute a category of legal subjects under general international law. It is interesting to observe how certain elements in VCLT 1986 that are reminiscent of the 'treaty conception', in particular the rule in Article 6, have been subsequently rationalised in a way that makes them align with the 'subject conception'. To complement Article 6, the participants in the 1986 Vienna Conference adopted a preambular clause that notes that 'international organizations possess the capacity to conclude treaties, which is necessary for the exercise of their functions and the fulfilment of their purposes'.[61] Karl Zemanek, who presided over the 1986 Vienna Conference, has put forth the view that it is 'a more convincing interpretation of the preambular paragraph

---

[57] Similarly, Amerasinghe, 'International legal personality revisited', 141.

[58] As Sette-Câmara affirmed in the debates on treaty-making capacity at the ILC, following the *Reparation for Injuries* opinion, 'there could be no doubt regarding the objective personality of international organizations': YILC 1973/I, p. 202.

[59] *Interpretation of the Agreement of 25 March 1951 between the WHO and Egypt* (Advisory Opinion) [1980] ICJ Rep 73, pp. 89–90. Whether the subjection of IOs to their own constitutions is a consequence of their being subjects of international law, however, is debatable.

[60] *Legality of the Use of Nuclear Weapons in Armed Conflict*, paras. 19 and 25.

[61] Preamble, VCLT 1986.

to suppose that IOs possess treaty-making capacity by virtue of general (customary) international law, if that capacity is necessary for the exercise of their functions and the fulfilment of their purposes', the inference being that Article 6 does not 'refer to the *source* of the treaty-making capacity but states the limit within which that capacity may be exercised'.[62]

In short, though the 'subject conception' is not self-evident – favouring it over the 'treaty conception' requires justification – it seems that there are, as argued by Dapo Akande, 'good reasons of practice and principle for concluding that the personality possessed by any international organization is objective and opposable to non-members', so that, 'once [general] international law ascribes personality to an organization, a subject of international law is created with its own rights and its own duties'.[63] The experience of the past decades, in which many international organizations were created to perform a variety of tasks without having their legal existence challenged by third parties, indicate that the structural change that the legal profession for many years hesitated to accept has indeed occurred, as reflected in the shift that one identifies not only in work of the ILC but also in academic commentary.

2.1.1.3   The Importance of Taking a Position

Whether one adheres to the 'treaty conception' or to the 'subject conception' is of direct consequence for the applicability of public international law to intergovernmental institutions on the international plane and for the possibility of analogising between States and international organizations.

If international organizations are mere treaty transactions, States remain free to establish whatever body corporates they wish, but the realm of existence of those is limited to the relations of the States creating and recognising them. International organizations can only be regarded as subjects of international law in a relative sense. It would also be correct to describe each international organization as genuinely unique in the eyes of international law, as they would not form a category of international legal subjects. If that were the case, organizations would

---

[62] K. Zemanek, 'The United Nations Conference on the Law of Treaties between States and International Organizations or between International Organizations: the unrecorded history of its "general agreement"' in K. H. Böckstiegel (ed.), *Völkerrecht, Recht der internationalen Organisationen, Weltwirtschaftsrecht: Festschrift für Ignaz Seidl-Hohenveldern* (Cologne: Heymann, 1988), p. 671. Similarly, Klabbers, *An Introduction*, p. 268.

[63] Akande, 'International organizations', p. 255.

relate to customary international law in the same way as any other treaty. The customary rules that apply to States would be relevant for the interpretation of constituent instruments on the ground that, as provided by Article 31(3)(c) VCLT 1969, 'any relevant rules of international law applicable in the relations between the parties' shall be taken into account.[64] Customary rules could also be relevant to the extent that constituent instruments explicitly incorporate them as applicable in the relations between organizations and members. Less clear would be the basis for interactions, on the international plane, between an international organization and third parties that 'recognise' it. If such relations are based upon the *ad hoc* acceptance by third parties of the existence of the international organization, the customary law of States can be hardly presumed as applying *ipso jure* or by analogy. The rules by which those relations will be governed must instead arise from an agreement between the entities concerned. The fiction of recognition would have to be taken one step further so that, for example, entering into relations is viewed as entailing the application of customary international law as a matter of 'choice of law'. The upshot of subscribing to the 'treaty conception' is having to accept that the codifications undertaken by the ILC or any similar efforts are no more than comparative studies of the practice and institutional arrangements of different international organizations. Their ambition can be no more than formulating general rules that will apply to international organizations on an *ad hoc* basis, as provided in constituent instruments and impliedly agreed in relations with third parties.

In contrast, under the 'subject conception', the path is open to viewing a series of international organizations that at first glance appear to be radically different as members of a category of international legal subjects that may receive a more or less uniform treatment under general international law. The question then arises of what that uniform treatment consists in – in other words, how the international law that applies to international organizations can be identified. One possibility is to refer to the inductive methodology to establish customary rules, together with all relevant 'subsidiary means', to ascertain which rules apply – to international organizations. Another, as explored in this study, is to consider the role that a systemic analogy between States and international

---

[64] Art. 5 VCLT 1969; see also, art. 5 VCLT 1986.

organizations may play in the development of a public international law of international organizations in situations where practice and *opinio juris* are limited or inconclusive. If international organizations form a category of subjects of international law proper, they can be meaningfully compared with the category of entities falling under the rubric of 'statehood'. To the extent that the two categories share relevant similarities, arguments for extending rules from one category to the other by analogy can be made.

Either way, any robust account of the applicability (or otherwise) of general rules to international organizations on the international plane requires one to take a position as to what their status under contemporary international law is. It is doubtful that registering disagreement without facing this issue straight on – a temptation for which many a commentator has fallen – remains a productive course of action in this day and age.

2.1.2   *In Search of a Unifying Principle*

If one ascribes to the 'subject conception' and accepts the premise that international organizations constitute a category of international legal subjects to which certain rights, duties and capacities are attached, one is left with the task of establishing the contours of that category. What counts as an international organization under general international law?[65]

2.1.2.1   Attempts to Define 'International Organization'

It is helpful to begin the enquiry by revisiting attempts to define international organizations in the context of codification projects carried out by the ILC. In codifying the law of treaties, the law of responsibility and the law of diplomatic relations, the Commission needed to adopt working definitions of international organizations. The way that its approach evolved over the decades is illuminating.

---

[65] It should be noted that this is a relevant question whether one adopts the 'subject conception' or the 'treaty conception'. The function that a definition of IO will perform is, however, different in either case. If IOs are seen as treaties, the definition will be helpful as a general description of a social phenomenon for pedagogic purposes. If IOs are seen as forming a category of legal subjects, the definition serves an ulterior purpose: affirming that an institution falls within the category will have legal implications, namely, determining the applicability to the institution of the legal regime that general international law reserves for members of that category.

A first, and rather minimalistic, definition is found in Article 2(1)(i) VCLT 1969: "'international organization" means an intergovernmental organization'.[66] Because in the 1960s the Commission was only dealing with agreements involving States, there was no need for it to come up with a more robust definition. In fact, the only reason why the Commission looked into the matter was that the project was also meant to apply to constituent instruments and other agreements adopted within international organizations.[67] The Commission's concern was to emphasise that the set of articles would apply solely to intergovernmental – as opposed to non-governmental – organizations.[68]

As it often happens with successful codification projects, the definition found in VCLT 1969 came to be regarded as authoritative in subsequent endeavours. In his third report on the relations between States and intergovernmental organizations, Special Rapporteur El-Erian proposed to define international organization as 'an association of States established by treaty, possessing a constitution and common organs, and having a legal personality distinct from that of the member States'.[69] This proposal was met with opposition at the Commission, and further debate was postponed to a later stage.[70] El-Erian eventually changed his mind, noting that 'an elaborate definition was not necessary for the time being since [the Commission] was not dealing ... with the status of international organizations themselves, but only with the legal position of representatives of States to the organizations'.[71] The VCLT 1969 formula was thus reproduced with no further discussion in the draft provision eventually adopted as Article 1(1) of the Vienna Convention on the Representation of States in their Relations with International Organizations of a Universal Character.[72]

The same happened when the ILC adopted the draft provision that would become Article 2(i) VCLT 1986. In the 1970s, however, the matter received greater attention. The Commission could no longer afford to be

---

[66] Art. 2(i) VCLT 1969.
[67] See art. 5 VCLT 1969.
[68] Commentary to art. 2, YILC 1966/II, p. 190, para. 14.
[69] YILC 1968/II, pp. 124–26.
[70] See Rosenne, YILC 1968/I, pp. 17–18, paras. 52–55. Sir Humphrey Waldock suggested that the Special Rapporteur's proposal be left 'aside for the time being', as the 1968–1969 Vienna Conference was expected to debate the question of the definition of IO in its second session in 1969 (ibid., p. 19, paras. 66–67).
[71] El-Erian (Sixth Report), YILC 1971/II, part one, p. 17, para. 43.
[72] See the records of the 1130th meeting of the ILC in YILC 1971/I, pp. 288–91.

completely agnostic as to the status of international organizations in international law, not least because the definition to be adopted would have a direct impact on the scope of the project.[73] Moreover, a few States commenting on the draft articles adopted on first reading had criticised the VCLT 1969 formula for its vagueness, suggesting that the Commission reformulate it with a view to including references to other relevant elements such as international legal personality.[74] The Commission nonetheless decided not to adopt a new definition on the grounds that the VCLT 1969 formula was 'adequate for the purposes of the draft articles'. The commentary points out that 'either an international organization has the capacity to conclude *at least* one treaty, in which case the rules in the draft articles will be applicable to it, or, despite its title, it does not have that capacity, in which case it is pointless to state explicitly that the draft articles do not apply to it.'[75]

When the ILC took on the topic of the responsibility of international organizations in 2002, it soon became clear that the phrase 'intergovernmental organization' could not provide a satisfactory definition. The same conclusion had been reached, a few years earlier, when the *Institut de droit international* studied the question of the liability of international organizations for damages caused to third parties. On the advice of Rapporteur Higgins, the *Institut* departed from the text of VCLT 1969 and defined international organizations as entities 'possessing an international legal personality distinct from that of its members'.[76] Higgins had initially proposed to define international organization more comprehensively, as 'an intergovernmental institution established by treaty under international law, having its own organs and possessing an international personality distinct from that of its members'. She had also suggested including a few criteria that would indicate whether any given institution possessed legal personality.[77] The more economical text

---

[73] Commentary to art. 2, YILC 1982/II, part two, p. 20, para. 20.

[74] See the comments of Canada and Romania in YILC 1981/II, part one, at 182 and 189.

[75] Commentary to art. 2, YILC 1982/II, part two, p. 21, para. 23.

[76] Art. 1, 'The Legal Consequences for Member States of the Non-fulfilment by International Organizations of their Obligations toward Third Parties', (1995) 66-I *Annuaire de l'Institut de droit international*.

[77] See the draft resolution of October 1994, (1995) 66-I *Annuaire de l'Institut de droit international*, p. 465. The criteria were the following: 'a) An international organization possesses international legal personality when its constituent instrument so provides or by necessary implication by reference to its structure, powers, purposes and functions. b) The existence of a *volonté distincte*, as well as the capacity to enter into contracts, to own property and to sue and be sued, is evidence of international legal personality.'

finally adopted by the *Institut* may not have gone into that amount of detail, but it constituted a first step towards the adoption of a more substantive definition.

At the ILC of the 2000s, Special Rapporteur Gaja followed the lead of the *Institut* by suggesting that the Commission abandon the VCLT 1969 formula. He considered that, looking for a definition that was 'functional' for the purposes of the project, 'one [had] to start from the premise that responsibility under international law may arise only for a subject of international law'. After all, 'international law cannot impose on an entity "primary" obligations or "secondary" obligations in case of a breach of one of the "primary" obligations unless that entity has [international] legal personality'.[78] Thus, he initially suggested defining an international organization as 'an organization which includes States among its members insofar [as] it exercises in its own capacity certain governmental functions'.[79] While the phrase 'in its own capacity' was employed to indicate that international organizations were legal persons distinct from the member States, the phrase 'governmental functions' was proposed with a view to keeping 'some homogeneity in the object of the Commission's enquiry'.[80] The intention was to establish a parallel between the category of acts that give rise to State responsibility and the category of acts that would give rise to the responsibility of international organizations. The phrase 'governmental functions' was criticised, however, as members thought that the functions exercised by the various international organizations were too different in nature to fall under one such rubric.[81] As Brownlie pointed out, the phrase was also misleading as regards States, because 'Governments did all sorts of things', from 'railways to private enterprises', which meant that 'governmental functions' might not be 'useful as a factor of differentiation'.[82] In contrast, the majority of members favoured the inclusion of the notion of legal personality, urging the Special Rapporteur to state it in clearer terms.[83] Consequently, the Commission ended up adopting the following definition:

[78] Gaja (First Report), YILC 2003/II, part one, p. 110, para. 15.
[79] Ibid. 115, para. 34.
[80] Ibid. 113, para. 26.
[81] See the records of the debate in YILC 2003/I, pp. 5–33.
[82] Brownlie, YILC 2003/I, p. 5, para. 7.
[83] Pellet, YILC 2003/I, p. 9, para. 17; Candiotti, ibid., p. 12, para. 47; Pampou-Tchivounda, ibid., p. 3, para. 56; Momtaz, ibid., pp. 20–21, para. 48; Galicki, ibid., p. 24, para. 19; Addo, ibid., p. 25, paras. 28–29. Koskenniemi (ibid., p. 15, para. 1), Mansfield (ibid., p. 26,

'international organization' means an organization established by a treaty or other instrument governed by international law and possessing its own international legal personality. International organizations may include as members, in addition to States, other entities.[84]

2.1.2.2   International Legal Personality as a Unifying Principle?

That, after decades of hesitation, the ILC adopted a definition emphasising the element of international legal personality is revealing in many respects. The Commission was unconvinced that it should define international organizations on the basis of the character of the acts that they perform, as their purposes and functions are simply too diverse to provide a unifying principle for the category of entities that the draft articles purport to address.[85] It thus favoured a more abstract notion: the quality of holding rights and obligations on the international plane. By doing so, the Commission followed an approach which is common in the literature, where international legal personality is usually taken as a starting point for the analysis of the status of international organizations under international law.[86] This approach can be traced back to the *Reparation for Injuries* case, where the ICJ deemed it necessary to establish that the United Nations had international legal personality to answer the question of whether it could bring claims on the international plane.[87]

However, the use of international legal personality as a unifying principle is misleading. That is because the term has been construed in different ways, with some writers viewing it as a source of entitlements and duties, and others as a purely formal concept.[88] The confusion stems

para. 38) and Xue (ibid., p. 88, para. 51) expressed reservations as to the use of the concept of legal personality.

[84] Art. 2(a) ARIO. The same definition was adopted by the Commission in its work on identification of customary international law, as explained in the commentary to Conclusion 4: ILC Report 2018, A/73/10, at 158, footnote 691.

[85] The argument according to which different legal regimes should apply to different categories of IOs is discussed in Section 4.1.

[86] E.g., M. Rama-Montaldo, 'International legal personality and implied powers of international organizations' (1970) 44 BYIL 111, 138.

[87] *Reparation for Injuries*, p. 178.

[88] Within the ILC, see the statement by Koskenniemi: 'Legal personality [is] the consequence of rights, obligations and powers, not their source ... there [is] no *a priori* concept of legal personality': YILC 2003/I, p. 15, para. 1. In the literature, see e.g., Sands and Klein, *Bowett's Law of International Institutions*, pp. 476–77 and R. Portmann, *Legal*

from the fact that the literature tends to elide the distinction between the general notion of legal personality as discussed in legal theory, and the structural norms that may define categories of legal persons in contingent legal systems.

From a jurisprudential point of view, the proposition that an entity possesses legal personality means that this entity is elected by the legal system as a focal point for the attribution of rights, obligations and capacities.[89] Kelsen has persuasively shown that legal persons are not ontological realities in the same way as beings and things, but rather 'personified unit[ies] of a set of legal norms', that is to say, centres of imputation of legal norms that the legal system itself constitutes.[90] This means that, in the abstract, a legal subject is merely an addressee of legal norms. Legal personality does not have an *a priori* content, but is better understood as a status that follows from the possession of rights and obligations – as a consequence rather than a cause.[91] Thus, at this level of analysis, to affirm that international organizations have international legal personality means to affirm that they are addressed by rules of the international legal system. It does not answer the question of what specific rights, obligations and capacities these organizations possess.

That said, existing legal systems invariably comprise structural norms that regulate legal personality by creating categories of legal subjects to whom a defined legal regime is attached. At the domestic level, human beings are typically characterised as 'natural' legal persons at birth,[92] and from this legal status a number of rights, duties and capacities under private and public law follow, including the possession of fundamental rights and (subject to specific age and health requirements) the capacities to contract, marry and make a will. The same happens with corporations and with public agencies, when legal systems stipulate procedures

Personality in International Law (Cambridge: Cambridge University Press, 2010), pp. 278–80.

[89] Hence the schematic definition of international legal personality as the capacity to bear rights and obligations under international law; e.g., Akande, 'International organizations', p. 251 and Crawford, *Brownlie's Principles of Public International Law*, p. 115.

[90] Kelsen, *General Theory of Law and State*, (n 50) 93. The thrust of Kelsen's work on legal personality is to separate the 'is' from the 'ought', *sein* from *sollen*, and to point out that legal subjects are constituted by the system, i.e., that they are not ontological entities.

[91] See the comprehensive articulation of the 'formal conception' of legal personality in Portmann, *Legal Personality*, pp. 173–96.

[92] See e.g., §1 of the German Civil Code (Bürgerliches Gesetzbuch): 'Die Rechtsfähigkeit des Menschen beginnt mit der Vollendung der Geburt' <http://dejure.org/gesetze/BGB/1.html> accessed 12 February 2018.

74   THE FOUNDATIONS OF THE ANALOGY

whereby myriad legal persons can be established, each receiving its own predefined package of duties and entitlements under relevant statutes and case law.

International law is no different from municipal law in this respect. First and foremost, it recognises a concept of statehood, ascribing to territorial entities that fall under the category of 'State' a set of rights, duties and capacities, including the right to self-determination, the duty of non-intervention and the capacity to conclude treaties.[93] Likewise, it is nowadays well accepted that international law confers a number of rights and imposes a number of obligations on individuals, as provided by customary international law and treaties in the fields of human rights and international criminal law.[94] Thus, when the United Kingdom and Ratko Mladić are described as 'subjects of international law', what is meant is that, given their membership in existing categories of international legal persons, certain previously defined legal regimes will be applicable to each of them.

The same is true for international organizations, although here the use of terminology is less straightforward. Historically, the term 'international legal personality' has been employed to describe the general status of international organizations under international law. As Wilfred Jenks put it, 'the concept of legal personality is so much more widely understood in the majority of countries than any newer terminology that for practical purposes it would seem more convenient to continue using it to define the status of public international organizations as legal entities'.[95] The problem is that the international legal lexicon lacks a term of art that specifically relates to international organizations in the same way that the term 'statehood' relates to States.[96] Yet, the fact that the use of the term 'legal personality' in the specific context of international organization scholarship transcends its proper meaning in

---

[93] Lists of well-accepted general rights and duties of States can be found in the 1933 Montevideo Convention on the Rights and Duties of States and in the 1949 Draft Declaration on the Rights and Duties of States, annexed to UNGA Res. 375 (IV) (1949).

[94] For an overview, K. Parlett, *The Individual in the International Legal System* (Cambridge: Cambridge University Press, 2011), in particular pp. 274–77 and 337–39. See also A. A. Cançado Trindade, *The Access of Individuals to International Justice* (Oxford: Oxford University Press, 2012), pp. 1–16.

[95] C. W. Jenks, 'International legal personality of international organizations' (1945) 22 BYIL 267, 271.

[96] Klabbers occasionally uses the term 'organizationhood' to refer to the status of international organizations in international law: *An Introduction*, p. 48.

legal theory is a cause of misunderstandings. For the sake of clarity, in investigating the position that international organizations occupy in the international system, it is preferable to adopt the phrase 'status of international organizations under international law' as an umbrella concept.

Possession of international legal personality cannot thus, without more, serve as a unifying principle for the category that international organizations form under general international law. It is either circular, when (confusingly) seen as a synonym for whatever status international organizations enjoy under international law, or hollow, when (accurately) viewed as the formal attribute of possessing rights and obligations on the international plane which derives from that status.

2.1.2.3   International Legal Autonomy as a Unifying Principle

The search has thus to focus on a more substantive attribute that is shared by the various entities belonging to the category of international organizations. The definition adopted by the *Institut de droit international* provides a helpful starting point. International organizations are described as entities 'possessing an international legal personality *distinct from that of their members*'. A legal identity that is separate from that of members hints at a characteristic shared by most of the entities that we usually refer to as international organizations: the possession of legal autonomy on the international plane. When defining international organizations, the opinion of commentators tends to converge on two aspects. First, international organizations are institutions created by States – and, occasionally, other entities – by treaty or another instrument governed by international law. Second, international organizations are described as legally autonomous, under international law, from the States that create them.[97] Institutionally, this legal autonomy is

[97] E.g., Virally, 'Definition and classification', p. 51 (IOs are 'an association of States, established by agreement among its members and possessing a permanent system or set of organs ... '); Seidl-Hohenveldern, *Corporations*, p. 72 ('An international organization will be a subject of international law if it has been established by a meeting of the wills of its member States ... and if the member States have enabled the organization to have rights and duties of its own under international and domestic law and to express a will not necessarily identical with the will of each of them, such will to be expressed by an organ not subject to instructions of any single member State'); Schermers and Blokker, *International Institutional Law*, pp. 37–47 (IOs are 'forms of cooperation (1) founded on an international agreement; (2) having at least one organ with a will of its own; (3) established under international law'); Sands and Klein, *Bowett's Law of International Institutions*, pp. 15–16 (noting general agreement as to the following characteristics: 'its membership must be composed of states and/or other international

operationalised by the establishment of at least one organ empowered to express a *volonté distincte* for the organization.[98] Legally, international organizations are viewed as autonomous in that they are not subject to the jurisdiction of any of their members.[99]

In this vein, Finn Seyersted refers to international organizations as 'self-governing communities', and introduces a concept that is helpful for understanding what legal autonomy entails: the notion of *organic jurisdiction*.[100] Possessing organic jurisdiction means being governed by one's own 'public law', to the exclusion of the public law of other entities, and keeping a legal monopoly over the relations between one's organs and officials.[101] International organizations enjoy organic jurisdiction because they exercise 'legislative, administrative and judicial jurisdiction over their organs and the members hereof as such'.[102] On occasion, international organizations are given powers that go far beyond organic jurisdiction, in which case they exercise public authority over member States (e.g., the extensive regulatory powers of the European Union), territory (e.g., the transitional administration set up by the UN in Kosovo under UNSC Resolution 1244/99), and even individuals not acting in their service (e.g., the exercise of criminal jurisdiction by the International Criminal Court). But because this 'extended jurisdiction in substantive matters'[103] varies from organization to organization, what

organisations; it must be established by treaty or other instrument governed by international law, such as a resolution adopted in an international conference; it must have autonomous will distinct from that of its members and be vested with legal personality; and it must be capable of adopting norms (in the broadest sense) addressed to its members'); and Brölmann, *The Institutional Veil*, p. 20 ('the core aspects seem to be that an international organisation is established by international law, or by subjects of international law; that it is governed by international law, rather than incorporated in a national legal order; and that it has a degree of autonomy'). Nigel White's textbook, by contrast, adopts a broader conception of international organization that is not tied to the idea of legal autonomy: N. White, *The Law of International Organisations* (Manchester: Manchester University Press, 2005), pp. 1–2.

[98] E.g., Seidl-Hohenveldern, *Corporations*, p. 72.
[99] As argued by Seyersted, *Common Law*, p. 42. Compare with Brölmann, *The Institutional Veil*, p. 20: '[The] existence [of an international organization] is based on the act of uncontested international actors, and it has independence vis-à-vis its component elements (member states).'
[100] Seyersted, *Common Law*, pp. 70–72.
[101] Ibid., p. 82.
[102] Ibid., p. 97.
[103] To borrow Seyersted's terminology; see chapter six of his *Common Law of International Organizations*.

is common to *all* of them is the exclusive jurisdiction that they enjoy over their internal arrangements.

Understanding legal autonomy under general international law as the attribute shared by a range of entities whose institutional set-ups radically differ provides the key to viewing international organizations as a unified category of international legal subjects. Just as the notion of sovereign equality allows international law to articulate the concept of statehood, legal autonomy allows it to articulate the concept of the status of international organizations under international law.

Legal autonomy also sheds light on the processes whereby international organizations are created,[104] and, in particular, on the question of whether members must confer international legal personality on them.[105] As Klabbers emphasises, organizations are established through a series of deliberate acts on the part of their members – they are not created by chance.[106] If international organizations are seen merely as treaty transactions, the specific intention of the parties to create them as legal persons is crucial, as the existence of legal personality is no more than a matter of treaty interpretation. When they are seen as legal subjects under general international law, however, their status cannot solely derive from their constituent instrument, but rather from whatever criteria the rule of incorporation implicit in the international legal system prescribes for their creation. The decisive element is thus the institutional design that the parties to the constituent instrument set up: insofar as members endow the institution with legal autonomy, shielding it from their own territorial, personal and organic jurisdictions, the result will be the creation of an international organization. This is what the ICJ appears to have suggested in *Reparation for Injuries* when it pointed out that 'the Organization was intended to exercise and enjoy, and is in fact exercising and enjoying, functions and rights which can only be explained on the basis of the possession of a large measure of international personality and the capacity to operate upon an international plane'.[107] This is also

---

[104] Whether an IO may be created without the participation of at least one State is a contentious issue. In its latest definition, the ILC requires that there be at least one member State: commentary to art. 2, YILC 2011/II, part two, pp. 50–51, paras. 11–12.

[105] Klabbers, 'Presumptive personality', pp. 231–35.

[106] Klabbers, *An Introduction*, p. 11.

[107] *Reparation for Injuries*, p. 179. The Court, however, pointed out that '[i]t must be acknowledged that its Members, by entrusting certain functions to it, with the attendant duties and responsibilities, have clothed it with the competence required to enable those functions to be effectively discharged'.

probably what Giorgio Gaja and Rosalyn Higgins had in mind when they noted, respectively, that the characterization of an organization as a subject of international law is a 'question of fact' and an 'objective reality'.[108]

But where does one draw the line dividing institutions that are legally autonomous from their members from those that are not? First of all, legal autonomy must be accompanied by a certain degree of factual autonomy. If the *volonté distincte* of the organization is purely nominal, or if an organization is *de facto* subjected to the legal system of their members, it cannot be said to enjoy legal autonomy.[109] Thus, institutions managed in conjunction with the organs of a member State may not fall within the category enjoying the status of international organization under international law.[110] The *Reparation for Injuries* case, again, provides some guidance, with the Court pointing to the recommendatory and dispositive powers of the United Nations, its privileges and immunities and its participation in international agreements to ascertain that it must enjoy international legal personality.[111] The conferral of legal autonomy to the organization would be, to use Higgins' words, a 'necessary implication by reference to its structure, powers, purposes and functions'.[112] More recently, in its judgment in *Pulp Mills*, the Court affirmed that a river commission that had been set up by Argentina and

---

[108] Gaja (First Report) YILC 2003/II, part one, p. 111, para. 19; Higgins, (1995) 66-I *Annuaire de l'Institut de droit international*, p. 276. In his first Report, Gaja suggested that the acquisition of 'objective legal personality ... would depend on the actual establishment of the organization', as 'an organization merely existing on paper cannot be considered a subject of international law' (ibid.). But here a qualification should be made. The existence of an international organization would be 'a question of fact' in the same way that the creation of States may be described as 'a question of fact'. It is more accurate to say that the creation of States and international organizations is the result of a legal operation that is completed once certain factual conditions are fulfilled. In the case of States, statehood emerges when a territorial community, under government, effectively exercises territorial, personal and organic jurisdiction to the exclusion of other States, provided that by doing so it has not violated any fundamental rules of international law: Crawford, *The Creation of States*, pp. 88 and 106–07. In the case of international organizations, the status of an international organization would emerge when an institution is created by States with the means to operate with legal autonomy from its members.

[109] On the factual autonomy of IOs and its connection to legal personality: Verdirame, *The UN and Human Rights*, pp. 32–34, 60–63.

[110] Seyersted refers to these institutions as organizations of the *type dependant*. Seyersted, *Common Law*, pp. 19–21.

[111] *Reparation for Injuries*, pp. 178–79.

[112] Draft article 2(a), (1995) 66-I *Annuaire de l'Institut de droit international*, p. 421.

Uruguay to promote the optimal and rational use of the Uruguay River constituted an 'international organization with legal personality'.[113] This suggests that the threshold in practice may be relatively low, raising questions as to how to deal with borderline cases.

2.2 The Relevant Similarity between States and International Organizations

It was argued above that it is a condition for an analogy between States and international organizations that organizations be seen as a category of international legal subjects under general international law. There must be, in other words, a 'status of international organizations under international law' that can be meaningfully compared with statehood. Once that condition is satisfied, the plausibility of the analogy depends on a judgement as to whether statehood and that status share a 'relevant similarity' that justifies extending to international organizations rules originally adopted for States. On that basis, an analogy-warranting rule connecting States and international organizations has to be formulated and, to the extent that it is justified by analogy-warranting rationales, applied in cases where there is uncertainty as to the rights, obligations and capacities of international organizations.[114]

This section looks into the crucial 'relevant similarity' between States and international organizations. Counter-arguments and controversies surrounding the possibility of transposing particular rules to international organizations will be addressed in the chapters that follow.

2.2.1 Legal Autonomy and the Capacity to Operate on the International Plane

In *Reparation for Injuries*, the ICJ described the UN as 'a subject of international law ... capable of possessing international rights and duties' and derived from this status the 'capacity to maintain its rights by bringing international claims', including claims against third parties.[115] Significantly, the Court viewed the *'capacity to operate upon an international plane'* as a corollary of the possession of international

---

[113] *Pulp Mills on the River Uruguay (Argentina v. Uruguay)* [2010] ICJ Rep 14, para. 89.
[114] On the structure of reasoning by analogy, see Section 1.1.2.
[115] *Reparation for Injuries*, p. 179.

legal personality by the organization.[116] The Court was there hinting at the basic normative implication arising from the status of international organizations under international law. While the functions of international organizations are determined by their constituent instruments, general international law ascribes to these organizations a general capacity to operate on the international plane, which is a corollary of the legal autonomy that they enjoy as personified entities set up by States.

That international legal autonomy, coupled with the capacity to operate on the international plane, constitutes the relevant similarity between States and international organizations *qua* subjects of international law. In his seminal work on international organizations, Seyersted suggested that 'the only criterion which is common to the two types of subjects of international law is the fact that they have organs which are sovereign (or self-governing) or not subject to the jurisdiction of any one other organized community'.[117] He argued that 'although [international organizations] in fact are very different from States and have much less extensive jurisdiction and resources than these, they are from an external point of view not as different from States as has been generally assumed'.[118] That led him to posit that 'when the difference in nature [between international legal subjects does] not require different legal rules, the rules which have been developed in relations between States may usually be applied by analogy to other sovereign communities, to the extent that their activities call for the application of such rules'.[119] The same type of reasoning can be discerned in *Reparation for Injuries* when the Court compares the UN's capacity to operate on the international plane with the capacity that 'certainly belongs to the State'. That the Court concluded that the UN could bring a claim similar to that made 'between two political entities, equal in law, similar in form, and both the direct subjects of international law' (i.e., States) attests to its acceptance of the proposition that the two categories of international subjects share a fundamental characteristic.[120]

The analogy-warranting rule underpinning the analogy between States and international organizations can thus be formulated in the following terms: 'self-governing legally autonomous entities, operating on the

[116] Rama-Montaldo, 'International legal personality', 138.
[117] Seyersted, *Common Law*, p. 44.
[118] Ibid., p. 400.
[119] Ibid., p. 396.
[120] *Reparation for Injuries*, pp. 177–78.

international plane and outside the jurisdiction of any other self-governing entity, are subject, in their external relations, to the same rules of general international law'. This rule can then be honed and applied to various contexts. For example, as regards the law of treaties, it can be postulated that the legal regime that applies to States also applies to international organizations to the extent that the latter are also legally autonomous entities making international agreements. That explanation is superior to the 'general principle of consensualism' on which Special Rapporteur Reuter relied to justify extending the rules in VCLT 1969 to the treaties concluded by international organizations. That principle, for Reuter, constituted 'the basis of any treaty commitment and [entailed] the legal equality of the parties'.[121] But that 'legal equality of the parties', which Reuter presumed without never quite justifying, rests on a view of States and international organizations as comparable entities whose *pacta*, made on the international plane, *sunt servanda*.

As regards the law of international responsibility, it can be similarly proposed that the secondary rules laying down the conditions and consequences of the internationally wrongful acts of States extend to international organizations, insofar as the latter are also legally autonomous entities which may breach obligations assumed on the international plane. There would be indeed no reason to distinguish, as the Commission so often states in the commentary to the ARIO, between States and international organizations. The capacity to be held internationally responsible is the sister principle of the 'capacity to bring an international claim' that the International Court affirmed in *Reparation for Injuries*. This was confirmed in the *Cumaraswamy* case, when the Court said that 'the United Nations may be required to bear responsibility for damage arising' from acts performed by itself or its agents acting in their official capacity.[122] Unsurprisingly, the premise underlying the work of the ILC on the responsibility of international organizations did not generate much debate.[123]

---

[121] Reuter (Tenth Report) YILC 1981/II, part one, p. 46, para. 5.

[122] *Difference Relating to Immunity from Legal Process of a Special Rapporteur of the Commission on Human Rights* (Advisory Opinion) [1999] ICJ Rep 62, para. 66.

[123] That has not always been the case, though. When the ILC reoriented its efforts for the codification of the law of State responsibility in the early 1960s, Roberto Ago favoured excluding international organizations from the scope of the project, noting that it was 'questionable whether such organizations had the capacity to commit international wrongful acts': YILC 1963/II, p. 229.

Similar lines of argument would justify, at least *prima facie*, extending to international organizations other rules of international law that are engaged as those organizations act on the international plane.[124]

2.2.2 Justifying the Relevant Similarity

Every analogy-warranting rule must be confirmed by analogy-warranting rationales which demonstrate that the rule in question 'effects an *acceptable sorting* of particular items, actual or hypothetical, thought relevant by the legal reasoner'.[125] The question then arises of what normative reasons justify extending rules from one internationally legally autonomous category of legal persons to the other. It may be argued that because international law is the only set of rules that apply on the international plane, the rules that apply in the relations between States must also apply to the relations involving international organizations. After all, what other rules would apply?

This is an assumption requiring further elaboration. Even if international organizations are viewed as legal persons under general international law, this does not necessarily mean that they have to be subject to the customary rules devised by States and for States.[126] Rather, normative considerations militating in favour of assimilation must be taken into account. Subject to the debates surrounding the precise legal status of international organizations discussed in this chapter, it is undeniable that under contemporary international law States have the right to act collectively by establishing body corporates set up to pursue goals of international cooperation. Such body corporates may exercise, so far as international law is concerned, all the rights and capacities that States can exercise individually. There does not seem to be any limit – except for those imposed by peremptory norms of general international law[127] – to the tasks that

---

[124] See further the discussion in section 7.1.
[125] Brewer, 'Exemplary reasoning', 1021.
[126] Somewhat uncritically, this is a position often stated in general works on IOs: e.g., Schermers and Blokker, *International Institutional Law*, pp. 996–97 and Sands and Klein, *Bowett's Law of International Institutions*, pp. 461–64. As Klabbers pointed out, 'the discipline may claim … that international organizations are subjects of international law, and thus also subject to international law, but it remains unclear which international law, and why: there is no plausible theory of obligation': Klabbers, 'The Paradox', 165.
[127] Art. 53 VCLT 1969.

international organizations can fulfil.[128] To press the point, one has only to look at the wide-ranging external relations conducted by the European Union in lieu of its members, or to the fact that States have delegated to international organizations mandates that range from collective self-defence (e.g., the North Atlantic Treaty Organization) to economic policy (e.g., the Organisation for Economic Co-operation and Development).

But the rule of incorporation implicit in contemporary international law does not – and could not, without more – authorise States to create body corporates operating outside the overarching legal system under which States operate individually.[129] States may, of course, modify the rules between themselves within the confines of the institutional framework established by a constituent instrument, so that, on the institutional plane, the organization can do much more than each of them would have been allowed to do individually. For instance, under international law, no State has the power to change another's domestic law, but the European Union is entitled to adopt regulations that have precisely this effect vis-à-vis its member States. But when it comes to relations taking place on the international plane – the outside world, as it were – if international organizations were not bound by the rules that apply to States under international law, the implication would be that States are entitled to circumvent their international obligations or enhance their rights by setting up a body corporate to act in their stead. That would be an untenable position, with widespread implications for the coherence of the international system. As Guglielmo Verdirame has noted, comparing the position of international organizations with that of new States:

> Subjecting international organisations to [general international law], not-withstanding the absence of any evidence of them specifically consenting to each rule of it, is consistent with the approach adopted in the 1950s and 1960s towards newly independent states. Then too the view was taken that the international legal personality that followed from statehood had automatic obligatory consequences in respect at least of general custom.

---

[128] According to a comment submitted by the IMF, '[t]here is no principle of international law that limits States' ability to set up international organizations to act collectively and on behalf of the membership': A/CN.4/545 (2004), p. 10.

[129] See, in this respect, International Law Association, 'Accountability of International Organisations', Final Report (2004), p. 18: 'States cannot evade their obligations under customary law and general principles of law by creating an IO that would not be bound by the legal limits imposed upon its Member States'. Also, F. Morgenstern, *Legal Problems of International Organizations* (Cambridge: Grotius, 1986), p. 32.

It would, after all, be extremely disruptive for the international legal system to tolerate the presence of actors that are endowed with legal personality, and thus with the legal capacity to operate upon the international plane, but are exempt from a body of universally or almost universally accepted rules ... The view that international organisations are bound by customary international law by virtue of their legal personality ensures systemic coherence.[130]

A similar systemic consideration underpins the very notion of international responsibility. In the draft articles on State responsibility adopted by the ILC on first reading, a provision was included to affirm the capacity of States to be held internationally liable. The commentary to that provision noted the following:

> States establish themselves as equal members of the international community as soon as they achieve an independent and sovereign existence. If it is the prerogative of sovereignty to be able to assert its rights, the counterpart of that prerogative is the duty to discharge its obligations. The principle that no State which by its conduct has committed a breach of an international obligation can escape the consequence, namely, to be regarded as having committed an internationally wrongful act which entails its responsibility, is the corollary of the principle of the sovereign equality of States.[131]

---

[130] Verdirame, *The UN and Human Rights*, pp. 71–72. Making a similar point: K. Daugirdas, 'How and why international law binds international organizations' (2016) 57 *Harvard International Law Journal* 325, 357–58 and A. Reinisch, 'Sources of international organizations' law: why custom and general principles are crucial' in S. Besson and J. D'Aspremont (eds.), *The Oxford Handbook of the Sources of International Law* (Oxford: Oxford University Press, 2017), pp. 1016–18. As regards the proposition that new States are bound by customary international law, the standard – and authoritative – view is as follows: 'Membership of the international community carries with it the duty to submit to the existing body of such rules, and the right to contribute to their modification or development in accordance with the prevailing rules for such processes. Thus, new States which come into existence and are admitted into the international community thereupon become subject to the body of rules for international conduct in force at the time of their admittance': R. Jennings and A. Watts, *Oppenheim's International Law*, 9th edn (Oxford: Oxford University Press, 1992), p. 14. See also T. Franck, *The Power of Legitimacy among Nations* (New York: Oxford University Press, 1990), pp. 190–91 (noting that 'new States are deemed to be obliged to comply with the duties of Statehood not because they agree to do so, but because they have satisfied requirements for the recognition of their right to membership in the community. The obligations, so to speak, come with the rights').

[131] YILC 1973/II, p. 177, para. 2. Draft article 2 was later deleted on second reading for the sake of simplification.

A system in which States were able to contract out of their obligations vis-à-vis a third party by establishing an entity that is not bound by the same default rules as they are would effectively negate the idea of State responsibility. In a comment submitted to the Commission, the European Commission observed that 'the duty of reparation also arises for an international organization for breaches of their obligations because of the fact that they were allowed to participate in the conduct of international relations as a subject of international law in the first place'. '[I]t would indeed be absurd', the European Commission added, 'if one category of actors (States) would face more severe legal consequences for internationally wrongful acts than another category of actors (international organizations)'.[132]

Thus, the notion that States may collectively do what they can do individually, but that they cannot do so by creating entities that would operate outside the system of customary international law, serves as an analogy-warranting rationale justifying why a common legal regime should apply to States and the legally autonomous entities operating on the international plane that they themselves create. If like cases are to be treated alike, so that gaps in the law are filled in the way that best ensures the coherence of the legal system, extending rules of general international law from States to international organizations by analogy in situations of uncertainty must be, in principle, admissible.

2.3   Concluding Remarks

In this chapter, I argued that the possibility of analogising between States and international organizations is tied to a view of international organizations as forming a category of international legal subjects comparable, for certain purposes, to that composed by States. This requires favouring a 'subject conception' over a 'treaty conception' of international organization, that is, postulating the existence of a rule of incorporation under which States may establish subjects of international law operating on the international plane. If international organizations are instead regarded as treaty transactions, each organization will constitute, from the perspective of general international law, a unique entity that exists only vis-à-vis its member states on the basis of the *pacta sunt servanda* principle. As a consequence, there can be no public international law proper governing

---

[132] A/CN.4/593 (2004), p. 6.

the activities of international organizations. While both conceptions are theoretically plausible, and though proving the existence of a rule of incorporation in international law poses an epistemological challenge, the 'subject conception' offers a better rationalisation of existing practice and precedent.

The 'subject conception' presupposes the existence of a principle unifying international organizations into a category of legal subjects in the same way that sovereign equality brings self-governing territorial communities under the rubric of statehood. The crucial attribute of the status of international organizations under international law is legal autonomy, that is, exemption from the jurisdiction of any other self-governing entity. Legal autonomy, externalised through the capacity to operate on the international plane, also constitutes the relevant similarity that invites a comparison between statehood and the status of international organization under international law. The rules of international law that apply in the external relations between States can thus be in principle extended to the external relations of international organizations.

PART II

Objections to the Analogy

In Part I, I argued that the analogy between States and international organizations is plausible if – and to the extent that – the latter can be conceptualised as a category of international legal subjects that, endowed with legal autonomy, operate on the international plane. If this premise is accepted, analogical reasoning offers a justification for extending rules of general international law from States to international organizations. But the question of whether States and international organizations are indeed 'relevantly similar' has to be further probed. In the debates that took place when the International Law Commission was carrying out its projects on treaties and responsibility, States and organizations often argued the opposite. For example, the International Monetary Fund made the following contention:

> [W]e do not necessarily agree that rules on State responsibility should be applied to international organizations. The differences between the legal status of States and that of international organizations are significant, as are the differences among international organizations. Furthermore, it seems to us that any analysis of the responsibility of international organizations must take into account the provisions of the international agreements by which individual organizations were created.[1]

Three main strands of principled argument against analogising between States and international organizations can be identified in international legal discourse. The first points to structural differences between States and international organizations and is covered in Chapter 3. The second views international organizations as 'special' subjects of international law to be distinguished from the 'general' subjects and is dealt with in Chapter 4. The third strand of argument emphasises the layered structure of international organizations as corporate bodies constituted and governed by States and is dealt with in Chapter 5.

---

[1] IMF, A/CN.4/545 (2004), p. 6.

3

Structural Differences between States and International Organizations

Some of the most glaring differences between States and international organizations are of a structural character. International organizations do not possess territory or a population. Political organs where representatives from member States sit and secretariats composed of international civil servants hardly resemble national parliaments and executive branches. As the International Law Commission observed in the General Commentary to the ARIO, '[i]nternational organizations are quite different from States' and '[t]here are very significant differences among international organizations with regard to their powers and functions, size of membership, relations between the organization and its members, procedures for deliberation, structure and facilities'.[1] To what extent do such structural differences affect the applicability of general international law to international organizations, thus justifying departures from an analogy with States?

3.1 'International Organizations Have No Territory'

The fact that international organizations are not, unlike States, territorial units makes the international law that applies to the acquisition, use and disposal of territory generally inapplicable to them. While the land in which their headquarters are located is typically accorded special status, and may be largely exempted from the domestic jurisdiction of the host State, headquarters agreements do not confer on international organizations international legal title over territory. On the contrary, those agreements may even condition the exercise of rights of property under domestic law. The headquarters agreement between the UN and the United States provides, for example, that '[t]he United Nations shall not dispose of all or any part of the land owned by it in the headquarters

---

[1] General commentary, YILC 2011/II, part two, p. 47, para. 7.

district without the consent of the United States', absent which the United States 'shall buy the land in question from the United Nations'.[2]

That international organizations lack territory generated debate on the possibility of extending to them two provisions of VCLT 1969. The first is Article 29, which prescribes that 'a treaty is binding upon each party in respect of its entire territory'. The second is paragraph 2 of Article 62, according to which a fundamental change of circumstances may not be invoked as a ground for terminating a treaty establishing a boundary.

Discussing the first provision, Special Rapporteur Reuter pondered the question of whether international organizations are unitary entities in the same way as States.[3] He referred to the position of the various subsidiary organs that international organizations establish and to 'connected organs' that, though not established under the rules of the organization, operate within the institutional framework. The issue was whether those subsidiary and connected organs could conclude treaties autonomously, or whether any such treaties would be binding on the parent organization.[4] A related problem was whether treaties concluded by the parent organization were binding on such organs. In the commentary to the set of articles adopted on first reading, the Commission suggested that there was a link between subsidiary and connected organs and the parent organization,[5] which would justify adopting a clause, functionally analogous to Article 29 VCLT 1969, recognising the 'organic scope' of treaties concluded by international organizations. The Commission refrained from adopting such a provision, however, on the ground that the topic was not ripe for codification.[6] Article 29 VCLT 1986 thus replicates the text of VCLT 1969, containing a rule that applies exclusively to States.

Debate on the second provision '– relating to treaties that establish boundaries – entailed far greater controversy. Two questions arose from the debate about whether or not Article 62(2)(a) VCLT 1969 should be extended to international organizations. First, could international organizations be party to treaties establishing a boundary (and, if so, what would constitute a boundary)? Second, if it is accepted that international

---

[2] Agreement regarding the Headquarters of the United Nations, 26 June 1947, section 22.
[3] Reuter (Fourth Report), YILC 1975/II, part one, p. 41, para. 7. The same question, as regards the proposition that IOs are not unitary entities insofar as they are composed of States, is discussed in Chapter 5.
[4] Ibid., p. 41, para. 7.
[5] Commentary to art. 29, YILC 1982/II, part two, p. 40, para. 3.
[6] Ibid., p. 40, para. 3.

organizations can be party to such treaties, should the 'stabilising effect' conferred by Article 62(2)(a) benefit those treaties as well?

In Reuter's opinion, '[t]erritory . . . is so closely linked to State sovereignty that it is inconceivable that States would abandon to an organization the right to dispose of their territorial rights without losing the status of State'.[7] While Reuter conceded that States could 'make the future of part of their territories dependent on a decision of an international organization (or of a jurisdictional body)', he thought that it was 'quite a different thing to delegate to such entities the right to dispose of [State] territory by treaty'.[8] Accordingly, the Special Rapporteur proposed to limit the exception to the *rebus sic stantibus* rule contained in Article 62(2)(a) VCLT 1969 to treaties between two or more States and one or more international organizations. Several members of the Commission agreed with Reuter, though it was suggested that there would be no harm in leaving the door open for future development, should international organizations start to engage in boundary agreements.[9] As Pinto noted, under the 1982 UN Convention on the Law of the Sea, the Commission on the Limits of the Continental Shelf and the International Sea-Bed Authority could actively participate in the delineation of the continental shelf of a party, and agreements concluded between the Authority and the State in question could possess a territorial character.[10] This example from practice raised the question of whether maritime lines in general, and lines delimiting a State's continental shelf from the deep sea-bed in particular, constituted 'boundaries' in the sense of VCLT 1969. While the Commission accepted that the term 'could conceivably be taken more broadly to designate the various lines which fix the spatial limits of the exercise of different powers',[11] the majority of delegations at the Vienna Conference favoured the traditional understanding of boundaries as the 'political boundaries which delimited the territory of a State'.[12]

But even if a broader meaning of boundary had been adopted, it was suggested that the stabilising effect of Article 62(2)(a) should not shield agreements through which international organizations might come to establish a boundary. To Reuter, 'a boundary treaty celebrated by an

[7] Reuter (Ninth Report), YILC 1980/II, part one, p. 135, para. 4.
[8] Ibid., p. 135, para. 4.
[9] Vallat, YILC 1980/I, p. 12, para. 14.
[10] Pinto, YILC 1980/I, p. 9, paras. 41–42, and p. 13, para. 24. The same point was made by India at the Vienna Conference: UNCLT 1986/I, 156, para 33.
[11] Commentary to art. 62, YILC 1982/II, part two, p. 60, para. 5.
[12] Switzerland, UNCLT 1986/I, p. 157, para. 142.

international organization – a possibility that could arise in the future – should [not] constitute a "stabilized treaty"' because international organizations were 'very fluid by [their] own nature'.[13] In the end, Article 62(2) VCLT 1986 is meant to apply only to the State boundaries established by a treaty between States in which an international organization happens to participate because, for example, the treaty envisages functions to be performed by the organization, such as guaranteeing the boundary.[14]

It is thus apparent that, when it comes to territorial matters, the analogy between States and international organizations is defeated by the fact that the two categories of legal subjects present a crucial structural difference. But should international organizations in the future somehow acquire territorial rights by treaty or otherwise, the question of the applicability to international organization of rules on territorial acquisition, use and disposal by States would be reopened. Whether their 'fluid nature', to use Reuter's phrase, invites the adoption of special rules would be at the core of the debate.

3.2 'International Organizations Have No Population'

That international organizations have no population means that some of the rules of general international law that apply to States will not be extended to them by analogy. This is true, for example, of rules the application of which is premised upon the political bond of nationality. As the International Court observed in *Reparation for Injuries*, '[i]t is not possible, by a strained use of the concept of allegiance, to assimilate the legal bond which exists . . . between the Organization on the one hand, and the Secretary-General and the staff on the other, to the bond of nationality existing between a State and its nationals'.[15] The absence of a social and political community of individuals over which an organization exercises personal jurisdiction entails that a wide range of rules – for example, the nationality principle in State jurisdiction and political rights in international human rights law – are either inapplicable to that organization, or at least require considerable adjustments.

Yet, as international organizations evolve and take up new tasks and competences, the picture gets more complicated. For one, the concept of

---

[13] YILC 1980/I, p. 14, para. 34. Similarly, Poland, UNCLT 1986/I, p. 138, para. 2.
[14] Commentary to art. 62, YILC 1982/II, part two, p. 61, para. 11.
[15] *Reparation for Injuries Suffered in the Service of the United Nations* (Advisory Opinion) [1951] ICJ Rep 174, p. 182.

'European citizenship' established under the framework of the European Union creates a novel category of political bond[16] which, though not identical to nationality,[17] raises new questions as to the applicability of rules of general international law to the EU. One such question concerns the possibility for the EU, as an international organization, to exercise diplomatic protection by espousing a claim of an EU citizen on the international plane against a third State.[18] Article 3(5) of the Treaty on the European Union provides that [i]n its relations with the wider world ... the Union shall ... contribute to the protection of its citizens'. Article 20(2)(c) of the Treaty on the Functioning of the EU includes among the privileges of European citizenship 'the right to enjoy, in the territory of a third country in which the Member State of which they are nationals is not represented, the protection of the diplomatic and consular authorities of any Member State on the same conditions as the nationals of that State'. It is not clear whether, as a matter of EU law, those provisions are meant to impose an obligation of exercising diplomatic protection on EU member States as opposed to a much less demanding duty to provide consular assistance. But it has been suggested in the literature not only that they are, but also that they can be construed as empowering the EU itself to espouse a claim of a citizen on the international plane.[19]

From the perspective of international law, can the proposition that the EU is entitled to exercise diplomatic protection be accepted? An analogy with States for that purpose can be rejected if one construes the 'nationality of claims' rule narrowly, as necessarily requiring a political bond between an individual and a State. But a narrow view of

---

[16] See art. 20, Treaty on the Functioning of the European Union, 25 March 1957, (2010) OJ C 83/47, which establishes EU citizenship, comprising rights such as that of residing within the territory of any member State and to vote and stand as candidates in elections to the European Parliament and in municipal elections in the member State where any given EU citizen reside.

[17] As clarified in art. 20(1) TFEU, '[c]itizenship of the Union shall be additional to and not replace national citizenship'.

[18] Art. 1 of the ILC's Articles on Diplomatic Protection defines diplomatic protection as 'the invocation by a State, through diplomatic action or other means of peaceful settlement, of the responsibility of another State for an injury caused by an internationally wrongful act of that State to a natural or legal person that is a national of the former State with a view to the implementation of such responsibility': YILC 2006/II, part two, p. 26.

[19] F. Forni, 'Diplomatic protection in EU law: what's new under the sun?' (2014) 9 *The Hague Journal of Diplomacy* 150 (examining cases in which EU action vis-à-vis third parties went beyond 'functional protection' of EU officials).

nationality might fail to do justice to the rationale of the right of diplomatic protection under international law. As the International Court of Justice stated in the *Nottebohm* case, 'nationality is a legal bond having as its basis a social fact of attachment, a genuine connection of existence, interests and sentiments, together with the existence of reciprocal rights and duties'. That bond entitles a State 'to exercise protection vis-à-vis another State, if it constitutes a translation into juridical terms of the individual's connection with the State which has made him its national'.[20] Could the same idea not be captured by legal bonds that might develop between a highly integrated international organization and individuals subject to its jurisdiction? The case law of the Permanent Court has explained that 'by taking up the case of one of its subjects and by resorting to diplomatic action or international judicial proceedings on his behalf, a State is in reality asserting its own rights – that is to say, its right to ensure, in the person of its subjects, respect for the rules of international law'.[21] That an organization in a similar position ought to be denied that right is far from evident. These are, of course, uncharted waters, but what this discussion shows is that structural differences between States and international organizations can become less relevant as those organizations evolve and increasingly exercise functions that are similar to those of the State.

A similar intuition would seem to underlie the most polemic ruling that the International Court gave in the *Reparation for Injuries* advisory opinion. The UN General Assembly asked the Court whether the United Nations could bring a claim not only for injury that it had itself suffered, but also in relation to injury suffered by its envoy, Folke Bernadotte, who had been assassinated by a group with links to the State of Israel. The Court conceded that 'the analogy of the traditional rule of diplomatic protection of nationals abroad [could not] justify in itself an affirmative reply' and that it was 'faced with a new situation' that 'could only be solved by realizing that the situation is dominated by the provisions of the Charter considered in the light of the principles of international law'.[22] It then affirmed the existence for the organization of a right of 'functional protection', which was required '[t]o ensure the independence

---

[20] *Nottebohm Case (Liechtenstein v. Guatemala),* Second Phase [1955] ICJ Rep. 4, p. 23.
[21] *Serbian Loans (France v. Yugoslavia)* [1929] PCIJ, Series A No. 20, p. 17.
[22] *Reparation for Injuries,* p. 213.

of the agent, and, consequently, the independent action of the Organiza-tion itself.[23]

The Court's finding on functional protection prompted the vigorous dissent of three judges who thought that the majority had gone too far in analogising between States and international organizations. Judge Hackworth stated that 'a theory, based upon supposed analogy, that organizations, not States and hence having no nationals, may act as if they were States and had nationals' was unwarranted.[24] To this day, the right to functional protection remains somewhat uncertain and unexplored.[25] But the Court's intuition that the UN should have a right 'to secure respect for undertakings entered into towards the Organiza-tion' to enable its agents to perform their duties is not necessarily off the mark. Perhaps, rather than a situation that is relevantly similar to that covered by the rules of diplomatic protection, the question standing before the Court did concern 'a new situation': whether autonomous entities operating on the international plane are entitled to bring claims on behalf of their agents. A State which happened to employ a person who did not bear its nationality might need or wish to bring a claim in 'functional protection' if that person were injured in its service. This is a case where the question raised by the comparison between States and international organizations is not simply whether an existing rule can be extended from one category to the other, but whether a new rule should be adopted for *both categories* on the basis of relevant principles or policy considerations.

That international organizations do not have a population with which they are linked by the political bond of nationality is not an objection, of course, to extending to an organization the rules of general international law that create rights for individuals. There has been a progressive acceptance of the proposition that customary rules in the field of human

---

[23] That, the Court thought, arose 'by necessary intendment out of the Charter' (at 183), a line of reasoning that can explain why such a right would arise on the institutional plane, but not why that should be the case on the international plane.

[24] Diss. op. Hackworth, p. 203. Also: diss. Op. Badawi Pasha, p. 216 and diss. op. Krylov, pp. 218–19.

[25] John Dugard (Fifth Report), YILC 2004/II, part one, pp. 49–50, para. 17. The ILC decided to exclude the issue of functional protection from the purview of its project on diplomatic protection: YILC 2006/II, part two, p. 26, para. 3.

rights can be extended to international organizations insofar as the latter's activities affect individuals.[26]

3.3 'International Organizations Have No Centralised Government'

The internal set-ups of States and international organizations are so varied that attempts at generalisation are doomed to fail. Yet, there are models of political organisation by which both categories are characterised. The government of a State is typically organised in branches comprising executive, legislative and judiciary functions,[27] while the classic model of international organizations comprises a plenary organ, a non-plenary organ performing executive functions, and a secretariat composed of international civil servants.[28] Do the institutional particularities that characterise each of the categories of international legal subjects present a challenge to analogising between States and international organizations?

3.3.1 Representation and Attribution of Conduct

In the case of the law of treaties, this question was raised in connection with Article 7 VCLT 1969, which prescribes that, 'in virtue of their functions and without having to produce full powers', Heads of State, Heads of Government and Ministers for Foreign Affairs are all considered 'as representing their State ... for the purpose of performing all acts relating to the conclusion of a treaty'. Extending this rule to international organizations posed two challenges.

First, while the proposition that certain representatives can commit the State *ex officio* is well established,[29] it is less certain that there are categories of representatives of international organizations similarly

---

[26] Benvenisti, 'The law of global governance', pp. 119–21; Sands and Klein, *Bowett's Law of International Institutions*, pp. 476–77; G. Verdirame, *The UN and Human Rights*, pp. 70–72. See also *Prosecutor v. Rwamakuba*, Case No. ICTR-98-44C-T, Decision on Appropriate Remedy (2007), para. 48.

[27] For a perspective from State theory, see H. Kelsen, *General Theory of Law and State* (Cambridge: Harvard University Press, 1945), pp. 269–82.

[28] E.g., Schermers and Blokker, *International Institutional Law*, pp. 290–351 (who view the 'large similarities when comparing the functions of some of the organs to those of organs of other organizations' as an example of 'unity within diversity' at 290).

[29] *Arrest Warrant of 11 April 2000 (Democratic Republic of the Congo v Belgium)* [2002] ICJ Rep 3, para. 53; *Armed Activities on the Territory of the Congo (Democratic Republic of the Congo v Rwanda)* (Jurisdiction and Admissibility) [2006] ICJ Rep 5, para. 46.

entitled to represent the organization on the international plane. From the outset, Special Rapporteur Reuter preferred not to formulate an analogous provision, noting that:

> organizations have no agents specializing in external relations grouped together under the authority of a senior official who is himself a specialist and is in turn subordinate to a supreme head, who, like the Head of State, has general powers of representation. Not only are there radical differences between the general structures of the international organizations themselves; this absence of specialized representatives means that there is also a difference between the case of organizations and the case of the State.[30]

Thus, the Commission rejected a suggestion by Canada to insert a reference to the 'executive head' of the international organization in the draft article being discussed. While this was in part justified by structural differences,[31] the commentary also takes a normative stance by affirming the need to uphold 'the principle that each organization has its own highly individualized structure, and that it decides, according to its own rules, on that capacity, status and title of the person responsible for representing it without powers'.[32] Thus, the decision not to formulate a rule on *ex officio* representatives analogous to that applicable to States was buttressed by the idea that international organizations have special characteristics.

Second, once the Commission decided not to adopt a rule on *ex officio* representatives for international organizations, the question arose of whether that meant that the agents of an organization were required to produce full powers at every occasion. If so, the rule contained in paragraph 1(b) of Article 7 VCLT 1969, dispensing full powers when

---

[30] Reuter (Second Report), YILC 1973/II, pp. 84–85, para. 59.

[31] Commentary to art. 7, YILC 1982/II, part two, p. 26, para. 8.

[32] Ibid., p. 27, para. 15. In a similar vein, the ILC sought to differentiate between States and IOs by adding to draft art. 67 a provision requiring that instruments issued by IOs to declare invalid, terminate, withdraw from or suspend the operation of a treaty be accompanied by full powers. This constituted a departure from art. 67 VCLT 1969, pursuant to which State representatives may be 'called upon' to produce full powers. The Special Rapporteur suggested that '[i]f international organizations seem to be treated more strictly than States', that was because they had no *ex officio* representatives comparable to those of States: Reuter (Ninth Report), YILC 1980/II, part one, p. 140, para. 3. The distinction was ultimately deleted on second reading, the Commission having concluded that 'it was difficult to justify requiring production of powers where the agent making the communication was at the same time the agent authorized to issue powers': commentary to art. 67, YILC 1982/II, part two, p. 66, para. 3.

those can be inferred from 'the practice of the States concerned or from other circumstances', should not be extended to international organizations. Certain members were sceptical of the existence of a 'general practice', common to international organizations, that would justify retaining this rule.[33] But the Commission decided that because Article 7(1)(b) VCLT 1969 referred to the practice of individual States in their relations with others – not to some general practice of States – it was appropriate that international organizations be also covered by the rule.[34] At the Vienna Conference, the Soviet Union proposed an amendment to the ILC draft which would have required representatives of international organizations to produce full powers at all times.[35] The reason was that they 'knew of no treaties where the presentation of full powers (with the exceptions set out in article 7, paragraph 2, of the Vienna Convention) was not an obligation on all the parties'.[36] The Council of Europe and the United Nations disagreed, replying that the practice of not requiring full powers in certain circumstances had consolidated over four decades of treaty-making by international organizations.[37] Their position ultimately prevailed, and the Conference rejected the Soviet amendment.

A related point concerning perceived structural differences between States and international organizations involved the use by the Commission, on first reading, of the phrase 'communicate consent to be bound by a treaty'. Instead of the standard phrase 'express consent' that VCLT 1969 employs, the Commission had favoured the phrase 'communicate consent' to describe the act whereby representatives of an organization express agreement to a treaty on its behalf.[38] Soviet member Leonid Ushakov had pushed for this distinction, arguing that only State representatives could be empowered to bind the State and thus genuinely *express* its consent. In contrast, representatives of international organizations could only be allowed to *communicate* the consent expressed by the competent political organ.[39] This overly formalistic position was later abandoned, and for good reason. States and international organizations are both intellectual constructs that act through persons and flesh and bone: the notion that there are inherent differences in their respective

---

[33] Ushakov, YILC 1975/I, p. 209, para. 12; Ago, ibid., p. 213, para. 48.
[34] Reuter, YILC 1975/I, p. 218, para. 65.
[35] UNCLT 1986/II, p. 67, para. 42.
[36] Soviet Union, UNCLT 1986/I, p. 71, para. 33.
[37] Council of Europe, ibid., p. 72, para. 58; United Nations, ibid., p. 73, para. 68.
[38] E.g., art. 47 as adopted on first reading: YILC 1981/II, part two.
[39] E.g., Ushakov, YILC 1982/I, p. 138, para. 17.

institutional architectures that mean that the agents of one can 'express' consent on its behalf while the agents of the other can only 'communicate' such consent cannot stand scrutiny.

In the context of the codification and progressive development of the law of responsibility, differences in internal set-up between States and international organizations permeated the debate on the rules of attribution of conduct. The general rule of attribution contained in Article 4 ARS covers the acts of organs performing legislative, executive and judicial functions, whether these belong both to the central government or to territorial subunits compounding the State. Because this terminology cannot be readily employed for international organizations, Article 6 ARIO prescribes, more economically, that the conduct of an organ or agent will be attributed to the organization 'whatever position the organ or agent holds in respect of the organization'.[40] Likewise, institutional differences between States and international organizations led the Commission not to extend to the ARIO Articles 5 and 8 ARS, on attribution of conduct of persons or entities exercising elements of governmental authority, and attribution of conduct directed or controlled by a State, respectively. The Commission adopted instead an expansive definition of 'agent' covering officials or other persons or entities that are 'charged by the organization with carrying out, or helping to carry out, one of its functions, and thus through whom the organization acts'.[41] According to the commentary, entities that have been empowered to exercise functions of the organization and entities that the latter directs or controls are to be regarded as 'agents' of the under that expansive definition.[42] In short, though particularities regarding the internal setups of international organizations led to some textual and structural departures from the ARS, the general principle underlying the general rule of attribution for States was extended to organizations, which will be liable for the actions and omissions of all persons acting on their authority or under their control.

3.3.2 Silence and the Acquisition and Loss of Rights

Given the particularities of the internal set-ups of international organizations, can their silence have the same legal effects as the silence of States?

---

[40] Commentary to art. 6, YILC 2011/II, part two, p. 56, para. 8.
[41] Article 2(d) ARIO.
[42] Commentary to art. 6, YILC 2011/II, part two, p. 56, paras. 10–11.

This was an issue arising in the discussion of a number of provisions in the codification of the law of treaties and the law of responsibility. Some proposals to treat States and international organizations differently were rejected, while others were accepted.

According to Article 36(1) VCLT 1969, which fleshes out the *pacta tertii* rule, a third State is presumed to assent to the rights created by a treaty for its benefit 'so long as the contrary is not indicated'. Special Rapporteur Reuter proposed to extend this rule to international organizations, but the Commission decided otherwise. Because the decision-making of the political organs of an international organization was different from – and in many respects more complex than – that of State governments, it was decided that the assent of a third organization to a treaty right was not to be presumed.[43] As a result, Article 36 VCLT 1986 provides that this assent 'shall be governed by the rules of the organization'. That being the case, construing the internal law of the organization is needed for establishing whether the organization has tacitly accepted a right provided by a treaty between third parties.

Pursuant to Article 45(b) VCLT 1969, a State may lose its right to invoke a ground for invalidating, terminating, withdrawing from or suspending the operation of a treaty by acquiescing to the treaty's validity. During the codification of the law of treaties concerning international organizations, Reuter made alternative proposals: either to replicate the rule contained in the Vienna Convention in its entirety ('solution A') or to drop it completely ('solution B').[44] The choice to be made by the Commission was described in the following terms:

> solution B has, as it were, the effect, if not the purpose, of protecting the organization against its own conduct, that is, it treats the organization in the same way that private law treats all those who by reason of their youth or weakness are treated as 'incapacitated'. Solution A, on the other hand, which is designed to protect the co-contractants of the organization, draws all the inferences of the participation of an international organization in international relations.[45]

The normative concern which animated 'solution B' was that, given the structural differences between States and international organizations, silence on the part of the political and administrative organs of an

[43] Ushakov, YILC 1977/I, p. 132, para. 15; Schwebel, ibid., p. 133, para. 19; Riphagen, ibid., p. 134, para. 25.
[44] Reuter (Eighth Report), YILC 1979/II, part one, p. 131.
[45] Ibid., p. 131, para. 3.

organization should not be construed as acquiescence. Some members of the Commission were convinced by the analogy that Reuter drew between international organizations and 'incapacitated persons' and suggested that, being the 'weaker party', organizations indeed deserved protection.[46] Others rejected this view by pointing to situations in which international organizations can hardly be viewed as the weaker party, such as when a State facing public debt asks the International Monetary Fund for a loan.[47] The draft article proposed by the Commission reached a compromise between the two positions, prescribing that, for the loss of a right to invoke a ground for invalidating, terminating, withdrawing from or suspending the operation of a treaty to take effect, the organization 'must by reason of the conduct of the competent organ be considered as having renounced the right to invoke that ground'.[48] On the one hand, the basic principle that applies to States was extended to international organizations 'for the security of the organization's treaty partners, and even out of respect for the principle of good faith'.[49] On the other hand, the term 'renunciation' was employed to reflect the idea that '[w]ith regard to States, it [is] sufficient for the conduct to indicate acquiescence – in other words, a sort of passive attitude – whereas for international organizations, the conduct must be considered as signifying renunciation', an attitude 'more active than acquiescence'.[50]

At the Vienna Conference, amendments were proposed to realign the text of Article 45(2)(b) with VCLT 1969 or at least to omit the reference to the 'competent organ' of an international organization.[51] France defended the Commission's text, stating that 'the distinction ... between acquiescence and renunciation was a wise one and should be maintained', for '[t]he silence of an international organization might, because of the complexity of the organization's structure, be due to factors quite other than the competent organ's implicit assent'.[52] Other delegations did not think that any such differentiation between States and international organizations was tenable from a legal point of view.[53] All amendments were then sent to the Conference's drafting committee,

---

[46] E.g., Sucharitkul, YILC 1979/I, p. 79, para. 5.

[47] Schwebel, ibid., pp. 81–82, para. 20.

[48] Art. 45(b) VCLT 1986.

[49] Commentary to art. 45, YILC 1982/II, part two, p. 51, para. 5.

[50] Reuter, YILC 1982/I, p. 129, para. 11.

[51] UNCLT 1986/II, p. 72, para. 96.

[52] UNCLT 1986/I, p. 123, para. 13.

[53] E.g., Netherlands, UNCLT 1986/I, p. 128, paras. 27–28.

which, without much explanation, chose to retain the Commission's text, now found in Article 45(2)(b) VCLT 1986.[54]

In the context of the codification the law of responsibility, the issue of loss of rights arose when the Commission considered the rule in Article 45(b) ARS, according to which '[t]he responsibility a State may not be invoked if ... the injured State is to be considered as having, by reasons of its conduct, validly acquiesced in the lapse of the claim'. In contrast to what happened in the 1970s, the issue of whether an international organization could forfeit a right by acquiescence was not the subject of substantive debate at the Commission – at least not in plenary.[55] Article 46 ARIO thus replicates the text of Article 45 ARS, confirming that the silence of an international organization may entail the loss of a right to invoke responsibility. That said, the commentary softens this position somehow by specifying that 'special features of international organizations make it generally difficult to ... assess whether acquiescence on the part of the organization has taken place' and that 'acquiescence on the part of an international organization may involve a longer period than the one normally sufficient for States'.[56] Still, the change in approach from the project on treaties to the project on responsibility is clear. In the ARIO, any structural differences between States and international organizations are only relevant as part of the interpretative context in which the rule in Article 46 is to be applied, and do not necessarily affect the applicable legal regime. The opposite seems to be the case with Articles 36 and 45(2)(b) VCLT 1986.

A similar debate took place when the ILC considered two provisions of VCLT 1969 which impose time-limits for States to act. Those are Article 20(5), establishing a presumption of acceptance of reservations if the parties to a treaty do not raise an objection within twelve months; and Article 65, which prescribes a three-month period for a party to a treaty wishing to oppose another's notification of invalidity, termination, withdrawal from or suspension of the operation of the treaty to place its objection.

---

[54] UNCLT 1986/I, p. 22, para. 52.

[55] When art. 46 (then draft art. 45) was adopted on first reading, the Chairman of the Drafting Committee reported that '[s]ome members had been of the opinion that, given the nature and structure of international organizations, they should not be easily considered as having waived a claim or acquiesced in its lapse': Comissário Afonso, YILC 2008/I, p. 89, para. 51.

[56] Commentary to art. 46, YILC 2011/II, part two, A/66/10, p. 87, para. 2.

As regards Article 20(5), a member of the Commission maintained that 'the time-limit of twelve months would not be sufficient because, in some international organizations, the competent organs held only two sessions each year'.[57] Contradicting the Special Rapporteur's opinion,[58] the drafting committee adopted a provision on objections to reservations that imposed the twelve-month limit for States, but did not extend it to international organizations, thus leaving a gap to be filled by future practice.[59] The Commission expressed the hope, in the commentary, that 'practice would have no great difficulty in producing remedies for the prolongation of a situation whose drawbacks should not be exaggerated'.[60] However, the gap was heavily criticised at the 1986 Vienna Conference, where delegations pointed to the uncertainty that it introduced into the law of reservations.[61] Amendments were then proposed either to make the twelve-month limit applicable to international organizations, adopt a more generous time-limit, or adopt a default time-limit while providing for some flexibility for organizations whose political organs do not hold annual sessions.[62] Although international organizations participating in the Conference were not opposed to the adoption of a time-limit, they advocated for a more flexible rule than that applicable to States in the light of 'the very real differences that existed in the nature and functioning of States and international organizations'.[63] Without much explanation, the Conference decided to realign the draft with VCLT 1969, so that Article 20(5) VCLT 1986 does not distinguish between States and international organizations.

In contrast, while similar objections were made to extending to international organizations the three-month deadline imposed by Article 65 VCLT 1969,[64] the Commission did not seriously consider adopting a special rule for organizations in this regard. Rather, as Special Rapporteur

---

[57] Ushakov, YILC 1981/I, pp. 51–52, para. 6. Ushakov, in fact, thought that 'it was impossible to formulate a rule whereby silence on the part of an international organization would be tantamount to acceptance of a reservation' (ibid., para. 8).

[58] Reuter (Tenth Report), YILC 1981/II, part one, pp. 62–63, paras. 80–81.

[59] Díaz González (reporting for the Drafting Committee), YILC 1981/I, p. 264, para. 29.

[60] Commentary to art. 20, YILC 1982/II, part two, p. 36, para. 6.

[61] China, UNCLT 1986/I, p. 104, para. 45; Morocco, ibid., para. 110, para. 34.

[62] See the amendments proposed by Austria, China and Australia, UNCLT 1986/II, 70, para. 70.

[63] FAO, UNCLT 1986/I, p. 109, para. 25. FAO and UNIDO observed that their competent organs normally met every two years: UNIDO, ibid., pp. 106–07, para. 72; and FAO, ibid., p. 109, para. 2.

[64] Ushakov, YILC 1980/I, p. 21, para. 34.

Reuter pointed out, the time-limit ought to be retained because 'there was always, within an organization, one organ which was permanently in session and could duly raise an objection' to a notification of invalidity, termination, withdrawal from or suspension of the operation of the treaty'. Adopting a longer period for international organizations, he added, 'would amount to creating serious discrimination against States and in favour of international organizations'.[65]

3.4   Assessing the Significance of Structural Differences

Structural differences between States and international organizations can provide convincing reasons for departing from analogical reasoning in the identification of the rules that apply to international organizations under general international law. Thus, for example, the fact that international organizations do not possess territory means that they are not 'relevantly similar' to States for the purpose of transposing rules concerning territory, and the fact that they do not possess a population means that they are not 'relevantly similar' to States for the purpose of transposing rules concerning nationality. It can be questioned, however, whether such structural differences are substantive objections to the analogy as opposed to mere limitations on the relevance of certain rules of general international law to international organizations. The former would be the case if territory and population were treated as exclusive features of statehood, so that any intergovernmental institution that acquired territory or the power to rule over a population on a permanent basis would cease to be an international organization and become a State. But such a rigid conception of what States and international organizations are might lack nuance. If an organization were to conclude a treaty of cession to acquire an island for its headquarters or develop novel political bonds with the population of its member States (as is increasingly happening with the EU), it might still remain a self-governing territorial and political community that does not – nor purports to – exercise all the functions of a State. In such cases, there would be little difficulty in extending to international organizations by analogy rules that normally are only relevant for States.

As the debates at the ILC and at the 1986 Vienna Conference suggest, there is an even greater risk of overplaying differences in institutional

---

[65] Reuter, YILC 1982/I, pp. 153–54, para. 56. Ushakov denied that there was a 'problem of discrimination . . . because States and international organizations were two entirely different subjects of law' (ibid., p. 154, para. 49). Similarly, Balanda, ibid., p. 154, para. 50.

architecture, which should not necessarily affect the legal regime applicable to international organizations. If, like States, organizations are legally autonomous entities operating on the international plane, they must be expected to exercise their treaty-making capacity while complying with the 'rules of the game'. As Reuter remarked:

> [It was not] possible to establish a privileged status for international organizations that would be justified by their organic weakness. If the security necessary for legal relations was not to be destroyed, the principle must be that whoever participated in such relations was bound by his conduct.[66]

This was why proposals that would have given to international organizations a larger time-limit to perform certain acts – or left those issues unregulated – were ultimately rejected.[67] If the time frame for action is laid down in advance, with a view to promoting legal security in treaty relations, it should be up to each organization to devise internal mechanisms to cope with the requirements imposed by the law of treaties. Doing otherwise would result in arbitrary discrimination between the two categories of legal subjects.

A similar position is implied in the ILC's reluctance to engage with two arguments raised by international organizations in the context of the responsibility project. The first concerned the possibility of responsibility by omission. The International Monetary Fund put forth the view that a significant difference between States and international organizations was that that the latter's omissions may result from 'the application of the organization's decision-making process under its constitutive charters'.[68] The Fund was referring to political stalemates that may prevent the adoption of resolutions and decisions without which the organization is unable to take action. Dismissing the argument, Special Rapporteur Gaja noted that 'difficulties with compliance due to the political decision-making process are not the prerogative of international organizations'.[69] Indeed, the foreign ministries of States often have their

---

[66] Reuter, YILC 1981/I, p. 53, para. 20.

[67] As Reuter pointed out, '[i]f the rule that silence amounted to tacit acceptance after twelve months applied to States acting on their own, States acting collectively through an international organization would be favoured by being given an indefinite time in which to make their positions known': YILC 1981, p. 50, para. 51.

[68] IMF, A/CN.4/545 (2004), p. 13.

[69] Gaja (Third Report), YILC 2005/II, part one, p. 9, para. 9. Similarly, Kabatsi noted that '[i]t would be unfortunate if those organizations were allowed to shirk their responsibility by claiming that they had been unable to comply with their international obligations

hands tied due to political stalemates or judicial decisions blocking courses of action.

The second argument concerned the obligation to provide full reparation arising from the commission of an internationally wrongful act. Twelve organizations suggested that upholding the principle of full reparation 'could lead to excessive exposure taking into account that international organizations in general do not generate their own financial resources but rely on compulsory or voluntary contributions from their members'.[70] As a member of the Commission noted, departing from the principle would amount to the 'negation of international law'.[71] Why should a corporate entity through which States act collectively be exempted from liability for wrongful acts on the international plane? Whatever institutional weaknesses organizations may suffer from should be of no concern to third parties. Furthermore, it is evident that the ILC could not have departed from the principle of full reparation without clear prompts in the practice or *opinio juris* of States. But as the Special Rapporteur noted, no State had criticised the Commission's approach to the content of the responsibility of international organizations.[72] The Commentary thus states that:

> It may be difficult for an international organization to have all the necessary means for making the required reparation. This fact is linked to the inadequacy of the financial resources that are generally available to international organizations for meeting this type of expense. However, that inadequacy cannot exempt a responsible organization from the legal consequences resulting from its responsibility under international law.[73]

In short, when it comes to differences in architectural structure, objections to the analogy between States and international organizations become are far from compelling. The rejection of the notion of acquiescence for international organization in the context of treaties provides the odd example of a departure from VCLT 1969 justified on the basis of an institutional difference. Whether this departure has stood (or should stand) the test of subsequent practice and precedent is hard to tell.

owing to difficulties in their internal decision-making process': YILC 2005/I, p. 87, para. 42. For a more nuanced position, though ultimately agreeing with the Special Rapporteur's approach, Pellet, ibid., p. 70, para. 51.

[70] Joint Submission, A/CN.4/637 (2011) 30.
[71] Pellet, A/CN.4/SR.3084 (2011), p. 7.
[72] Gaja (Eighth Report), A/CN.4/640 (2011), p. 25, para. 74.
[73] Commentary to art. 31, YILC 2011/II, part two, p. 77, para. 4.

4

International Organizations as 'Special Subjects'

The phrase 'principle of speciality' became part of the legal discourse on international organizations when the International Court of Justice coined it in the *Nuclear Weapons (WHO Request)* advisory opinion in 1996.[1] While the Court employed it to emphasise the limited competences that organizations have under their constituent instruments, the notion of 'speciality' has been invoked to convey a range of ideas.[2] This is evident in the debates at the International Law Commission concerning the codification and progressive development of the law of treaties and responsibility, where the 'special character' of international organizations was taken to mean not only that the 'special subjects' must be distinguished from the 'general subjects', but also that international organizations are different from each other.[3] As the General Commentary to the ARIO observes:

> International organizations are quite different from States, and in addition present great diversity among themselves. In contrast with States, they do not possess a general competence and have been established in

---

[1] *Legality of the Use of Nuclear Weapons in Armed Conflict* (Advisory Opinion) [1996] ICJ Rep 66, para. 25. See E. Lauterpacht, 'Judicial review of acts of international organizations' in L. B. Chazournes and P. Sands (eds.), *International Law, the International Court of Justice and Nuclear Weapons* (Cambridge: Cambridge University Press, 1999), p. 99 at note 12, suggesting that the term was borrowed from French administrative law. Indeed, neither the ICJ nor its predecessor had ever used it before.

[2] Two terminological clarifications must be made at this juncture. First, while this chapter discusses a range of arguments for differentiation between States and IOs under the umbrella of speciality, the term was not current during the codification of the law of treaties in the 1970s. Second, for reasons of clarity, the phrase 'principle of speciality' is used in the sense that it was originally coined in *Nuclear Weapons (WHO Request)*, that is, to refer to the notion of IOs as subjects with limited competences as discussed in Section 4.3.

[3] As McRae pointed out, the term speciality was used to 'refer to the divergence between the draft articles on responsibility of international organizations and the articles on state responsibility, and to refer to differences between international organizations *inter se*': A.CN.4./SR.3081 (2011), p. 7.

order to exercise specific functions ('principle of speciality'). There are
very significant differences among international organizations with regard
to their powers and functions, size of membership, relations between the
organization and its members, procedures for deliberation, structure and
facilities, as well as the primary rules including treaty obligations by which
they are bound. Because of this diversity and its implications, the draft
articles where appropriate give weight to the specific character of the
organization, especially to its functions.[4]

But what does it mean to 'give weight to the specific character' of an
international organization? Does that 'specific character' displace the
proposition that States and international organizations are analogous
for the purpose of the law of treaties, the law of responsibility and other
subfields of international law? Those are questions that can only be
tackled when one 'unpacks' the notion of speciality and considers the
various propositions associated with it. This chapter addresses three such
propositions: (i) that international organizations are different from one
another and must thus be treated differently; (ii) that the 'secondary' or
'derivative' subjects of international law must be distinguished from the
'primary' or 'original' subjects and (iii) that general international law
should reflect the fact that international organizations, unlike States, are
entrusted with limited competences by their constituent instruments.
The chapter then discusses the connection between the notions of speciality and *lex specialis* and assesses the extent to which speciality may
provide an interpretative framework for the application of general international law to international organizations.

4.1   Different Rules for Different International Organizations?

The view that international organizations are fundamentally unequal
entities in the eye of international law, which results from the adoption
of a 'treaty conception' of the status of international organizations, has
been discussed in Chapter 2 and needs not be reconsidered here.[5] But an
important question arises even if one subscribes to the 'subject conception' and accepts that international organizations form a category of
legally autonomous entities operating on the international plane. Given
the differences in terms of mandate, institutional set-up and membership
that exist among international organizations, do they form a unitary

---

[4] General commentary, YILC 2011/II, part two, p. 47, para. 7.
[5] See section 2.1.

category of legal subjects? Or could it be rather argued that existing organizations must be divided into subcategories to which different sets of rights, duties and capacities accrue?[6] If the latter is true, attempts to analogise between States and international organizations that do not take into consideration the particularities of each subcategory will be defeated.

4.1.1   Universal and Regional Organizations

A first distinction that comes to mind is that between international organizations of universal character – that is, organizations aspiring to universal membership, such as the United Nations – and international organizations of regional scope – that is, organizations with limited membership, such as the European Union. The ILC adopted that distinction in preparing the set of articles that take the form of the 1975 Vienna Convention on the Representation of States in their Relations with International Organizations of a Universal Character (not yet in force). The Commission's objective was not, however, to establish separate regimes for different categories of international organizations. Instead, the decision to delimit the scope of the project reflected the Commission's hesitation to deal with problems arising from the status of regional international organizations under international law.[7] A saving clause was added to Article 2 with a view to clarifying that the 1975 Convention was without prejudice to 'the application to the representation of States in their relations with . . . other organizations of any of the rules set forth in the Convention which would be applicable under international law independently of the Convention'. In the commentary, the Commission noted that the purpose of this clause was 'to give due recognition to the fact that certain provisions in the draft articles are or are likely to become

---

[6] For classifications adopted for pedagogic purposes, see generally H. Schermers and N. Blokker, *International Institutional Law: Unity within Diversity*, 5th edn (Leiden: Nijhoff, 2011), pp. 50–59. A classic study on the subject is M. Virally, 'Definition and classification of international organizations: a legal approach' in G. Abi-Saab (ed.), *The Concept of International Organization* (Paris: Unesco, 1981), pp. 56–64.

[7] This attests to the influence of the 'treaty conception' of IOs back in the 1960s. As the Special Rapporteur explained, 'the study of regional organizations raised a number of problems, such as recognition by, and relationship with, non-member States, which would call for the formulation of special rules for those organizations': El-Erian (Second Report), YILC 1967/II, p. 148, para. 89.

customary international law', which suggests that the Commission was envisaging rules capable of more general application.[8]

Half a decade later, when it embarked on the codification of the law of treaties concerning international organizations, the Commission declined to follow the path that had been taken for the topic of representation. Special Rapporteur Reuter favoured the broad definition adopted in VCLT 1969 – '"international organization" means an intergovernmental organization' – because he wanted to ensure that the project would encompass all organizations that conclude treaties. In his words:

> the goal of codification is the unification of legal rules as well as the stabilization of their development. How much authority with regard to the law of treaties would be carried by codification instruments which disregarded, for example, agreements concluded by regional organizations?[9]

The issue of the inequality between subcategories of international organizations arose when the ILC pondered the legal character of the treaties that they conclude between themselves. In a striking passage in the debates, Reuter affirmed that 'treaties between international organizations were, paradoxically, more akin to treaties between States than to treaties between one or more States and one or more international organizations, since they involved entities of a similar nature and standing'.[10] To his mind, from the perspective of the law of treaties, differences between international organizations interacting on the international plane had to be treated as internal matters pertaining to each organization but having no bearing on the validity and application of the agreement. In Reuter's words:

> since a treaty between a universal organization and a regional organization . . . has a legal value and since its legal regime cannot depend either on the law of the universal organization or on the law of the regional organization, it must be admitted that the treaty derives this value from general international law . . . There is therefore no reason to

---

[8] Commentary to art. 2, YILC 1971/II, part one, p. 287, para. 3. The Convention was ultimately unsuccessful due to its overly generous conferral of immunities against the interests of host States: J. G. Fennessy, 'The 1975 Vienna Convention on the Representation of States in Their Relations with International Organizations of a Universal Character' (1976) 70 AJIL 62, 71–72.
[9] Reuter (Third Report), YILC 1974/II, part one, p. 142, para. 3.
[10] Reuter, YILC 1981/I, p. 3, para. 6.

exclude from the sphere of application of the draft articles treaties to which organizations in any particular category are parties: to do so would be to confuse general international law with the law peculiar to each organization or, at best, with comparative law.[11]

Therefore, the distinction between universal and regional organizations in international discourse has been more descriptive than prescriptive. It does not seem to have resulted in the diversification of legal regimes applying to international organizations.

4.1.2   Regional Integration Organizations

Speciality as an argument for distinguishing between international organizations was a polemic topic in the codification and progressive development of the law of responsibility. The debate revolved around whether 'supranational organizations' such as the European Union should be addressed by different rules from those applying to 'classical intergovernmental organizations'. This was a point that the European Commission repeatedly made in its comments on the draft articles being prepared by the ILC:

> Unlike classical intergovernmental organizations, the European Community (EC) constitutes a legal order of its own, with comprehensive legislative and treaty-making powers, deriving from transfer of competence from the member States to the Community level.[12]

As the European Commission emphasised, a concept of 'regional (economic) integration organization' has emerged in international legal discourse.[13] It is used in multilateral treaties such as the 1994 Energy Charter Treaty and the 2006 UN Convention on the Rights of Persons with Disabilities to refer to organizations to which members 'have transferred competences' over the areas regulated by the agreement in question.[14] In fact, it is usually organizations belonging to this category that are allowed to become party to important multilateral treaties otherwise reserved for States.[15] Paasivirta and Kuijper have argued that the relevant

[11] Reuter (Third Report), YILC 1974/II, part one, p. 143, paras. 7–8.
[12] European Community, A/CN.4/545 (2004), p. 10.
[13] Ibid.
[14] Compare art. 1(3), Energy Charter Treaty with art. 44, 2006 Convention on the Rights of Persons with Disabilities.
[15] E.g., 1982 UN Convention on the Law of the Sea, open to 'intergovernmental organization[s] constituted by States to which its Member States have transferred

multilateral treaty practice evidences 'wide "third-party" recognition of special features' of the category, so that it has now become 'a significant legal fact for the purposes of international law'.[16] But how would the legal regime applicable to regional integration organizations differ from that applicable to other international organizations? It has been suggested that a consequence of the emergence of that new category is that third parties must recognise 'a division of powers between the organization and its members.'[17]

This has consequences for how conduct is to be attributed to the organization. In the debates at the ILC, the European Commission advocated for the adoption of a special rule of attribution for the EU. Because of the level of integration achieved between the EU and its member States, and given that the latter have transferred to the Union exclusive competences that they are no longer in a position to exercise, it was suggested that acts taken by members in the implementation of their obligations under EU law should be attributed to the Union alone.[18]

The position of the EU finds support in panel reports adopted by the World Trade Organization's dispute settlement mechanism and in the writings of commentators.[19] In *EC – Geographical Indications*, a WTO panel accepted the argument advanced by the then European Communities to the effect that member States could 'act *de facto* as organs of the Community, for which the Community would be responsible under WTO law and international law in general'.[20] This approach was not followed, however, by the European Court of Human Rights in various

competence over matters governed by this Convention, including competence to enter into treaties in respect of those matters' (arts. 1 and 4, Annex IX); and 1994 Agreement establishing the World Trade Organization, according to which the EU is a founding member of the WTO (art XI) and 'customs territory possessing full autonomy in the conduct of its external commercial relations' are eligible to apply for accession (art., XII(1)).

[16] E. Paasivirta and P. J. Kuijper, 'Does one size fit all?: the European Community and the responsibility of international organizations' (2007) 36 *Netherlands Yearbook of International Law* 169, 210.

[17] Ibid., p. 211.

[18] A/CN.4/556 (2005), p. 6.

[19] Notably, Paasivirta and Kuijper, 'Does one size fit all?', 212–15, F. Hoffmeister, 'Litigating against the European Union and its member States: who responds under the ILC's draft articles on international responsibility of international organizations?' (2010) 21 EJIL 723, 739–47, and S. Talmon, 'Responsibility of international organizations: does the European Community require special treatment?' in M. Ragazzi (ed.), *International Responsibility Today* (Leiden: Nijhoff, 2005), pp. 419–21.

[20] *EC – Protection of Trademarks and Geographical Indications for Agricultural Products and Foodstuffs*, WT/DS174/R, 20 April 2005, para. 7.98.

cases concerning alleged human rights violations by member States in the implementation of EU rules. Instead, the European Court has consistently maintained that acts committed by member States remain within its jurisdictional purview, implying that those acts are not attributable to the Union alone.[21]

Given the conflicting positions in the case law, the ILC stated that 'it seem[ed] preferable at the current stage of judicial developments not to assume that a special rule has come into existence to the effect that, when implementing a binding act of the European Community, State authorities would act as organs of the European Community'.[22] As a result, the Commission did not formulate a special provision on attribution for regional integration organizations. In the commentary to the general clause on *lex specialis* in Article 64 ARIO, however, the Commission conceded that such a rule could exist as a special rule of international law.[23] But that places the burden on the EU to prove the existence of the special rule, presumably on the basis of State practice and *opinio juris* regarding the relations between the Union and third parties. It is interesting, in this connection, to note that in the on-going negotiations for the accession of the EU to the European Convention on Human Rights, the parties involved have drafted a protocol that departs from the special rule of attribution suggested by the European Commission in the debates at the ILC.[24] Under the draft protocol of accession, individuals are to file a case against the entity whose organs have breached the Convention, and a co-respondent mechanism has been devised to allow for the joint participation of the EU and its member States whenever such breaches are linked to the implementation of EU law.[25]

---

[21] E.g., *Bosphorus Hava Yollari Turizm ve Ticaret AS v. Ireland* (App no 45036/98) ECHR 2005-VI, para 137. On the difference in approach between WTO panels and the ECtHR: Hoffmeister, 'Litigating against the European Union', pp. 738–39.

[22] YILC 2005/II, part two, p. 45, para. 7.

[23] Commentary to art. 64, YILC 2011/II, part two, pp. 102–03, paras. 2–5.

[24] See G. Gaja, 'The "co-respondent mechanisms" according to the Draft Agreement for the Accession of the EU to the ECHR' (2013) 2 *ESIL Reflections*, para. 3 <www.esil-sedi.eu/sites/default/files/ESIL%20Reflections%20-%20Gaja_0.pdf> accessed 29 Jan 2018.

[25] Art. 1(4), Draft revised agreement on the accession of the European Union to the Convention for the Protection of Human Rights and Fundamental Freedoms <www.echr.coe.int/Documents/UE_Report_CDDH_ENG.pdf > accessed 29 January 2018. The process of accession has come to a halt after the Court of Justice of the European Union decided, *inter alia*, that the draft agreement would 'affect the Union's competences as defined in the Treaties': Opinion 2/13 (2014).

Another debate on the possibility of adopting special rules for regional integration organizations took place when Special Rapporteur Gaja suggested adding a new substantive provision to Article 57, concerning countermeasures 'taken by States or international organizations other than an injured State or organization'. That new provision would have recognised the right of a 'regional economic integration organization' to take countermeasures on behalf of its members when the latter transfer to the organization competences affecting the obligations concerned.[26] The reasoning behind the Special Rapporteur's proposal was that, by transferring competences to international organizations, States might find themselves 'unable to take effective countermeasures'.[27] This proposal was not well received by the Commission, though, one of the reasons being the use of the concept of 'regional economic integration organization'. It was pointed out in the debate that the terminology implied that the right to take countermeasures on behalf of members would only accrue for regional organizations of a very specific kind, a solution that would discriminate against other organizations to which States may also transfer competences.[28] It was also suggested that there were no reasons 'why an entity denominated a regional economic integration organization should be given special status', for that would not be 'consonant with current law'.[29] The Commission thus rejected the Special Rapporteur's proposal.[30]

4.1.3   The Challenge of Establishing Subcategories

The possibility of devising 'specific rules for different categories of international organizations' was considered at the beginning of the responsibility project, on the ground that it might be 'unreasonable to look for general rules applying to all intergovernmental organizations'.[31] However, as work on the topic progressed, the Commission refrained

---

[26] Gaja (Sixth Report), YILC 2008/II, part one, pp. 28–30.

[27] Ibid., p. 29, para. 60.

[28] As Nolte observed, '[a]n air-traffic control organization, for example, might not be linked to a regional economic integration organization but might still have certain exclusive powers which would have to be used in order to implement certain countermeasures': YILC 2008/I, p. 36, para. 34; also, Pellet, ibid., pp. 40–41, para. 8; Wisnumurti, ibid., p. 46, para. 41; Kolodkin, ibid., p. 47, para. 51.

[29] Vasciannie, YILC 2008/I, p. 55, para. 42.

[30] Candioti (reporting for the Working Group on countermeasures), A/CN.4/SR.2978 (2008) 18.

[31] YILC 2002/II, part two, 94, para 472.

from discussing specific categories except in cases when it considered the position of the EU and regional integration organizations. As the first reading of the ARIO was coming to an end, Donald McRae reopened the debate on the Commission's methodology, suggesting that there might be a need to establish distinct regimes for different international organizations.[32] This occurred when the Commission was discussing the issue of the responsibility that arises for members in connection with an organization's conduct. McRae offered the following comment:

> The Commission might be creating rather than solving problems by treating smaller international organizations with limited capacities and processes for dealing with the consequences of international responsibility in the same way as the United Nations, an organization that could clearly handle issues of responsibility. In fact, the Commission might be formulating rules that would work admirably for some international organizations, but which would be unrealistic for many smaller organizations ... A possible alternative solution would be to distinguish between different organizations, or different types of organizations. Would it not be more appropriate to have different rules on responsibility, at least as far as reparation was concerned, given that organizations themselves differed vastly in scope, mandate and capacities?[33]

The suggestion to reorient the responsibility project at that stage was met with fierce opposition.[34] Should the Commission have taken it more seriously, though? Part of the explanation of why the Commission extended rules from the ARS international organizations was the sparseness of practice and precedent concerning the general rules that apply to their responsibility. That approach can be justified on the view that, as legally autonomous entities operating on the international plane, international organizations are analogous to States. But when one tries to move beyond that general proposition and formulate special rules for different categories of organizations, one is at a loss to find in the sparse practice and precedent any meaningful guidance as to what might be the legally relevant criteria for dividing organizations into subcategories.[35] As

---

[32] YILC 2007/I, p. 131, para. 81.

[33] Ibid.

[34] E.g., Pellet, YILC 2007/I, p. 138, para. 88.

[35] See J. Klabbers, 'Unity, diversity, accountability: the ambivalent concept of international organisation' (2013) 14 *Melbourne Journal of International Law* 1 (concluding that '[t]he law, it seems, is structurally incapable of making principled decisions relating to the different nature of different organisations' (at 21). Also, N. Blokker, 'Preparing articles on responsibility of international organizations: does the International Law Commission take international organizations seriously? A mid-term review' in J. Klabbers and

Stephen Vasciannie observed, 'there was next to no practice in the area of responsibility suggesting that there should be one set of rules for one class of organization and a different set for others'. 'Such a differential approach', he continued, 'would amount to progressive development and would be in need of clear policy support'.[36] If disagreement dissuaded the Commission from adopting special rules for the only subcategory that seems to be emerging (that of regional integration organizations), there was even less basis for carving out other subcategories. Any attempt to distinguish between organizations would have provided the occasion for accusing the Commission of arbitrariness.

That being said, there is no reason why differences between international organizations should not be a major driving force for future legal development. Just as domestic systems embrace different categories of corporate entities to which different legal regimes apply, the law of international organizations could – and perhaps should – become more detailed and sophisticated as time passes. That could involve the emergence of separate regimes for 'universal' and 'regional' organizations, and/or of special rules for highly sophisticated 'regional integration organizations'. In the meantime, viewing international organizations as a single category that can be, as appropriate, analogised with States provides a provisional framework for discussing the application of general international law to them.

4.2   International Organizations as 'Derivative Subjects' of International Law

A recurring theme in the debates within the ILC and at the 1986 Vienna Conference was that international organizations could not be assimilated to States insofar as the former are the 'original' or 'primary' subjects of international law while the latter are 'derivative' or 'secondary' subjects.[37]

A. Wallendahl (eds.), *Research Handbook on the Law of International Organizations* (Cheltenham: Elgar, 2011), p. 335 (noting that asking whether the great variety of organizations would require a great variety of responsibility regimes is akin to 'asking how it should be possible, given the great variety of states ..., that there is only one uniform set of articles on state personality').

[36] Vasciannie, YILC 2007/I, p. 137, para. 4.

[37] In the context of the treaties project, e.g., Reuter, YILC 1979/I, p. 133, para. 13 (noting that 'it was a fact that there were original members of the international community – States – and derivative members. States could create legal entities – international organizations – which formed part of the international community and through which they

This is a distinction serving both descriptive and normative goals. On the descriptive side, it captures the fact that international organizations are the creation of States and that, as a result, some sort of order of priority between the two categories of legal subjects is unavoidable.[38] Just as member States have the right to set up an international organization, they are entitled to reform or dissolve it; no State has a comparable right over another State. On the normative side, the distinction reflects an anxiety to put international organizations in their place, as it were, by emphasising that whatever degree of 'personality' they enjoy under international law falls short of the comprehensive set of rights, duties and capacities that originate from statehood.[39]

Perceptions relating to the distinction between 'original' and 'derivative' subjects of international law are sometimes too vague to result in

could act'). In the context of the responsibility project, e.g., Galicki, A/CN.4/SR.2935 (2007), p. 25 (stressing that '[a]n organization's status as a subject of international law was not original, but derived from the status of its member States as subjects of international law') and Fomba, YILC 2005/I, p. 82, para. 9 (to whom 'the key issue [was] how to interpret the relations between States and international organizations in their capacity as primary and secondary subjects of international law'). At the Vienna Conference, this was commonly argued by States belonging to the Socialist bloc and some developing countries; see e.g., Ukraine, UNCLT 1986, p. 117, para. 54. In the literature, see H. Mosler, 'Réflexions sur la personnalité juridique en droit international public' in Baugniet (ed.), *Mélanges Offerts à Henri Rolin* (Paris: Pedone, 1964), pp. 240–43, and the survey in C. Osakwe, 'Contemporary soviet doctrine on the juridical nature of universal international organizations' (1971) 65 AJIL 502.

[38] According to Mosler, States are necessary subjects without which the idea of international law is inconceivable. In contrast, IOs are subjects derived from the will of States, which cannot 'threaten the functioning of the legal order *as a whole*': Mosler, 'Réflexions', p. 240.

[39] The initial reluctance of States to draft clauses explicitly conferring international legal personality on international organizations attests to this normative concern. For example, Article 104 of the UN Charter, which bestows on the UN 'such legal capacity' in the territory of the member States 'as may be necessary for the exercise of its functions and the fulfilment of its purposes', is conspicuously silent on the matter of international legal personality. As noted by Williams, there seems to be 'a potency of unknown quality in such a name [international legal personality]; such a name must by prudent persons be avoided, whatever rash lawyers might propose': J. F. Williams, 'The legal character of the bank for international settlements' (1930) 24 AJIL 665, 671. See also C. W. Jenks, 'International legal personality of international organizations' (1945) 22 BYIL 267, 270. In the past few decades, there has been a tendency to include clauses on international legal personality in constituent instruments. See e.g., art. 34, 1994 Additional Protocol to the Treaty of Asunción on the Institutional Structure of MERCOSUR; art. 3, 2007 Charter of the Association of South-Asian Nations; art. 47, Treaty on European Union.

principled objections to assimilating the two categories for the purpose of applying rules of general international law on the international plane. I deal with those as a case of 'normative contestation' in Chapter 7. Others overlap with the 'principle of speciality' discussed later in this chapter.[40] The focus of this section is on the objection to a full analogy between States and international organizations in a fundamental field of enquiry: the making of general international law. The international plane on which intergovernmental institutions operate is the domain of sovereign equals – States – whose customs are regarded as a source of obligations. Does the fact that international organizations are legally autonomous entities operating on that plane entail that they are entitled to partake in international law-making on the same footing as their creators?

4.2.1 International Organizations and the Formation of Custom

Orthodoxy has it that rules of customary international law are formed when States adhere to certain practices with the conviction that the law requires them to do so.[41] Underlying the 'two-element test' that the case law of the PCIJ and the ICJ has developed to identify rules of custom is the notion that States are the makers of international law. While custom is created and experienced by States collectively, so that the assent of no individual State is essential for the emergence of a given rule, the link between custom and the consent of States is evident in prevailing accounts of international law-making. This is a predictable feature of a decentralised system whose main organising principle is the sovereign equality of States.

Because of the high stakes involved, the issue of how custom is created provides a test case for the analogy between States and international organizations. There is no doubt that the participation of States in the work of international organizations can provide evidence of State practice and *opinio juris*.[42] More than that, the emergence of international

---

[40] See section 4.3.
[41] E.g., *Continental Shelf (Libyan Arab Jamahiriya/Malta)*, Judgment [1985] ICJ Rep 13, para. 27.
[42] See e.g., conclusions 6(2) and 10(2) of the draft conclusions on identification of customary international law completed by the ILC in 2018: ILC Report 2018 (Advance Version), A/73/10, pp. 145–46.

organizations had a tremendous impact on how custom is made.[43] Georges Abi-Saab distinguishes between the 'traditional custom' that the international legal system has inherited from its formative period and the 'new custom' that has developed with the help of international institutions.[44] While most traditional rules of customary international law originated from a lengthy process of consolidation of State practice and *opinio juris*, more recent rules are the product of relatively centralised and deliberate law-making processes under the auspices of the United Nations and other international organizations.[45] In the formation of this 'new custom' – of which the law of the outer space, the law of self-determination and new aspects of the law of the sea are examples – the starting point for the creation of new rules was a detailed set of provisions that a majority of States endorsed by, *inter alia*, voting in favour of resolutions of the UN General Assembly or adopting conventions in diplomatic conferences.[46] This means that *opinio juris* was often expressed before the required general practice took shape: first States indicated that they were inclined to consider the negotiated rule as required by law, and then State practice started to coalesce.[47] This rejuvenation of the process for the formation of custom would not have been possible without the contribution of international organizations.

But if international organizations are legally autonomous entities operating on the international plane to which rules of custom can be extended by analogy, are they also in a position to contribute to the formation of custom through their own practice and *opinio juris*? This question was briefly debated by the ILC in the 1970s, when the Commission considered extending to international organizations the rule in Article 38 VCLT 1969, according to which the *pacta tertiis* principle does not preclude 'a rule set forth in a treaty from becoming binding upon a third State as a customary rule of international law, recognized as

---

[43] Generally: Alvarez, *International Organizations as Law-Makers*, especially pp. 591–95.
[44] Abi-Saab, 'La Commission du Droit International, la codification et le processus de formation de droit international' in United Nations, *Making Better International Law: Proceedings of the United Nations Colloquium on Progressive Development and Codification of International Law* (1998), pp. 195–97.
[45] Ibid., pp. 196–97. This phenomenon is also illustrated by René-Jean Dupuy's colourful metaphor of a 'coutume sage' being opposed to a 'coutume sauvage': R. J. Dupuy, 'Coutume sage et coutume sauvage' in S. Bastid (ed.), *Mélanges Offerts à Charles Rousseau: La Communauté Internationale* (Paris: Pedone, 1974), pp. 75–87.
[46] On the advantages of generating custom through multilateral forums: J. Charney, 'Universal international law' (1993) 87 AJIL 529, 546–47.
[47] See Dupuy, 'Coutume sage et coutume sauvage', p. 84.

such'. The Commission did not, however, express a clear-cut view, with Special Rapporteur Reuter noting that:

> It might be argued that international organizations [do] not play any part, at least so far as rules of general international law [are] concerned, since the general customary rules applicable to an international organization [are] recognized by all member States. It might also be argued that, in the process of developing a rule of general customary law, an international organization, as a subject of international law, [is] entitled to establish by its behaviour that it considered that that rule [exists] so far as it [is] concerned.[48]

The topic was taken up by the ILC in its recently completed study on the identification of customary international law. Conclusion 4 states that '[i]n certain cases, the practice of international organizations also contributes to the formation, or expression, of rules of customary international law'.[49] In the commentary, the Commission emphasises that States, as 'the primary subjects of the international legal system... possessing a general competence', 'play a pre-eminent role' in the formation of custom.[50] That said, it acknowledges the relevance of the practice of international organizations in three cases.[51] First, the Commission is of the view that if 'member States have transferred exclusive competences to the international organization . . . the practice of the organization may be equated with the practice of those States'.[52] This proposition caters to the case of the European Union, given that, in the fields where the EU enjoys exclusive competence, its members are prohibited under EU law from taking action individually.[53] The justification on which the Commission bases its position is compelling: if the practice (and *opinio juris*) of international organizations exercising exclusive competences were not equated with that of their members, the latter 'would themselves be deprived of or reduced in their ability to contribute to State practice'.[54] Second, and more generally, the Commission recognises that the practice

---

[48] Reuter, YILC 1977/I, p. 146, para. 38.
[49] ILC Report 2018 (Advance Version), A/73/10, p. 157.
[50] ILC Report 2018 (Advance Version), A/73/10, p. 158, para. 2.
[51] For a pointed analysis of the conclusions as adopted on first reading: N. Blokker, 'International organizations and customary international law: is the international law commission taking international organizations seriously?' (2017) 14 IOLR 1.
[52] ILC Report 2018 (Advance Version), A/73/10, p. 159, para. 6.
[53] See Article 3, TFEU.
[54] Wood (Third Report) A/CN.4/682 (2015), p. 53, para. 77.

of international organizations can influence the formation of custom when they exercise powers that are 'functionally equivalent to the powers exercised by States', such as serving as depositaries for treaties or deploying military forces.[55] Third, the Commission observes that the practice of organizations may be relevant with respect to customary rules that are 'addressed specifically to them', such as 'those on their international responsibility or relating to treaties to which [they are] parties'.[56]

The clear implication of the Commission's conclusion is that international organizations are entitled, alongside States, to create custom. At the same time, the Commission has taken pains to emphasise that 'caution is required in assessing the weight' of the practice of international organizations.[57] The caveat was prompted by the reactions of some States at the Sixth Committee of the UNGA, were concerned that the Commission was putting the practice of international organizations on the same footing as State practice.[58] The commentary thus notes that 'the more directly a practice of an [organization] is carried out on behalf of its member States, the greater weight it may have', and proposes the following factors for assessing the relevance of that practice:

> the nature of the organization; the nature of the organ whose conduct is under consideration; whether the conduct is *ultra vires* the organization or organ; and whether the conduct is consonant with that of the member States of the organization.[59]

Because the ILC does not elaborate on those factors, it is not altogether clear whether differences between the relevance of practice of States and the practice of international organizations for the formation of custom would be a matter of degree, or whether there is a more fundamental qualitative difference between the two. On the one hand, it is surely the case that international organizations have fewer opportunities than States to contribute to the creation of customary rules. Their contribution is in practice limited to fields in which they are empowered to act, and much of the 'internal practice' deriving from action taken on the institutional plane may not be relevant for the formation of general

---

[55] ILC Report 2018 (Advance Version), A/73/10, p. 159, para. 6.
[56] Ibid., p. 159, para. 5.
[57] Ibid., p. 160, para. 7.
[58] Wood (Fourth Report), A/CN.4/695 (2016), p. 6, para. 19. See also, Wood (Fifth Report), A/CN.4/717 (2018), pp. 16–18.
[59] ILC Report 2018 (Advance Version), A/73/10, p. 159, para. 7.

rules of international law.[60] On the other hand, factors such as 'whether the conduct is *ultra vires* the organization or the organ' and 'whether the conduct is consonant with that of the member States of the organization' hint at more fundamental differences between State practice and the practice of international organizations. The underlying question is whether the actions and omissions of political and administrative organs of intergovernmental institutions has any truly independent value for the creation of custom, or whether it has to be rationalised as an expression of the collective action of member States. One thing is to accept that the practice of international organizations can shed light on and fill gaps in the practice of its members and to regard that practice as representative of that particular group of States. Another is to view international organizations as additional players the practice of which can be uncritically added to that of their member States for the purpose of determining whether practice is sufficiently 'general' or 'settled'.

Which of the views is then to be favoured? The notion that the practice of international organizations can mean more than the expression of the collective action of its member States was opposed by some ILC members. A member emphasised that 'it was solely the practice of States that created the rules of custom', while 'the practice of international organizations should be consulted only in the contact of evidence, not creation, of a rule'.[61] Another described the practice of international organizations as a 'subsidiary form of practice', which 'contributed to the formation of customary rules to the extent that it reflected general or collective State practice'.[62] This view is appealing because allowing international organizations any greater role would contravene the principle of sovereign equality and upset the political structure on which the international legal system is built.[63] States would be entitled to increase their

---

[60] The distinction between external and internal relations is aptly captured in Wood (Third Report) A/CN.4/682 (2015), p. 48, para. 7. As regards the codification of the law of treaties, Reuter doubted that 'a rule concerning the institutional mechanisms of an international organization could be generally extended to all organizations, each of which had its own system and its own rules', because '[t]he relations between an organization and its member States were not a matter that lent itself to the development of customary rules': YILC 1982/I, p. 126, para. 41. See also, France, UNCLT 1986/I, p. 123, para. 43.

[61] Huang, A/CN.4/SR.3226 (2014).

[62] Hmoud, A/CN.4/SR.3251 (2015), p. 9. Along the same lines, Gevorgian, A/CN.4/SR.3226 (2014), p. 13.

[63] For a normative defense of the traditional sovereignty system on the grounds that, despite being 'flawed', 'stretched' and 'strained', it is at present the most 'realistic system for the management of enduring inequalities and of other pathologies of the international system

influence over the creation of custom by establishing additional entities whose practice would add to their own, resulting in double counting.[64]

There are thus limits to the role that the practice of international organizations may play in the development of customary rules that apply to States under the current international legal system. But is the same true when one considers the role of that practice in the creation or confirmation of rules applying to international organizations themselves (the third category identified by the ILC)? A survey of the codification projects that culminated with the adoption of VCLT 1986 and the ARIO reveals that most of the practice that the ILC was able to gather in support of the proposed rules comprised acts of international organizations themselves. While the insufficiency of practice was a common theme in the debates, it was never suggested that the practice that could be actually found was not of the kind that could serve as evidence of emerging or existing rules of customary international law. Indeed, if customary rules specifically applying to the functioning of international organizations are ever to emerge, this will have to occur through the accumulation of practice and precedent involving international organizations themselves.[65] But, these being uncharted waters, a number of questions remain. Are the practice and *opinio juris* of different international organizations to be treated equally? How relevant can factors such as size and representativeness of membership be in assessing the relevance of that practice?

In short, even if there are good reasons to accept that the practice of international organizations as such contributes to the formation of custom, that is not because international organizations are analogous to States, but rather because doing otherwise would exclude from the picture practice stemming from the collective action of States. The structure of the international legal system challenges the analogy at the level of law-making, where perceptions as to the difference in status

---

of law and politics': B. Kingsbury, 'Sovereignty and inequality' (1998) 9 EJIL 599, especially pp. 616–25. See also, J. Crawford, 'Chance, order, change: the course of international law' (2013) 365 RdC 13, 86.

[64] It must be acknowledged, however, that by acting collectively through international organizations, States may enhance their prospects to push for, block or influence, in practice, the development of customary rules.

[65] For an argument on the role that the EU may play, through its own practice, in the development of customary rules that apply to IOs (or certain types of IOs): J. Odermatt, 'The development of customary international law by international organizations' (2017) 66 ICLQ 491, 503–10.

between States and international organizations – the 'secondary' or 'derivative' subjects of international law – are most persuasive.

4.2.2 International Organizations and the Formation of Peremptory Norms

The ILC's work on peremptory norms of general international law provides another example of difficulties in analogising between States and international organizations when it comes to international law-making. Article 53 VCLT 1969 defines *jus cogens* as follows:

> a peremptory norm of general international law is a norm accepted and recognized by the international community of States as a whole as a norm from which no derogation is permitted and which can be modified only by a subsequent norm of general international law having the same character.

The question arises of whether 'the international community of States as a whole', whose acceptance and recognition of certain rules make them non-derogable, is a closed club. Or does it instead encompass other entities, including international organizations? The more inclusive phrase 'international community as a whole' was used by the International Court of Justice in the *Barcelona Traction* case[66] and by the ILC in Article 48(1)(b) ARS, which provides that States other than the injured State have a legal interest in invoking responsibility for breaches of obligations 'owed to the international community as a whole'. That phrase encapsulates the view that the international community is 'no longer limited to States (if it ever was)'.[67] But in the commentary to the ARS the Commission takes pains not to disallow the terminology employed in VCLT 1969. 'The insertion of the words "of States" in article 53 of the Vienna Convention', the Commission explains, 'was intended to stress the paramountcy that States have over the making of international law, including especially the establishment of norms of a peremptory character'.[68]

This has been the ILC's approach when it comes to *jus cogens*. Considering the possibility of extending Article 53 VCLT 1969 to treaties

[66] *Barcelona Traction, Light and Power Company, Limited (Belgium v. Spain)*, Judgment [1970] ICJ Rep 3, para. 33.
[67] J. Crawford, *The International Law Commission's Articles on State Responsibility* (Cambridge: Cambridge University Press, 2002), p. 41.
[68] YILC 2001/II, part two, p. 84, para. 18.

involving international organizations, the Commission did not hesitate to conclude that international organizations were bound by *jus cogens*,[69] but refrained from adding international organizations to the definition of 'international community'. The prevailing sentiment was expressed by Francis Vallat, who pointed out that it was 'one thing to say that international organizations had international legal personality and the capacity to conclude treaties, but quite another to place international organizations in the same position as States in regard to peremptory norms of general international law'.[70]

The same tendency can be discerned in the current work of the ILC on *jus cogens*, still in its early stages.[71] Noting that 'the material advanced to illustrate recognition of norms as *jus cogens* remain State-developed materials, such as treaties and General Assembly resolutions', Special Rapporteur Dire Tladi has suggested that it is the 'the acceptance and recognition of "the international community of States as a whole" that is relevant'.[72] The Drafting Committee, though noting lack of consensus among members on the issue, agreed to retain for the time being the phrase used in VCLT 1969 'out of the concern that reconceiving the idea of the "international community of States" would represent a significant departure from the Vienna Convention and the Commission's own previous work on *jus cogens*, including prior understandings on language employed in the context of *jus cogens*, and that in connection with *erga omnes* obligations'. It added that 'the topic being considered concerned a source of international law, and, as such, it was still the case that acceptance and recognition by States was central to the concept of *jus cogens*'.[73]

Though the position of principle adopted by the ILC is defensible, there is some regrettable inconsistency between its treatment of the role of international organizations in the formation of *jus cogens* and of their

---

[69] Reuter, YILC 1979/I, p. 132, para. 4. An exception was Ushakov, who was 'not sure' whether peremptory rules 'were also binding on international organizations': ibid., p. 133, para. 7.

[70] YILC 1979/I, p. 133, para. 12.

[71] At the time of writing, the Special Rapporteur had submitted three reports to the Commission, proposing several draft conclusions that were being considered by the Drafting Committee: ILC Report 2018 (Advance Version), A/73/10, chapter VIII.

[72] Tladi (Second Report), A/CN.4/706 (2017), pp. 35–36, paras. 70 and 72.

[73] Statement of the Chairman of the Drafting Committee, 9 August 2016, available at <http://legal.un.org/docs/?path=../ilc/documentation/english/statements/2017_dc_chair man_statement_jc.pdf&lang=E> accessed 14 February 2018.

role in the formation of customary international law. The study on identification of custom openly embraces international organizations and accepts that their own practice may, in certain circumstances, contribute to the creation of custom; in contrast, the definition of 'international community of States' that the ILC has provisionally adopted seems to exclude any direct participation of international organizations in the emergence of peremptory norms of international law. This distinction is arbitrary: for one, in cases in which international organizations have been given exclusive competence, the same argument that favours equating their practice with that of their members should extend to 'acceptance' and 'recognition' of *jus cogens* norms. Special Rapporteur Tlati has emphasised that 'the practice of non-State actors is not irrelevant' as '[i]t may lead to recognition and acceptance by States of the peremptoriness of the norm, or may contribute to assessing such recognition and acceptance'.[74] While this more nuanced approach is promising, further work needs to be done, in the next few years, to elucidate the ways in which the practice of international organizations can be used as evidence of recognition and acceptance of *jus cogens* by 'the international community of States'.

4.2.3 International Organizations and Law-Making Treaties

The debate revolving around a deceptively technical provision in VCLT 1969 further illustrates differences between States and international organizations when it comes to international law-making. That provision is Article 9(2), pursuant to which the adoption of the text of a treaty in an international conference convened for that purpose takes place 'by the vote of two thirds of the States present and voting, unless by the same majority they shall decide to apply a different rule'. Because international organizations seldom participate in international conferences in which major multilateral treaties are adopted, some ILC members argued that international organizations should not enjoy a 'default right' to vote on the adoption of the text of treaties.[75] The prerogative to decide on the extent to which international organizations may participate in a conference should rather remain with States. In the end, this being a minority position, the Commission proposed replicating the rule in Article 9(2) VCLT 1969 in the set of draft articles that it sent to the 1986 Vienna Conference.

---

[74] Tladi (Second Report), A/CN.4/706 (2017), p. 36, para. 72.
[75] Pinto, YILC 1975/I, p. 221, para. 14.

The issue was, however, reopened at Conference, where several amendments to the ILC text were considered.[76] One of these amendments would have confined to States the right to vote on the adoption of treaties negotiated in international conferences, unless States by a two thirds majority decided otherwise.[77] The differences in status between States and international organizations justifying the amendment were described by the Egyptian delegation in the following terms:

> most delegations attached importance to distinguishing between States and international organizations in the matter of concluding treaties. It was the distinction between the creators and the created. States were sovereign; international organizations could not be placed on terms of equality with them with regard to voting, although organizations might express an opinion on the drafting of texts.[78]

But other delegations considered this view unacceptable. The Holy See blamed the disagreement on the reluctance on the part of States to 'recognize the international legal personality of international organizations when it came to the consequences of that legal personality' as a result of the 'mistaken idea, which was dying hard, that States, and only States, could legitimately be the subjects of international law'.[79] It further noted that it was 'only logical that an international organization destined to become a party to an international treaty on an equal footing with States should have the same say as States in the negotiations leading to the elaboration of the text and in its formal adoption'.[80]

The prevailing opinion at the Conference was favourable to extending to international organizations the default right to participate in the adoption of treaties in international conferences.[81] Somewhat incongruously, the provision now found in Article 9(2) VCLT 1986 was adopted by an

---

[76] UNCLT 1986/II, p. 68, para. 51.

[77] See ibid., Egypt's amendment.

[78] Egypt, UNCLT 1986/I, 82, para 70. The underlying normative concern was shared by the Soviet delegation: 'International organizations did not possess rights equal to those of States. In a particular case, the number of States casting an affirmative vote might be less than two-thirds of the entities present and voting, and there would then be a danger of international organizations imposing their will on sovereign States.' (ibid., p. 82, para. 69).

[79] Holy See, ibid., p. 83, para. 19.

[80] Ibid., para. 20.

[81] Art. 9 VCLT 1986 slightly departs from the text of its counterpart in VCLT 1969 insofar as it emphasises that international conferences have autonomy to adopt their voting procedures. But it preserves the residual rule in paragraph 2.

international conference the rules of which provided that only States could exercise decision-making powers, including voting on the adoption of the Convention's text.[82] The Austrian delegation explained this apparent contradiction in the following terms:

> The comparison was not valid, because the present Conference was a law-making conference and States were the only law-makers under international law. Paragraph 2 of article 9 dealt with a different situation. The paragraph related to the elaboration of a treaty between States and international organizations. In that situation, international organizations should be given decision-making powers with regard to the negotiation and adoption of the text.[83]

This comment points to a disconnect between rights that international organizations are understood to have under general international law, and rights that they are in a position to exercise in practice. It mirrors the debate on the relatively limited role that international organizations can play in the formation of customary rules and peremptory norms. The analogy with States may provide a reason not to adopt provisions that formally restrict the procedural rights of international organizations under the general law of treaties: being legally autonomous entities operating on the international plane, they should be put in a default position of equality with States for the purpose of concluding agreements. But it does not follow that the 'secondary' or 'derivative' subjects will be given the same opportunities of participation in multilateral law-making processes as States, especially if the resulting convention is one aiming to codify and progressively develop international law. Perceived differences between States and international organizations may influence the way in which their respective political roles are fulfilled in the creation of international obligations.

4.3   International Organizations as Subjects with Limited Competence

In *Reparation for Injuries*, the International Court distinguished international organizations from States in the following terms:

---

[82] See Rule 34, Rules of Procedure, UNCLT 1986/I, xxii. The fact that the Rules did not allow IOs to vote on the adoption of the Convention's text had been invoked as an argument against extending the rule in art. 9(2) VCLT 1969 by analogy: Egypt, UNCLT 1986/I, p. 82, para. 70.

[83] Austria, ibid., p. 83, para. 25.

> Whereas a State possesses the totality of international rights and duties
> recognized by international law, the rights and duties of an entity such as
> the Organization must depend upon its purposes and functions as speci-
> fied or implied in its constituent documents and developed in practice.[84]

The point was further articulated in *Nuclear Weapons (WHO Request)*:

> [I]nternational organizations are subjects of international law which do
> not, unlike States, possess a general competence. International organiza-
> tions are governed by the 'principle of speciality', that is to say, they are
> invested by the States which create them with powers, the limits of which
> are a function of the common interests whose promotion those States
> entrust to them.[85]

That international organizations are entities established to fulfil specific
purposes is of course one of their central features, and one that distinguishes them from States. At the core of perceptions as to the difference
between 'original' and 'derivative' subjects is the insight that, while States
are free to pursue their interests within the bounds of international law,
international organizations are set up by States to perform specific tasks
of international cooperation. From the perspective of their members, the
more fitting analogy would be with public agencies operating under a
public law framework,[86] which, constituted and constrained by law, have
to 'show their powers' before taking action.

The principle of speciality is undoubtedly a well-established principle
for the interpretation of constituent instruments and other internal rules
on the institutional plane.[87] It is also a basic tenet of the influential theory
of functionalism, which conceptualises international organizations and

---

[84] *Reparation for Injuries*, p. 180.

[85] *Legality of the Use of Nuclear Weapons in Armed Conflict*, para. 25.

[86] D. Sarooshi, 'The role of domestic public law analogies in the law of international
organizations' (2008) 5 IOLR 237.

[87] When applying speciality to the interpretation of the WHO Constitution, the ICJ
explored another dimension of the principle which, though not directly relevant to the
present enquiry, can be briefly noted. This is the notion that the constituent instrument of
a specialized agency of the UN must be construed in the light of the logic of division of
labour at the UN system. The insight is that the interpreter wishing to identify the
implicit powers that an IO can be truly deemed to possess must take into account the
governance framework in which the organization is inserted. On the subject, see
M. Bothe, 'The WHO request' in Chazournes and Sands, *International Law*, p. 108,
and J. Klabbers, 'Global governance before the ICJ: re-reading the WHA opinion' (2009)
Max-Planck Yearbook of United Nations Law 1, 17–19.

the law that applies to them by reference to their functions.[88] But can the principle of speciality produce legal effects on the international plane, that is, when international organizations maintain relations with the outside world?.

The pronouncements by the International Court on speciality are confusing in this respect because the Court does not distinguish between the international plane and the institutional plane. In *Reparation for Injuries*, a full answer to the question of whether the UN, as a body corporate, was entitled to bring an international claim against a third State would have had to consider two issues: whether the UN had that capacity under general international law, so that it could exercise it in relation to a non-member; and, if so, whether the UN could exercise that capacity in accordance with the UN Charter, which defines the competences that member States entrusted to the organization.[89] But the analysis of the Court conflates the question of what powers member States conferred on the UN – a question of 'internal UN law' – with the question of what capacities an institution such as the UN is entitled to exercise when acting on the international plane – a question of general international law. Moreover, expressions such as 'possession of the totality of international rights and duties' and 'general competence', employed to contrast States with international organizations, are deceptive. International organizations are sometimes given competence to perform acts that States themselves may no longer perform. For example, the 'totality of international rights and duties' of States include the prohibition on the unilateral use of force except in situations of self-defence:[90] it is an international organization – the United Nations – that has the competence to authorise or use force in response to threats to international peace and security.[91] In the European context, the EU has been given a batch of 'exclusive competences' which it alone can exercise, such as

---

[88] Critics of functionalism often do a better job describing the theory than their proponents. See the analysis in J. Klabbers, 'The transformation of international organizations law' (2015) EJIL 9, particularly pp. 15–36.

[89] Indeed, some of the most quoted advisory opinions on IOs that the ICJ issued, including *Certain Expenses of the United Nations* and *Nuclear Weapons (WHO Request)*, concerned the interpretation of the 'internal law' of the IOs concerned, and not the rules of general international law that apply to these organizations. This may have contributed to the tendency to conflate the international plane with the institutional plane.

[90] Article 2(4) UN Charter and *Military and Para-Military Activities in and against Nicaragua (Nicaragua v. USA)* (Merits) [1986] ICJ Rep 135, paras. 183–92.

[91] Chapter VII, UN Charter.

legislating on common commercial policy and on conservation of marine biological resources.[92] Thus, when the Court referred to the 'totality of international rights and duties', it can only have meant that States possess those rights, duties and capacities that accrue, as a default position, from the status of statehood. The question that the Court has not quite answered is whether the package of international rights and duties that accrues from the status of international organizations under international law is similar to that which applies to States, or whether it is conditioned by the principle of speciality also on the international plane.

Once one accepts that international organizations are personified entities under general international law, the restrictions laid down by their constitutional instruments cannot without more be taken to legally affect or govern their relations with third parties. That does not mean, however, that general international law has to remain indifferent to the content of the internal law of international organizations. It would be theoretically possible for the principle of speciality to transcend the sphere of constitutional interpretation and become a rule of international law having the effect that international organizations may only act within the bounds of their competences. It would then follow that their *ultra vires* acts can be challenged not only on the institutional plane but also on the international plane. If this were the case, the possibility to analogise between States and international organizations *qua* legally autonomous entities on the international plane would be conditioned by the principle of speciality.

4.3.1   The Case for a Wide-Reaching Principle of Speciality

The normative concern for emphasising principle speciality arises from the fear that international organizations may misuse or seek to unduly expand the competences that they are given by member States. Once animated by a desire to protect State sovereignty, this concern has acquired currency in recent times through the work conducted under research projects such as 'Global Administrative Law' and 'International Public Authority'.[93] Those endeavours point to the need to promote

---

[92] Art. 3, TFEU.

[93] B. Kingsbury, N. Krisch and R. Stewart, 'The emergence of global administrative law' (2005) 68 *Law and Contemporary Problems* 15; A. von Bogdandy, P. Damm and M. Goldmann, 'Developing the publicness of public international law: towards a legal framework for global governance activities' in A. von Bogdandy and others, *The Exercise*

accountability in global governance and propose to extend to international organizations standards of public law shared by the domestic systems of the world. This (re)turn to the notion of legality in global governance is in part the result of the realisation that international organizations are not always the 'good Samaritans' of global governance, but rather forces to be reckoned with in the same way as the governments of States.[94]

The very the articulation of the principle of speciality in the *Nuclear Weapons (WHO Request)* advisory opinion comes across as a reaction to the expansive interpretative approach to the powers of international organizations that the Court itself was instrumental in developing.[95] In *Reparation for Injuries*, the Court found that the UN 'must be deemed to have those powers which, though not expressly provided in the Charter, are conferred upon it by necessary implication as being essential to the performance of its duties'.[96] The emphasis on effectiveness found in this 'implied powers doctrine', used to infer a right of functional protection over agents of the UN, departed so much from the prevalent approach to treaty interpretation at the time (textual, restrictive and committed to the protection of sovereignty) that some judges observed that the Court was taking on a legislative role.[97] The doctrine was taken even further in *Certain Expenses of the United Nations*, in which the Court had to decide whether costs incurred by peacekeeping operations constituted expenses of the organization pursuant to Article 17 of the UN Charter.[98]

---

of Public Authority by International Institutions (Heidelberg: Springer, 2010), pp. 22–26. See also, generally, E. Benvenisti, 'The law of global governance' (2014) 368 RdC 47.

[94] See J. Klabbers, 'The life and times of the law of international organizations' (2001) 70 *Nordic Journal of International Law* 287 and Benvenisti, 'The law of global governance', 59–66.

[95] At least two advisory opinions of the PCIJ laid the foundations for this expansive approach: *Competence of the International Labour Organization to Regulate, Incidentally, the Personal Work of the Employer* (Advisory Opinion) [1926] PCIJ, Series B No. 13, p. 14, and *Jurisdiction of the European Commission of the Danube Between Galatz and Braila* (Advisory Opinion) [1927] PCIJ, Series B No. 14, p. 5.

[96] *Reparation for Injuries*, p. 182.

[97] See sep. op. Alvarez, ibid. 190–91; diss. op. Hackworth, ibid. 198–99; and diss. op. Krylov. Also: H. Lauterpacht, *The Development of International Law by the International Court* (London: Stevens, 1958), p. 274 (noting that 'in relation to the interpretation of the Charter of the United Nations the Court has repeatedly and on a large scale acted upon the principle of effectiveness – on a scale so large as to bring its pronouncements on the subject within the category of judicial legislation').

[98] *Certain Expenses of the United Nations* (Advisory Opinion) [1962] ICJ Rep 151, p. 152.

Absent any provisions on peacekeeping operations in the Charter, the Court observed that 'when the Organization takes action which warrants the assertion that it was appropriate for the fulfilment of one of the stated purposes of the United Nations, the presumption is that such action is not *ultra vires* the Organization.'[99] This presumption of *vires* has been invoked to justify the expansive measures that the UN Security Council has taken since the end of the Cold War, including the creation of international criminal tribunals[100] and the adoption of resolutions of a legislative character.[101]

While the principle of speciality does not negate the element of effectiveness in the implied powers doctrine, it shifts the emphasis from expansive interpretation to the need for taking conferral of powers seriously. In *Nuclear Weapons (WHO Request)*, the Court for the first and only time refused to acknowledge the existence of an implied power. Faced with a request by the World Health Organization for an advisory opinion on whether the use of nuclear weapons, given its potential impact on human health, was contrary to international law and to the WHO Constitution, the Court found that it had no jurisdiction to comply with that request because the issue of the legality of nuclear weapons did not arise within the scope of the activities of the organization, as required by Article 96(2) of the UN Charter.[102]

---

[99] Ibid., p. 168. (Emphasis added.)

[100] *Prosecutor v. Tadic* (Interlocutory Appeal on Jurisdiction) [1995] ICTY-94-1. Having stated that the UNSC was not '*legibus solutus*', the Appeals Chamber nevertheless confirmed the Council's competence to establish the ICTY. It noted that 'Article 39 leaves the choice of means and their evaluation to the Security Council, which enjoys wide discretionary powers in this regard' (paras. 28–40).

[101] Such as UNSC Res. 1373 (2001), imposing several obligations on States with regard to terrorism: S. Talmon, 'The Security Council as world legislature' (2005) 99 AJIL 175.

[102] *Legality of the Use of Nuclear Weapons in Armed Conflict*, paras. 21–24. Other cases suggest an awareness by the ICJ of legality concerns arising from the expansive interpretation of constituent instruments. In its first ever advisory opinion, the Court maintained that '[t]he political character of an organ cannot release it from the observance of the treaty provisions established by the Charter when they constitute limitations on its powers or criteria for its judgment': *Conditions of Admission of a State to Membership in the United Nations* (Advisory Opinion) [1948] ICJ Rep 57, 64. Putting this *dictum* to practice, the Court rejected the argument that the Assembly of the IMCO had discretion to choose the criteria pursuant to which 'the eight largest ship-owning nations' were to be identified. Rather, the Court found that the constituent instrument required the application of an objective criterion (registered ship tonnage): *Constitution of the Maritime Safety Committee of the Inter-Governmental Maritime Consultative Organization* (Advisory Opinion) [1960] ICJ Rep 150, 170–71.

The same normative concern that justifies the principle of speciality as a doctrine for the interpretation of the powers of international organizations under constituent instruments could underpin the use of speciality as a technique for controlling the exercise of 'public authority' also on the international plane. By embracing speciality, general international law could make respect for the internal rules of international organizations a part of the application of the law of treaties, the law of responsibility and other legal regimes. The following subsections consider how the ILC courted, but ultimately abandoned, this idea in its work on treaties and responsibility.

4.3.2 Speciality and the Observance and Invalidity of Treaties

The debate revolving around Article 6 VCLT 1986 provides the best illustration of an attempt to weave the principle of speciality into the fabric of general international law. One of the most disputed provisions in the ILC's work on treaties, Article 6 prescribes that '[t]he capacity of an international organization to conclude treaties is governed by the rules of that organization'. While the ILC did not mean for Article 6 to express a position as to the source of treaty-making capacity, which is tied to the more general question of the status of international organizations under international law, the provision constitutes a clear endorsement of the idea of speciality.[103] 'Every State possesses capacity to conclude treaties',[104] but the same is not true of every international organization; instead, 'every organization has its own distinctive legal image which is recognizable, in particular, in the individualized capacity of that organization to conclude treaties'.[105] Even the alternative formulation put forth by Reuter, which would have Article 6 state that treaty-making capacity is 'acknowledged in principle by international law', emphasised the notion of limited competences by providing that the extent of the capacity is 'determined by the relevant rules of each organization'.[106]

A similar idea is expressed in other provisions in VCLT 1986 that make reference to the internal law of international organizations. Articles 35(2), 36(2), 37(5) and 39(2) subject to the rules of the organization the expression of consent required for the acquisition of rights and

[103] Reuter (Second Report), YILC 1975/II, p. 82, para. 44. See Section 2.1.1.1.
[104] Art. 6 VCLT 1969.
[105] Commentary to draft art. 6, YILC 1982/II, part two, p. 24, para. 3.
[106] Reuter (Third Report), YILC 1974/II, part one, p. 150, para. 20.

obligations prescribed by treaties to which the organization is not a party, as well as for the amendment and modification of treaties.[107] Likewise, Article 65(4) prescribes that a notification of a claim of invalidity, termination, withdrawal from or suspension of the operation of a treaty, as well as objections thereto, 'shall be governed' by the rules of the organization making the notification or objection. As the corresponding provisions in VCLT 1969 do not contain any references to the internal law of States, it appears that the ILC and the 1986 Vienna Conference made a point of distinguishing between States and international organizations as regards those provisions. It is stated in the commentary to draft article 36(2) that a 'stricter regime' is warranted on the grounds that international organizations are 'not given unlimited capacity'.[108]

But what are the normative implications to be derived from provisions that stress that States entrust international organizations with limited competences? Do Article 6 and other provisions referring to the rules of the organization impose, as a matter of general international law, limits on the acts that international organizations may perform? If so, certain legal consequences must ensue, also as a matter of general international law, from the fact that the organization has acted *ultra vires*.

Under the law of treaties, the typical legal consequences arising from irregularities in the making or performance of treaties are invalidity, termination and suspension of the operation of a treaty, as provided in Part V of VCLT 1969. While irregularities concerning the making of treaties are treated as matters of invalidity, circumstances affecting performance are treated as matters of suspension or termination.[109] In the case of States, the only instance in which an irregular exercise of the

---

[107] In the case of draft art. 35, the text adopted on first reading provided that an obligation arose for a third IO 'if the parties to the treaty [intended] the provision to be a means of establishing the obligation in the sphere of its activities'. This was meant to stress that it was 'essential for an international organization not to go beyond the bounds of its competence' as implied in draft art. 6 (Reuter, YILC 1982/I, p. 26, para. 14). A member of the Commission, however, pointed out that the bounds of competence was an internal question that had little to do with the issue of the intention of the parties to establish an obligation for the IO: McCaffrey, YILC 1982/I, p. 29, para. 30–32.

[108] Commentary to art. 36, YILC 1982/II, part two, p. 43, para. 2. As discussed previously, militating in favour of a restrictive rule were also considerations relating to structural differences between IOs and States: see section 3.3.2.

[109] On invalidity, termination and the relationship the categories bear to each other, see M. Kohen and S. Heathcote, 'Article 42' in O. Corten and P. Klein (eds.), *The Vienna Conventions on the Law of Treaties: A Commentary*, v. II (Oxford: Oxford University Press, 2011), pp. 1018–21.

competence to conclude treaties as established under domestic law may be invoked as a ground of invalidity is that envisaged by Article 46 VCLT 1969. Pursuant to Article 46, a State may 'invoke the fact that its consent to be bound by a treaty has been expressed in violation of a provision of its internal law regarding competence to conclude treaties as invalidating its consent', provided that the violation was 'manifest and concerned a rule of its internal law of fundamental importance'. Article 46 thus opens a narrow window for States to rely on their internal law to free themselves from treaty obligations. The reason why the window is so narrow is not difficult to grasp: it is a corollary of the *pacta sunt servanda* principle that, as stipulated in Article 27 VLCT 1969, '[a] party may not invoke the provisions of its internal law as justification for its failure to perform a treaty'.

If Article 6 VCLT 1986 established a limitation under the general law of treaties on the capacity of international organizations to conclude treaties, then it would be expected that Articles 27 and 46 of the Convention would provide for meaningful legal consequences flowing from *ultra vires* treaty-making. That was precisely what some members of the Commission proposed.[110] The debate was particularly lively when the Commission considered the applicability to international organizations of the rule on 'internal law and observance of treaties' contained in Article 27 VCLT 1969. Soviet member Leonid Ushakov suggested that a provision be included 'to the effect that an organization was entitled not to perform obligations incompatible with its constituent instruments'.[111] At the 1986 Vienna Conference, the Soviet Union introduced an amendment which would have added to Article 27 the following paragraph:

> In the event of a conflict between obligations under the treaty concluded by an international organization and its obligations under the constituent instrument of the organization the obligations under that instrument shall prevail.[112]

The Soviet Union justified the amendment on the grounds that '[t]he position of international organizations was different [from that of States], and that recognizing a similar norm for them would run counter to the

---

[110] Sette-Câmara, YILC 1977/I, p. 107, para. 41; Njenga, ibid. pp. 107–08, para. 44; El-Erian, ibid., p. 110, para. 12.
[111] Ushakov, YILC 1981/I, p. 159, para. 15.
[112] UNCLT 1986/II, p. 71, para. 76.

limitations placed on them by earlier articles', notably Article 6.[113] However, this strong view on the legal effects of speciality failed to attract further support: the proposals by Ushakov and the Soviet Union were both rejected, the result being that Article 27(2) VCLT 1986, mirroring its counterpart in VCLT 1969, prescribes that '[a]n international organization party to a treaty may not invoke the rules of the organization as justification for its failure to perform the treaty'.[114]

Article 46 VCLT 1986 could have been a key provision for implementing the principle of speciality. Yet, the debate within the Commission was surprisingly straightforward, marked by the absence of proposals to abandon the strict rules laid down in VCLT 1969 for invalidity on the grounds of violation of provisions of internal law regarding the competence to conclude treaties. Members of the ILC instead focused on the narrower issue of whether the definition of the 'manifest violation of a rule of fundamental importance' that triggers the ground of invalidity had to be tweaked to cater to the needs of international organizations. On first reading, the Commission adopted a version of draft article 46 that omitted, as regards international organizations, the requirement that the rule violated be 'of fundamental importance'.[115] The reason was that 'international organizations should be protected even more than States

---

[113] Soviet Union, UNCLT 1986/I, p. 115, para. 40. The idea was also to reflect what the Socialist bloc perceived as a fundamental structural difference between domestic law and the rules of the organization. As Ushakov argued, while States were in a position to change their internal law to comply with what was required by treaties, modifications of the rules of the organization could only be achieved through amendments to the constituent instrument; accordingly, while States were 'masters of their internal law', IOs could not be said to be 'masters of their constituent instrument': YILC 1982/I, 11, paras. 22–23.

[114] Nothing prevents, of course, the parties to a treaty from inserting clauses recognising a special role for the internal law of an IO. The ILC adopted on first reading a provision envisaging the possibility that, 'according to the intention of the parties', performance of a treaty may be 'subject to the exercise of the functions and powers of the organization'. The intention was to cover agreements concluded with a view to implementing decisions by IOs: Reuter (Tenth Report), YILC 1981/II, part one, p. 158, para. 11. A member of the Commission questioned whether fleshing out what clauses the parties could or not include in a treaty was necessary: whether or not the parties intended that a treaty be subject to the rules of an organization would be an ordinary matter of treaty interpretation: Aldrich, YILC 1981/I, p. 165, para. 17–18. The Commission thus abandoned this proposal on second reading.

[115] YILC 1981/II, part two, p. 65. The Commission had also redefined the criterion that the violation be 'manifest' because the phrase 'normal practice', employed in VCLT 1969, was considered problematic in the case of IOs. It suggested defining a violation as manifest 'if it is or ought to be within the knowledge of any contracting State or any

in the event of a violation of the rules of the organization governing their competence to conclude treaties, all such rules being of fundamental importance'.[116] That change, which would have lowered the threshold for claims of treaty invalidity by international organizations, was discarded by the Commission on second reading without much discussion. Debate on the issue was however reopened at the 1986 Vienna Conference when a group of international organizations proposed an amendment that would have added the phrase 'including the rules of the constituent instrument of the organization' to the text of Article 46.[117] The amendment was met with fierce opposition,[118] revealing that States were averse to widening the scope of application of Article 46.

In the end, neither Article 27 nor Article 46 in the 1986 Vienna Convention prescribe legal consequences for cases in which an international organization exceeds its capacity to conclude treaties as defined in Article 6. Rather, they replicate the rules that had been adopted for States in the 1969 Vienna Convention. Despite the symbolic stance that Article 6 takes, there was clearly no appetite for exploring the implications that the view that international organizations have limited competences could have as a matter of general international law.

4.3.3 Speciality and Responsibility for Ultra Vires Conduct

The ARIO do not include a provision which, similar to Article 6 VCLT 1969, purports to limit the capacity of international organizations to commit internationally wrongful acts to conduct taken within the limits set by their constituent instrument. The capacity to incur responsibility is presumed both for States and international organizations as a corollary of their capacity to operate on the international plane. However, the question of whether *ultra vires* acts entail an organization's responsibility was

contracting organization'. The 1986 Vienna Conference realigned the text of art. 46(4) with that of VCLT 1969 on the grounds that the Commission had replaced an 'objective test' based on good faith and treaty-making practice with a 'subjective test' based on what the parties knew or ought to have known (e.g., Austria, UNCLT 1986/I, p. 130, para. 55). The Conference then discussed whether there was a 'normal treaty-making practice of international organizations' comparable to that of States. The Drafting Committee stated that a 'normal practice' of IOs 'might well develop in the future and that such developments should not be precluded': UNCLT 1986/I, p. 16, para. 88.
[116] Riphagen (reporting for the Drafting Committee), YILC 1979/I, p. 223, para. 11.
[117] UNCLT 1986/II, p. 73, para. 101.
[118] See the records of the 18th meeting of the Committee of the Whole, UNCLT 1986/I, pp. 134–39.

briefly discussed when the ILC considered the rule in Article 7 ARS.[119] Article 7 prescribes that the conduct of organs or persons empowered to exercise elements of governmental authority is attributable to the State even when the entity in question 'exceeds its authority or contravenes instructions'. While one can hardly challenge attribution of conduct to a State by contending that the conduct was *ultra vires* the competence of the State itself (as bearer of the 'totality of international rights and obligations'), a strong view on speciality would militate in favour of taking a different approach for international organizations. In fact, a member of the Commission suggested that acts of organs or agents falling outside the scope of the competences of the organization would be 'null and not an act of the organization'.[120] A similar position was taken by certain States and international organizations in the comments that they addressed to the Commission.[121] But the Commission remained unconvinced. In the words of Special Rapporteur Gaja:

> denying attribution of conduct may deprive third parties of all redress, unless conduct could be attributed to a State or another organization. The need to protect third parties requires an extension of attribution of conduct for the same reason that underpins the validity of treaties concluded by an international organization notwithstanding minor infringements of rules concerning competence to conclude treaties. While in that context it may be argued that protection of third parties should be limited to those that relied in good faith on the organ's or official's conduct, the same rationale does not apply in most cases of responsibility for unlawful conduct.[122]

On second reading, perhaps as a partial concession to its critics, the Commission departed slightly from the text of Article 7 ARS by adding

---

[119] There are, moreover, two provisions in the ARIO which make reference to the competences of IOs: art. 25, according to which organizations are permitted to invoke necessity to safeguard the interests of their member States and of the international community as a whole if 'the organization has, in accordance with international law, the function to protect the interest in question', and art. 49, pursuant to which an IO may only invoke responsibility for breaches of an *erga omnes* obligation 'if safeguarding the interest of the international community as a whole underlying the obligation breached is within the functions of the international organization invoking responsibility'. These provisions are discussed in Sections 7.2.3 and 7.2.4.

[120] Addo, YILC 2004/I, p. 30. See also the remarks of Rodríguez-Cedeño, YILC 2004/I, p. 81, para. 74, and Pellet, A/CN.4/SR.3082 (2011), p. 4.

[121] Poland, A/CN.4/547 (2004), p. 7; Interpol, A/CN.4/556 (2005), p. 26; ILO, A/CN.4/568/Add.1 (2006), p. 16; Czech Republic A/CN.4/636/Add.1 (2011), p. 11.

[122] Gaja (Second Report), YILC 2004/II, part one, p. 14, para. 53.

the requirement that the organ or agent act not only 'in an official capacity' but also 'within the overall functions of [the] organization'. As a result, Article 8 ARIO seems to be narrower in scope than Article 7 ARS. In the commentary, the Commission explains that the new phrasing was merely intended to make it 'clearer' that a 'close link between *ultra vires* conduct and the organ's or agent's functions' is necessary for attribution.[123] Rather than incorporating the principle of speciality into the provision on excess of authority and contravention of instructions, the goal of the Commission seems to have been achieving a more precise drafting than that found in the Articles on State Responsibility'.[124]

4.3.4 The Proper Scope of the Principle of Speciality

The debates at the ILC reveal some of the problems posed by any attempt to integrate into regimes of general international law the notion that international organizations, unlike States, have limited competences. Though there may be a case for using general international law to check on the exercise of powers by international organizations, there are at least two normative concerns pointing to the opposite solution. First, making the principle of speciality part of general international law would confer an undue benefit to international organizations, in that they might be able to rely on their internal law to get rid of international agreements or avoid responsibility for internationally wrongful acts. That, in turn, would make it easier for member States to make use of organizations to circumvent international obligations. Second, the implication of making speciality part of the general international law is to pave the way for third parties to invoke or rely on constituent instruments and other internal rules, which could constitute a form of destabilising interference with the activities of international organizations. That might be a solution creating more problems than it solves.[125]

---

[123] Ibid. 24, para. 4.

[124] The commentary makes it clear that '[e]ven if the act was considered invalid', because, e.g., it violates the rules of the organization, 'it may entail the responsibility of the organization'. It adds that '[t]he need to protect third parties requires attribution not to be limited to acts that are regarded as valid': commentary to art. 7, YILC 2011/II, part two, p. 57, para. 5.

[125] At the 1986 Vienna Conference, see the statements of the Council of Europe, UNCLT 1986/I, p. 97, para. 27, and Egypt, ibid., p. 102, para. 29.

The law of treaties provides the clearest example of how those concerns play out. Subjecting treaties concluded by international organizations on the international plane to the internal law of those organizations would have subverted the logic that underlies the legal regime of international agreements, characterised by principles that are geared towards promoting legal security and stability (*pacta sunt servanda* and good faith).[126] If the general law allowed for breaches of the internal law of international organizations to be invoked to avoid compliance with or invalidate a treaty, the law of treaties would protect international organizations and their members by making it safer for them to engage in irresponsible treaty making. It would, likewise, allow third parties to benefit from provisions that are, for them, *res inter alios acta*.

Ultimately, Article 6 VCLT 1986 is a symbolic provision with little or no substantive effect.[127] The notion that international organizations are subjects of limited competence governs relations on the institutional plane, where it constrains decision-making, paves the way for internal control and review, and is of great import for disputes between organizations and their members.[128] When it comes to the international plane, while engaging in external relations in the fulfilment of whatever mandates they may have been entrusted with, international organizations remain legally autonomous entities comparable to States. It is, in short, essential not to conflate the rights, obligations and capacities that international organizations may have *qua* international legal subjects – which will derive from the sources of international law applying to them on the international plane – and their competences under their constitutions.[129]

---

[126] As noted by the Special Rapporteur, the starting point should be that 'no international organization that concluded a treaty did so with the reservation that the treaty was concluded on the basis of a potestative clause unless that fact was expressly mentioned', as the 'adoption of any other solution would be tantamount to rendering meaningless the rule of *pacta sunt servanda*': Reuter, YILC 1981/I, p. 159, para. 15. Similarly, Riphagen YILC/I 1977, p. 112, para. 20.

[127] Criticising the multiple references to the 'rules of the organization' in VCLT 1986, Gaja remarked that 'it is not evident why the parallelism between States and international organizations has been broken', because '[s]hould the "rules of the organization" or the internal law be violated, the consequence is not necessarily the invalidity of the acceptance': G. Gaja, 'A "new" Vienna Convention on Treaties between States and International Organizations or between International Organizations: a critical commentary' (1988) 58 BYIL 253, 260–61.

[128] As discussed in section 6.2.1.

[129] Some commentators distinguish between the notions of 'capacity' (under general international law) and 'competence' (under institutional law): see G. Hartmann, 'The capacity of international organizations to conclude treaties' in K. Zemanek (ed.),

This is why, in the system put in place by VCLT 1986, all that Article 6 can achieve is to serve as a reminder that international organizations ought not to abuse their competences.

That said, the fact that a few specific provisions in VCLT 1986 and the ARIO make the application of rules of the law of treaties and responsibility hinge upon the rules of organization may give rise to controversy in disputes involving third parties. For example, Article 49(3) ARIO recognises the legal interest of international organizations to invoke responsibility for breaches of obligations owed to the international community as a whole only if 'safeguarding the interest of the international community as a whole underlying the obligation breached is within the functions of the international organization invoking responsibility'. What would the legal consequences flowing from *ultra vires* action by an international organization under Article 49(3) be? Could a third party challenge an organization's standing on the grounds of lack of a function to safeguard *erga omnes* obligations? That would provide an occasion for third parties to demand that an international organization abide by its constituent instrument, which, for them, is *res inter alios acta*. One should question the wisdom of elevating to the international plane, without convincing normative reasons, rules that are better left to apply and constrain the behaviour of international organizations on the institutional plane. The precise effects (if any) of sporadic attempts to incorporate the principle of speciality into the law of treaties and responsibility will have to be elucidated by future practice.

4.3.5   The Principle of Speciality, Lex Specialis *and the Relevance of General Rules*

While the principle of speciality cannot rebut the analogy between States and international organizations on the international plane, this does not mean that the extensive differences between the two categories of subjects do not have a bearing on the application of general international law to international organizations. On the contrary, there are at least three ways in which the fact that international organizations have limited competences affects the application of general rules.

Agreements of International Organizations and the Vienna Convention on the Law of Treaties (Vienna: Springer, 1971), pp. 149–50; and C. Brölmann, *The Institutional Veil in Public International Law: International Organizations and the Law of Treaties* (Oxford: Hart, 2005), pp. 90–94.

First, the 'internal law' of each organization governs the relations between international organizations and their members on the institutional plane, circumscribing the role that the general law of treaties, the general law of responsibility and any other customary rules extended by analogy may play in that realm. This point shall be covered in detail in Chapter 6.

Second, given the specific competences that each international organization is accorded under its constituent instrument, the occasion for many organizations to act on the international plane in a way that would trigger the application of rules of general international law may be severely limited. For example, it is difficult to imagine that rules on the taking of countermeasures will ever be relevant for entities such as the Universal Postal Union, or that the World Trade Organization will ever need to rely on the rules of international humanitarian law.[130] This is a point which Special Rapporteur Gaja has emphasised:

> The variety of international organizations is an undeniable fact which also contributes to explain why some draft articles do not offer precise answers to possible questions. It is also true that some draft articles are hardly relevant to certain organizations ... The draft articles at issue would apply to an organization only if the required conditions are met.[131]

Towards the end of the first reading of the ARIO, Michael Wood proposed a provision specifying that '[i]n applying [the ARIO] to a particular organization, any special considerations that result from the specific characteristics and rules of that organization shall be taken into account'.[132] That proposal went too far in emphasising speciality, begging the question of what '[taking] into account' ... 'specific characteristics and rules' would entail. If it was intended as a reminder that the articles are only applicable 'if the required conditions are met', the proposal would be trivial; if it was intended as a clause prescribing that special characteristics may be invoked to challenge an otherwise applicable provision, it would have introduced great uncertainty into the ARIO.[133]

---

[130] As the WTO pointed out, 'no claim was ever made against the World Trade Organization alleging violation of international law' possibly because the WTO 'is essentially a forum for negotiations and dispute resolution between its members': A/CN.4/545 (2004), p. 32.

[131] Gaja (Eight Report), A/CN.4/640 (2011), p. 5, para. 5.

[132] Wood, YILC 2009/I, p. 68, para. 28.

[133] As pointed out by Nolte, Wood's proposal could 'give rise to the practice of "special pleading" which would undermine the whole regime of international organizations': A.CN.4.SR.3080 (2011), p. 9.

While the Commission had good reasons to reject it, Wood's proposal expressed an important idea: that differences between States and international organizations and the latter's 'specific characteristics' are part of the factual framework under which the application of general international law international organizations takes place. Thus, the commentary to Article 54 ARIO, on proportionality of countermeasures, states that '[o]ne and the same countermeasure may affect a State or an international organization in a different way according to the circumstances', and that 'an economic measure that might hardly affect a large international organization may severely hamper the functioning of a smaller organization and for that reason not meet the test of proportionality'.[134] Likewise, the commentary to Article 46 ARIO points out that because of 'special features of international organizations', acquiescence to the loss of the right to invoke responsibility 'may involve a longer period than the one normally sufficient for States'.[135] That said, one should always distinguish between the issue of the relevance of certain general rules for an international organization and the issue of their applicability to the organization on the international plane. When speciality is rightly conceptualised as a principle of institutional law rather than as a principle of general international law, it becomes clear that 'particular IOs might be especially unlikely to contravene some general international law rules'; yet, that does not mean that such violations will be impossible, but merely improbable.[136]

Third, differences between States and international organizations mean that the *lex specialis* principle may be of great practical relevance for international organizations, bridging the gap between the rules that apply on the institutional plane and those that apply on the international plane.[137] The principle *lex specialis derogat legi generali*, reflected in

---

[134] YILC 2011/II, part two, p. 95, para. 3.
[135] Ibid., p. 87, para. 2.
[136] Daugirdas, 'How and why international law binds international organizations' (2016) 57 *Harvard International Law Journal* 325, 367.
[137] The ILC at times relied on the *lex specialis* principle to respond to criticisms that the ARIO were not taking into account the 'special characteristics' of international organizations: e.g., Gaja (Fifth Report), YILC 2007/II, part one, p. 7, para. 7. But *lex specialis* and the principle of speciality are different notions: as Pronto has put it, 'to equate *lex specialis* with the principle of speciality is to misconstrue the nature of the former, and to significantly constrain the scope of the latter. *Lex specialis* may be one way in which speciality is operationalized': A. Pronto, 'Reflections on the scope of application of the articles on the responsibility of international organizations' in M. Ragazzi (ed.), *Responsibility of International Organizations* (Leiden: Nijhoff, 2013), p. 158.

Article 55 ARS and Article 64 ARIO, is a 'technique of interpretation and conflict resolution' that governs the application of rules dealing with the same subject matter by giving priority to that which is more specific.[138] Given that most rules of general international law have the character of *jus dispositivum* – that is, can be derogated from with the exception of those belonging to the category of peremptory norms[139] – States and international organizations are free to agree to have their relations governed by special rules.[140] *Lex specialis* thus provides an option for international organizations to conclude treaties that depart from the general law whenever the character of their functions or other specificities so requires. For example, organizations concerned that the principle of full reparation for internationally wrongful acts may jeopardise the exercise of their functions can seek to conclude agreements limiting their responsibility – as, in fact, the United Nations often does in the context of peacekeeping operations.[141]

4.4 Concluding Remarks

In his Sixth Report, Special Rapporteur Gaja wearily remarked that critics of the ARIO used 'as a mantra the refrain that the Commission is basically replacing the term "State" with "international organization" in the articles on State responsibility'.[142] As the Commission did relatively little to elaborate on its methodology, that criticism was not exactly off the mark. But the Special Rapporteur would have had good cause to complain about the *other* set of mantras that permeated the debate at the Commission and beyond, namely that 'international organizations are special subjects of international law'; that 'international organizations

---

[138] Conclusions of the Work of the Study Group on the Fragmentation of International Law, YILC 2006/II, part two, p. 178, paras. 5–8.

[139] Ibid., para. 8.

[140] Thus, for example, in the practice of the WTO, responsibility for breaches includes the obligation of cessation but not that of reparation, and a sophisticated system of unilateral measures authorised by the Dispute Settlement Body replace the regime of countermeasures provided by the general law. Concerning the obligation to reparation, a more nuanced analysis is provided in S. Shadikhodjaev and N. Pak, 'Cessation and reparation in the GATT/WTO legal system: a view from the law of State responsibility' (2007) 41 *Journal of World Trade* 1237.

[141] United Nations, A/CN.4/637/Add.1 (2011), pp. 29–30. Also, commentary to art. 31, YILC 2011/II, part two, p. 77, para. 6.

[142] Gaja (Sixth Report), YILC 2008/I, part one, p. 19, para. 5.

have special characteristics'; that 'international organizations are governed by the principle of speciality'.

This chapter delved into some limits of the 'mantra of speciality'. The infinite variety of international organizations is not in itself a justification for postulating the existence of multiple legal regimes that would apply to different categories of organizations in the absence of relevant practice and precedent pointing in that direction. While the principle of speciality reflects the fact that international organizations are entrusted by their members with specific competences and functions, it is unclear what difference this can or should make at the level of general international law, especially when one considers the issue of the validity of *ultra vires* treaties and the extent of responsibility for *ultra vires* conduct. The history of the codification and progressive development of the law of treaties and responsibility of international organizations suggests that relying on internal particularities as a basis for distinguishing between States and organizations tends to introduce arbitrary distinctions based on policy arguments that are difficult to uphold.[143]

That said, the distinction between 'original' and 'derivative' subjects of international law points to at least one important difference between States and international organizations under general international law, and that concerns law-making. Though the ILC has rightly recognised that the practice of organizations may contribute to the formation of customary rules, that is only to the extent that that practice is representative of the practice of the organizations' member States. There is no indication that the emergence of international organizations has displaced the system of sovereign equality that lies at the core of prevailing conceptions of how general international law is made, even if it undeniably and decisively transformed the processes whereby the practice and *opinio juris* of States are expressed.

---

[143] As Alain Pellet conceded in a recent essay, 'it would probably have been difficult for the Commission to draw much more concrete consequences from the principle of speciality than it actually did': A. Pellet, 'International organizations are definitely not States: cursory remarks on the ILC Articles on the Responsibility of International Organizations' in Ragazzi, *The Responsibility of International Organizations*, p. 49. Also: M. Wood, '"Weighing" the Articles on Responsibility of International Organizations', ibid., p. 62.

5

International Organizations as 'Layered Subjects'

One of the most obvious differences between States and international organizations is that international organizations are created by States and typically governed by political organs in which States sit. Member States, who retain their separate existence as international legal subjects, are often required to implement – or collaborate in the implementation of – the organization's obligations on both institutional and international planes. That being so, the potential for States to influence the way in which their organization fulfils its mandate and discharges its international obligations should not be underestimated. Nor should the benefits that States reap from taking collective action through a body corporate.

In this respect, international organizations are not too different from those States that comprise subunits and organs with varying degrees of political and legal autonomy. In the case of federations, federated entities with exclusive competence to regulate subject matters to which international law applies may be capable of preventing the federal government from performing its international obligations. In the *LaGrand* case, for example, the United States found itself unable to comply with provisional measures indicated by the International Court of Justice because the Governor of Arizona refused to give effect to them.[1] Separation of powers under constitutions can also hinder compliance with international law, as is the case when, contrary to the advice of the executive branch, the judiciary disregards the jurisdictional immunities of foreign States.[2] Yet, international law mostly treats States as unitary actors,[3] the presumption

---

[1] *LaGrand (Germany v. United States of America)* (Judgment) [2001] ICJ Rep 466, paras. 111–16.

[2] As exemplified by *Jurisdictional Immunities of the State (Germany v. Italy; Greece intervening)* (Judgment) [2012] ICJ Rep 99.

[3] This view is captured, in international relations theory, by the 'billiard ball model', whereby '[e]ach state is represented by a government and is seen as an entity – a sovereign, independent unit', so that '[w]hat takes place within the boundaries of each is not the

being that international obligations apply to the State as a whole.[4] Likewise, breaches of international obligations committed by any organs or persons empowered to exercise governmental authority trigger the international responsibility of the State.[5] In the eyes of international law, rules concerning the allocation of competences and liability at the domestic level tend to be immaterial.

The issue that arises when one considers international organizations is whether, like States, they should be treated as unitary entities. It has been suggested and often assumed that because intergovernmental institutions possess separate legal personality, there is no formal intersection between their obligations and those of their members. As legally autonomous entities operating on the international plane, they would be subject, as is the case with States, to the *pacta tertii* rule and the principle of independent responsibility. But that might be taking the analogy too far. One thing is to say that States and international organizations are comparable, so that rules of general international law that bind States individually also bind their organizations on the international plane. Another is to suggest that, by acting collectively, States can circumvent their individual obligations, ignore treaty commitments assumed by the corporate entities that they set up and shield themselves from any individual liability resulting from collective wrongful conduct.

That international organizations can be described as 'layered', rather than unitary, subjects may thus provide a reason to resist assimilation with States as regards certain rules of general international law, particularly in the field of treaties and responsibility. Catherine Brölmann has described this as a question concerning the 'transparency of the institutional veil' of international organizations.[6] Organizations are sometimes viewed as legally autonomous 'opaque' subjects of international law, and sometimes as 'transparent' forums created to

---

concern of the others' (at 28): J. W. Burton, *World Society* (Cambridge: Cambridge University Press, 1972), pp. 28–35. Anne-Marie Slaughter has suggested that we are witnessing a shift from the conception of the unitary State to that of the 'disaggregated state', as State organs and their foreign counterparts start to interact directly with each other, without the intermediation of foreign offices: A. M. Slaughter, *A New World* Order (Princeton: Princeton University Press, 2008), pp. 12–15.

[4] Art. 29, VCLT 1969.

[5] Art 4, ARS. Also: *LaGrand (Germany v. United States of America)* (Provisional Measures) [1999] ICJ Rep 9, para. 28.

[6] C. Brölmann, *The Institutional Veil in Public International Law: International Organizations and the Law of Treaties* (Oxford: Hart, 2005), pp. 247–53.

facilitate cooperation between their members. This dichotomy creates a tension for those trying to make sense of how international law allocates obligations and responsibility between organizations and their members.[7]

By revisiting the ILC debates that led to the extension of the *pacta tertii* rule and the principle of independent responsibility to organizations and their members, this chapter discusses how a persuasive objection to a full analogy between States and international organizations was discarded in the light of emerging international practice and *opinio juris*. It also considers rules that have been proposed to mitigate the resulting strong separation between member States and their organizations by preventing the circumvention of international obligations.

5.1 The Push towards an Analogy between Unitary and Layered Subjects

5.1.1 International Organizations and the Relative Effect of Treaties

The maxim *pacta tertiis nec nocent nec prosunt*, as enshrined in Article 34 VCLT 1969, prescribes that '[a] treaty does not create either obligations or rights for a third State without its consent'.[8] Because treaties have only 'relative effect', they are *res inter alios acta* in relation to third parties, transactions that cannot affect the legal position of States that did not express their consent to be bound by them. The International Law Commission described the principle encapsulated in Article 34 as 'the expression of one of the fundamental consequences of consensuality',[9] to be extended to any treaty in which international organizations participate.

From the outset, the Commission never seriously considered departing from the *pacta tertiis* principle so as to provide, for example, that members would be *ipso jure* bound by treaties concluded by an organization or vice-versa. Special Rapporteur Reuter's starting point was that there could be 'no revision, but only adaptation, of the principles embodied in articles 34 to 38 of the Vienna Convention'.[10] Yet, he

---

[7] Ibid., pp. 4–5.
[8] See in general E. David, 'Article 34' in O. Corten and P. Klein (eds.), *The Vienna Conventions on the Law of Treaties: A Commentary*, v. II (Oxford: Oxford University Press, 2011), pp. 887–96.
[9] Commentary to draft art. 34, YILC 1982/II, part two, p. 42.
[10] Reuter (Sixth Report), YILC 1977/II, part one, p. 124, para. 25.

believed that 'the appearance of international organizations on the scene of international legal relations [gave] rise to some exceptions to this relative effect of treaties',[11] so that member States might occupy 'a position falling between that of a third State and that of a State party' to treaties concluded by the organization.[12] Reuter's intuition was sound: it does not follow from the fact that international organizations are legally autonomous entities operating on the international plane that member States can claim, vis-à-vis third parties, that they have no part in their organizations' treaty commitments. But a very strong view of international organizations as legally autonomous entities prevailed at the Commission.[13] It is curious that in a project where the ILC refrained from taking a position as to the status of international organizations in international law, its members had little difficulty accepting that, in the words of Leonid Ushakov, the legal personality of an international organization 'was its own and it possessed its own will, distinct from the will of its members taken separately or collectively', from which it 'followed that a treaty concluded by an international organization ... did not directly entail obligations for the member States'.[14]

As discussed later in this chapter, the scope of the *pacta tertiis* rule came into question when the Commission considered how the rules on the acquisition of treaty rights and obligations by third parties envisaged in Articles 35 and 36 VCLT 1969 should be adjusted to make sense of the relations between organizations and their members. The debate has led to an agreement to disagree at the 1986 Vienna Conference, which adopted a saving clause excluding from the purview of VCLT 1986 'any question that may arise in regard to the establishment of obligations and rights for

[11] Ibid., p. 121, para. 5.
[12] Reuter, YILC 1982/I, p. 26, para. 10.
[13] As Reuter noted: '[d]uring the Commission's debates on the corresponding draft articles, the proposed exceptions to that principle had been rejected because the rule seemed important enough to be stated generally and virtually absolutely': Reuter, YILC 1982/I, p. 26, para. 9.
[14] Ushakov embraced an analogy with States wholeheartedly, noting that the legal personality of an IO 'was its own and it possessed its own will, distinct from the will of its members taken separately or collectively', from which it 'followed that a treaty concluded by an international organization ... did not directly entail obligations for the member States'; YILC 1981/I, p. 173, para. 31. Affirming the autonomy of IOs, but taking a more nuanced approach: Reuter, YILC 1982/I, p. 26, para. 9 and Riphagen, YILC 1977/I, p. 137, para. 1.

States members of an international organization under a treaty to which that organization is a party'.[15] This saving clause notwithstanding, it is undeniable that the image of international organization found in VCLT 1986 is that of unitary entities that bear their rights and obligations independently of their members. According to Article 34, '[a] treaty does not create either obligations or rights or a third State or a third organization without the consent of that State or organization'. The legislative history of the Convention indicates that this vision did not only come from the dogmatism prevailing in the ILC, but also found support in the *opinio juris* of States and international organizations themselves.[16]

5.1.2 *International Organizations and the Principle of Independent Responsibility*

The law of State responsibility is premised upon the 'principle of independent responsibility', according to which 'State responsibility is specific to the State concerned'.[17] In other words, States are only liable for their own internationally wrongful acts. Only in exceptional cases, involving aid and assistance, direction and control, or coercion, can States incur responsibility in connection with the conduct of other States.[18] If international organizations are viewed as legally autonomous entities operating on the international plane, it can be argued that, like States, they must only responsible for their own breaches of international law. But the fact that international organizations are created and run by States, to perform tasks for their benefit, sheds doubt on the possibility to analogise between the two categories of legal subjects so bluntly. Do similarities between States and international organizations justify the conclusion that they should never respond for wrongful acts committed by their members, or that they must be liable for their own actions *to the exclusion of* their members?

---

[15] Art. 74(3) VCLT 1986.

[16] Having been enthusiastically upheld even by States of the 'Socialist bloc': e.g., Belarus, UNCLT 1986/I, p. 146, para. 11. Also, Iran, ibid., p. 147, para. 20; Japan, ibid., p. 175, para. 25; and Ireland, ibid., p. 177, para. 45.

[17] Commentary to chapter IV of Part I of the ARS, YILC 2001/II, part two, p. 64, para. 1.

[18] See arts. 16–18 ARS and commentaries, ibid. pp. 65–70.

5.1.2.1 Rules on Attribution of Conduct

With respect to attribution of conduct, the principle of independent responsibility can be applied without much controversy to international organizations once they are conceptualised as subjects of general international law. If their legal personality is separate from that of their members, the conduct of organs and agents of international organizations have to be imputed to the organizations directly. But a tricky question arises whenever members commit a wrongful act while implementing – or collaborating in the implementation of – an international obligation of the organization. In this case, to whom must the relevant conduct be attributed?

There are two ways to handle this question. A possibility is to assimilate member States implementing obligations of an international organizations to organs of that organization, so that conduct is *de jure* attributable, directly and exclusively, to the latter under the rule found in Article 4 ARS and Article 5 ARIO.[19] Another is to regard organizations and members as separate entities acting on the international plane which on occasion borrow each other's organs. If so, a rule analogous to Article 6 ARS – on attribution of 'conduct of organs placed at the disposal of a State by another State'[20] – has to be devised to allocate responsibility between the lending and borrowing entities.

The first solution was advocated by the European Commission.[21] Given the level of integration achieved at the European level, where the EU exclusively exercises competences that originally belonged with its members, the European Commission suggested that acts taken by members in the implementation of obligations under Union law should be attributed to the Union alone.[22] The ILC, however, favoured the second solution and thought that attribution of acts taken by the member States on behalf of the organization was comparable to the situations that

---

[19] According to art. 4 ARS, '[t]he conduct of any State organ shall be considered an act of that State under international law ... '; pursuant to art. 6 ARIO, '[t]he conduct of an organ or agent of an international organization in the performance of functions of that organ or agent shall be considered as an act of that organization under international law ... '.

[20] Art. 6 ARS provides that '[t]he conduct of an organ placed at the disposal of a State by another State shall be considered an act of the former State under international law if the organ is acting in the exercise of elements of the governmental authority of the State at whose disposal it is placed'.

[21] See Section 4.1.2.

[22] A/CN.4/556 (2005), p. 6.

Article 6 ARS was devised to cover. Finding it inappropriate to extend the language of Article 6 ARS to international organizations, the Commission formulated a separate test to ascertain whether an organ of a member 'is placed at the disposal of' the organization.[23] Pursuant to Article 7 ARIO:

> The conduct of an organ of a State or an organ or agent of an international organization that is placed at the disposal of another international organization shall be considered under international law an act of the latter organization if the organization exercises effective control over that conduct.

By adopting this formulation, the Commission seems to have departed from the approach taken in the ARS in one important respect. While the commentary to Article 6 ARS specifies that under this rule conduct is attributed to the borrowing State to the exclusion of the lending State,[24] in the commentary to the ARIO it is said that, '[a]lthough it may not frequently occur in practice, dual or even multiple attribution of conduct cannot be excluded'.[25] That this question was left open shows that the Commission was aware of the intricacy that often characterises the factual scenarios that Article 7 ARIO purports to regulate. For example, in the case of peacekeeping operations, the United Nations is vested with operational control over the dispatched troops, while contributing States retain certain disciplinary powers. It can thus be difficult to ascertain in practice which of the entities has exercised effective control over a particular act. Accordingly, it has been suggested that conduct may be attributed both to the organization and to the member if both concurrently exercise effective control.[26]

---

[23] Commentary to art. 7, YILC 2011/II, part two, p. 57, para. 4.

[24] Commentary to art. 6, YILC 2001/II, part two, p. 44, para. 2.

[25] Commentary to chapter II, Part Two, YILC 2011/II, part two, p. 56, para. 4. In a similar vein, Gaja (Second Report), YILC 2004/II, part one, p. 10, para. 31, and Gaja (Seventh Report), YILC/II, part one, pp. 82–83, para. 25.

[26] This was the position taken by the Supreme Court of the Netherlands in the *Nuhanovic* case: *The State of the Netherlands v. Hasan Nuhanovic*, Case 12/03324 LZ/TT, 6 September 2013, para 3.11.2. The Supreme Court confirmed the findings of the Court of Appeal in *Nuhanović v. Netherlands*, Appeal judgment, LJN:BR5388 reported in ILDC 1742 (NL 2011). The issue of dual/multiple attribution has been the subject of lively academic debate: see e.g., A. Nollkaemper, 'Dual attribution: liability of the Netherlands for conduct of Dutchbat in Srebrenica' (2011) 9 *Journal of International Criminal Law* 1143, especially at 1152–54; F. Massineo, 'Attribution of conduct' in A. Nollkaemper and I. Plakokefalor (eds.), *Principles of Shared Responsibility in International Law: An Appraisal of the State of the Art* (Cambridge: Cambridge University Press, 2014), p. 60;

In short, as regards attribution of conduct, the ILC extended to international organizations the rules originally adopted for States, the result being that the conduct of organs and agents of international organizations are attributable to the organization alone. However, it refrained from taking the analogy further so as to consider that members acting on the authority of the organization will always disappear behind the institutional veil and thus be assimilated into organs of the organization.[27] Rather, that will be the case only when the organization has effective control over the conduct of their members, without prejudice to dual or multiple attribution in complex situations. Independent responsibility was thus affirmed both for the organization *and* for its members.

Article 7 ARIO had been applied by the European Court of Human Rights[28] and domestic courts[29] even before the Commission completed the first reading of the draft articles. As such, it provides a rare example of a provision of the ARIO that is directly supported by judicial precedent.

5.1.2.2 Rules on Attribution of Responsibility

Although it is plausible to extend the rules of attribution from States to international organizations in that, as international persons with legal autonomy from their members, they take actions that ought to be attributable to them alone, it does not follow from that proposition that members should not be liable for conduct solely attributable to the organization. The system of international responsibility recognises, as 'exceptions to the principle of independent responsibility', 'exceptional cases where it is appropriate that one State should assume responsibility for the internationally wrongful act of another'.[30] The recognised cases of 'assumption of responsibility' for another State's wrongful act are aid and

---

and T. Dannenbaum, 'Dual attribution in the context of military operations' (2015) 12 IOLR 401.

[27] Advocating for this solution: C. Ahlborn, 'The rules of international organizations and the law of international responsibility' (2012) 8 IOLR 452.

[28] *Behrami v. France (App. No. 71412/01); Saramati v. France, Germany and Norway (App. No. 78166/01), Judgment of 2 May 2007*, paras. 133–34.

[29] *R. (on the application of Al-Jedda) (FC) v. Secretary of State for Defence* [2007] UKHL 58, 12 December 2007, paras. 5ff (Lord Bingham) and *Nuhanović v. Netherlands*.

[30] Commentary to chapter IV of Part I of the ARS, YILC 2001/II, part two, pp. 64–65, paras. 5–8.

assistance in; direction and control over; and coercion leading to the commission of the wrongful act.[31]

A question of State responsibility which the ARS did not tackle, and which was thus left for the ARIO, was whether the principle of independent responsibility should apply in cases involving wrongful conduct by international organizations. It could be argued that, because international organizations are not unitary entities like States, international responsibility entailed by conduct solely attributable to them should also be borne by the members, either jointly and severally or on a subsidiary basis. Whether or not this is a tenable proposition in law depends on the view one takes as to the content of the rule of incorporation in general international law, that is, on the character of the right that States enjoy to create corporate bodies operating on the international plane. Does it follow from that right that States are entitled to limit their individual responsibility?

This was arguably the most important question that the ILC had to answer when it codified and progressively developed the law of responsibility of international organizations. The Commission was inspired by the *Institut de droit international*'s work on the topic, culminating in a *Resolution on the Legal Consequences for Member States of the Non-fulfillment by International Organizations of their Obligations toward Third Parties* adopted in 1995.[32] For the *Institut*, no 'general rule of international law' exists 'whereby State members are, due solely to their membership, liable concurrently or subsidiarily, for the obligations of an international organization of which they are members'.[33] This position, which polarised commentators,[34] was presented as a rationalisation of existing practice and precedent as reflected in two series of cases.

---

[31] Arts. 16–18 ARS. The distinction between the concepts of 'attribution of conduct' and 'attribution of responsibility' is usefully discussed in J. Fry, 'Assumption of Responsibility' in Nollkaemper and Plakokefalor, *Principles of Shared Responsibility*, pp. 102–04.

[32] (1995) 66/II *Yearbook*, pp. 445–53.

[33] Art. 5(a), ibid.

[34] Affirming the principle of independent responsibility for IOs and members: P. Klein, *La Responsabilité des Organisations Internationales dans les Ordres Juridiques Internes et en Droit des Gens* (Brussels: Bruylant, 1998), p. 516; P. Sands and P. Klein, *Bowett's Law of International Institutions*, 6th edn (London: Sweet & Maxwell, 2009), p. 529; and H. Schermers and N. Blokker (eds.), *International Institutional Law: Unity within Diversity*, 5th edn (Leiden: Nijhoff, 2011), p. 1011. Contra: M. Hirsch, *The Responsibility of International Organizations towards Third Parties: Some Principles* (Dordrecht: Nijhoff, 1995), p. 148 and I. Brownlie, 'The responsibility of states for the acts of international organisations' in M. Ragazzi (ed.), *International Responsibility Today: Essays in Memory*

The first concerns proceedings instituted against the International Tin Council (ITC) by private parties before the English courts. When, in the mid-1980s, the ITC became unable to discharge its financial undertakings, the question arose of whether its member States were liable for the organization's debts. While the ensuing judgments focused on questions of English law, they have been taken as authority for the proposition that member States do not assume responsibility for wrongful acts committed by international organizations.[35] For example, in the judgment given by the Court of Appeal, Kerr LJ was unable to 'find any basis for concluding that it [had] been shown that there is any rule of international law, binding upon the member States of the ITC, whereby they can be held liable . . . for the debts of the ITC resulting from contracts concluded by the ITC in its own name'.[36] Likewise, Gibson LJ noted that '[n]othing [was] shown of any practice of States as to the acknowledgment or acceptance of direct liability for any States by reason of the absence of an exclusion clause'.[37]

The second series of cases relate to a dispute between Westland Helicopters Ltd. and the Arab Organization for Industrialization (AOI), which arose when the AOI defaulted on contractual obligations to set up a joint venture to manufacture helicopters in Egypt. The interim award given by the arbitral tribunal constituted to settle the dispute takes the

---

of Oscar Schachter (Leiden: Nijhoff, 2005), p. 359. Other authors have adopted a more nuanced position: Scobbie has suggested limited responsibility is a 'sensible, if potentially unwieldy, approach', which should not 'deter the further development of general principle in this matter': I. Scobbie, 'International organizations and international relations' in R. J. Dupuy (ed.), A Handbook on International Organizations, 2nd edn (Dordrecht: Nijhoff, 1998), p. 896.

[35] On the series of cases, see C. F. Amerasinghe, 'Liability to third parties of member states of international organizations: practice, principle and judicial precedent' (1991) 85 AJIL 259 (concluding that 'judicial precedents . . . strongly militate against the presumption that members are concurrently or subsidiarily liable for the obligations of the organization': at 279).

[36] J. H. Rayner (Mincing Lane) Ltd v. Department of Trade and Industry and Others [1988] 3 All ER 257; 80 ILR 47, 109. Confirming the Court of Appeal's judgment, Lord Templeman at the House of Lords stated that 'no plausible evidence was produced of the existence of such a rule of international law' making members liable for debts of their IOs: J. H. Rayner (Mincing Lane) Ltd v. Department of Trade and Industry [1989] 3 WLR 969; 81 ILR 670, 679–80.

[37] J. H. Rayner (Mincing Lane) Ltd v. Department of Trade and Industry and Others [1988] 3 All ER 257, 80 ILR 47, 174. Nourse LJ, dissenting from the majority, found that while the ITC had 'separate personality in international law', 'its members [were] jointly and severally, directly and without limitation liable . . . if and to the extent that [liability is] not discharged by the ITC itself': ibid., 147.

opposite approach than that found in the ITC cases. Rather than affirming that the four States constituting the AOI were not liable for acts of the Organization, the tribunal observed that because those States did not expressly exclude their liability 'third parties which have contracted with the AOI could legitimately count on their liability', a proposition that would stem 'from general principles of law and from good faith'.[38] This pronouncement, made at the jurisdictional phase of the dispute, proved to be an outlier. It was later successfully challenged before the Swiss courts, which found that the arbitral tribunal had lacked competence to hear claims against Egypt.[39] According to the Federal Supreme Court of Switzerland, the predominant role of the AOI's members could not 'undermine the independence and personality of the Organization, nor lead to the conclusion that when organs of the AOI deal with third parties they *ipso facto* bind the founding States'.[40]

The applicability of the principle of independent responsibility to international organizations and their members would seem to find support in this convoluted case law, coupled with the absence of past instances in which States were held liable for the wrongful conduct of organizations. That was the position that Special Rapporteur Gaja presented to the ILC. Following in the *Institut*'s footsteps, Gaja suggested that 'once it was admitted that an international organization had a legal personality separate from that of its members, the latter could not be deemed to share a common identity with the organization'.[41] That being the case, '[i]f an organization assumed an obligation, it rested only with the organization and a breach thereof entailed only the responsibility of the organization'.[42] The proposal to distinguish sharply between the responsibility of organizations and their members gave rise to a heated debate. The majority of members concurred with the Special Rapporteur, with Alain Pellet noting that '[t]he reasoning based on logic, doctrine and

---

[38] *Westland Helicopters Ltd v. Arab Organization for Industrialization*, Interim Award Regarding the Jurisdiction ('*Compétence*') of the Arbitral Tribunal, 5 April 1984 (1994) 80 ILR 600, 613.

[39] In fact, the award was successfully challenged by Egypt before Swiss courts, which decided that the arbitral tribunal was incompetent to rule on the rights and obligations of the member States of the AOI.

[40] *Arab Organization for Industrialization v. Westland Helicopters*, Judgment of 19 July 1988 (1994) 80 ILR 652, 658 (upholding the decision of the Court of Justice of Geneva on the matter).

[41] Gaja, YILC 2006/I, p. 153, para. 52.

[42] Ibid.

jurisprudence that lay behind [the principle of independent responsi-
bility] seemed fully convincing'.[43] But a vocal minority, spearheaded by
Ian Brownlie, described the application of the principle of independent
responsibility to international organizations and their members as:

> contrary to existing general international law and to all the principles of
> the law of treaties and the law of State responsibility because its applica-
> tion could allow States to circumvent their obligations by concluding a
> multilateral treaty establishing an international organization.[44]

This minority noted that independent responsibility raised normative
concerns because it would allow States to avoid their international
obligations by creating a separate corporate entity with limited liability.
Other members did not take as strong a position, but suggested that
further exceptions to the principle of independent responsibility should
be formulated,[45] in particular a rule on residual responsibility in cases of
default by international organizations.[46]

The debate between Pellet and Brownlie illustrates the doctrinal and
normative questions facing the Commission. Once international organizations are seen as legally autonomous entities operating on the international plane, there may be good reasons to apply the principle of
independent responsibility to them. But there is nothing 'logical' about
analogising between States and international organizations in this context. Indeed, as Brownlie pointed out, one can hardly describe as logical
the view that 'a multilateral treaty could be adopted which presented an
international legal person' with full limitation of responsibility for the
States creating it.[47] Viewing international organizations as subjects of
international law does not imply that States have a right to 'combine
forces in organizations possessing a separate legal personality'[48] at the
expense of the rights of third parties. If the rationale for the analogy is
that States are entitled to do collectively what they can do individually, it
does not follow that they can act collectively by excluding their individual

---

[43] Pellet, YILC 2006/I, p. 156, para. 12. Also, Matheson, ibid., p. 160, para. 33; Mansfield,
ibid., p. 161, para. 41; Economides, ibid., p. 173, para. 42; Ojo, YILC 2007/I, p. 130,
para. 66; Petric, ibid., p. 140, para. 36.

[44] Brownlie, YILC 2006/I, p. 157, para. 17. Also, Yamada, YILC 2006/I, p. 169, para. 8 and
Kemicha, YILC 2006/I, p. 171, para. 14 (though ultimately endorsing Gaja's proposal as a
'clever compromise').

[45] Eouurumuiu, YILC 2006/I, p. 153, para. 6

[46] Rao, ibid., p. 158, para. 2; and Economides, ibid., p. 173, para. 42.

[47] Brownlie, ibid, p. 167, para. 51.

[48] Ibid., p. 161, para. 1.

liability. Arguing that States are entitled to create a body corporate that will contract its own obligations and incur liability on its own right is one thing, arguing that this means that they can thereby limit their individual responsibility is quite another.

Yet, applying the principle of independent liability to international organizations and their members does have its attractions. A separation between the obligations and responsibility of organizations and members may not be dictated by logic or supported by a systemic analogy between the two categories of legal subjects, but it is a solution which promotes the former's autonomy and provides an incentive for action in the collective interest. The normative arguments supporting the principle of independent responsibility were articulated by the *Institut* as follows:

> Important considerations of policy, including support for the credibility and independent functioning of international organizations and for the establishment of new international organizations, militate against the development of a general and comprehensive rule of liability of member States to third parties for the obligations of international organizations.[49]

In a similar vein, Gaja observed that a rule of joint or subsidiary responsibility for member States would deeply affect decision-making within international organizations. Members might be 'prompted to intervene . . . , thereby robbing the organization of the independence it was granted by its constituent instrument'.[50] That could have a detrimental effect on the willingness of States to act collectively via international organizations, especially when the latter's political organs provide for decision-making by majority vote instead of unanimity. Although it is a mistake to treat international organizations as the 'harbingers of international happiness'[51] – the ITC and the AOI surely were not – it is

---

[49] Art. 8, (1995) 66/II *Yearbook*, p. 451. Also, E. Paasivirta, 'Responsibility of a member state of an international organization: where will it end? (2010) 7 IOLR 49, 51.

[50] Gaja, YILC 2006/I, p. 153, para. 53. In a similar vein, Mansfield, YILC 2006/I, p. 161, para. 41. In the literature, it has been contended that the 'relatively unaccountable nature of international organizations may be a key structural feature as far as their importance to states is concerned, not something that has come about by accident': R. Wilde, 'Enhancing accountability at the international level: the tension between international organisation and member state responsibility and the underlying issues at stake' (2006) 12 *ILSA Journal of International and Comparative Law* 395, 411.

[51] See J. Klabbers, 'The life and times of the law of international organizations' (2001) 70 *Nordic Journal of International Law* 287, 288.

undeniable that they perform a crucial role in global governance that the law should not set out to undermine.[52] Just as regimes of limited liability have their attractions in the domestic context, the same can be true of international law.

In the end, the position defended by Pellet and the Special Rapporteur carried the day. Even if the existing practice on member State responsibility remains somewhat haphazard,[53] the crucial factor explaining the ILC's decision to endorse the principle of independent responsibility was the guidance that it received from the relevant stakeholders, that is, the *opinio juris* that coalesced in the debates. Similar to what happened at the 1986 Vienna Conference as regards the applicability of the *pacta tertii* rule between international organizations and their members, States and international organizations expressed unequivocal support for the notion that each international legal person has to bear its own responsibility.[54] While one should be cautious in drawing conclusions from what delegations say or fail to say at the Sixth Committee of the UNGA,[55] the absence of opposition to the approach taken by the Commission in this particular instance speaks volumes. No other question arising during the drafting of the ARIO affected the individual interests of States as much as that of whether they should bear responsibility for the acts of international organizations, and the fact that the approach proposed by the Special

---

[52] For an energetic argument against member State responsibility, see N. Blokker, 'Member State responsibility for wrongdoings of international organizations: beacon of hope or delusion?' (2015) 12 IOLR 319.

[53] A. Geslin, 'Réflexions sur la repartition de la responsabilité entre l'organisation internationale et ses etats membres' (2005) 109 RGDIP 539, 542–62; M. Zwanenburg, *Accountability of Peace Support Operations* (Leiden: Nijhoff, 2005), p. 84.

[54] As the Special Rapporteur noted in his Seventh Report, '[t]here was wide support for restricting the responsibility of member States, as provided in article 29 [now 62]': YILC 2009/I, p. 89, para. 84. Clear support for the principle was expressed in comments submitted by Germany, A/CN.4/556 (2005), p. 65 (surveying State practice) and A/CN.4/636 (2011), p. 39; International Monetary Fund, A/CN.4/545 (2004), p. 10; Interpol, A/CN.4/568 (2006), p. 14; International Labour Organization, A/CN.4/568/Add.1 (2006), p. 24; Unesco, ibid., 23; and European Commission (A/CN.4/582, 24). Likewise, general support was expressed in debates at the Sixth Committee: A/CN.4/577 (2007), p. 15, para. 41.

[55] As Berman notes, 'i[t] takes a soothsayer to discern whether widespread silence is an encouraging token of confidence in the ILC or a worrying sign of disengagement from its work': F. Berman, 'The ILC within the UN's legal framework: its relationship with the Sixth Committee' (2007) 49 GYIL 107, 120.

Rapporteur remained unchallenged in the process – despite the strong normative critique offered by some members – is revealing. It indicates the plausibility of affirming that, as a matter of customary international law, a rule has emerged to the effect that member States are not as such liable for the internationally wrongful acts of their organizations.[56] This outcome is reflected in the adoption by the ILC of Article 62 ARIO. Article 62 reads as follows:

1. A State member of an international organization is responsible for an internationally wrongful act of that organization if:
   (a) it has accepted responsibility for that act towards the injured party; or
   (b) it has led the injured party to rely on its responsibility.
2. Any international responsibility of a State under paragraph 1 is presumed to be subsidiary.

The ARIO follow the methodology adopted in the ARS of only specifying the scenarios in which a State or an international organization will be responsible, without specifying the circumstances in which they will not.[57] The general principle expressed in Article 62 is thus to be distilled from an *a contrario* reading of paragraph 1. As the commentary clarifies, the applicability of the principle of independent responsibility to international organizations and their members 'is clearly implied', and 'membership does not as such entail for member States international responsibility when the organization commits an internationally wrongful act'.[58]

---

[56] See also C. Brölmann, 'Member states and international legal responsibility: developments of the institutional veil' (2015) 12 IOLR 358, 363–68 (coming to the conclusion, at 380, that as regards subsidiary responsibility of member States 'the institutional veil is, and has been, consistently opaque'). The *Jurisdictional Immunities* case illustrates how the attitude of States in the context of codification projects can be significant. The ICJ considered that 'the absence of any statements by States in connection with the work of the International Law Commission regarding State immunity and the adoption of the United Nations Convention' were significant factors militating against a finding that the exception in the law of State immunity for torts committed in the territory of the host State applied to the conduct of 'the armed forces and other organs of a State in the conduct of armed conflict': *Jurisdictional Immunities of the State*, para. 77.

[57] As explained in the commentary to art. 62 as adopted on first reading, 'the Commission found that it would be inappropriate to include in the draft a provision stating a residual, and negative, rule': YILC 2009/II, part two, p. 74, para. 2.

[58] Commentary to art. 62, YILC 2011/II, part two, p. 100, para. 2.

5.2 Calibrating the Analogy between Unitary and Layered Subjects

The 1986 Vienna Convention and the 2011 Articles on the Responsibility of International Organizations analogise international organizations with States by prescribing that their obligations and responsibility are borne by them alone. They thus reject the view that the layered character of international organizations provides a reason to distinguish them from States by not extending to them the *pacta tertii* rule and the principle of independent responsibility. Though this solution is neither required nor justified by a systemic analogy between the two categories of international legal subjects, it is based on the (limited) practice in the field and on the *opinio juris* of States and international organizations as expressed during the debates for which the codification projects provided an occasion.

The picture that emerges, therefore, is that of an international legal system where any group of States enjoys the right to set up corporate bodies which are exclusively responsible for the performance of their international obligations. Needless to say, such a wide right presents a considerable potential for abuse. In awareness of that, the ILC considered a number of provisions that mitigate – or would have mitigated – some of the normative concerns that arise when one takes the analogy this far. The provisions discussed by the Commission concern acceptance by members of rights, obligations and responsibility of organizations; responsibility in cases where organizations or their members are attempting to circumvent its international obligations; and the need to enable organizations to perform their international obligations.

5.2.1 Acceptance of Rights, Obligations and Responsibility

5.2.1.1 Acceptance of Rights and Obligations by Member States

The single most controversial issue that the Commission dealt with in its work on the law of treaties was that of the position of members vis-à-vis treaties concluded by international organizations. The debate revolved around draft article 36*bis*, a provision without a counterpart in VCLT 1969 that Special Rapporteur Reuter proposed in his Sixth Report.[59]

---

[59] YILC 1977/II, part one, pp. 128–33. A robust historical account and discussion of art 36*bis* is provided by C. Brölmann, 'The 1986 Vienna Convention on the Law of Treaties: the history of draft article 36*bis*' in J. Klabbers (ed.), *Essays on the Law of Treaties* (The Hague: Nijhoff, 1996), pp. 121–40.

Reuter contended that the notion that organizations have 'separate legal personality' had to be tempered by factual considerations. First, considerable uncertainty ensued from the fact that the constituent instruments of most international organizations were vague as regards their competence to conclude treaties.[60] Second, international organizations, unlike States, often lacked 'the financial and human resources to ensure the effective performance of [their] own obligations'.[61] In the light of these 'factual considerations', it would be 'fairly natural that both partners of the organization and the member States should want member States to be associated with the obligations of the organization'.[62] Thus, rather than subverting the *pacta tertiis* rule making the 'institutional veil' transparent and members co-contractors alongside their organizations, what Reuter and the Commission tried to achieve in the various incarnations of draft article 36*bis* was a more flexible regime for the acceptance of rights and obligations. In particular, Reuter thought that the close connection between organizations and members would warrant a mitigation of the rigid requirement posed by Article 35 VCLT 1969 that acceptance of an obligation by a third party be expressly given 'in writing'. This is how he described the choice standing before the Commission:

> either it finds that member States must be protected in the most strictly formal manner with respect to any commitment that might arise from their membership in the organization, because vis-à-vis its treaty commitments they are third parties in the fullest sense of the term – in which case article 36*bis* should be eliminated on principle – or it considers that the solidarity and close ties which exist between an organization and its member States justify their giving their assent in a less formal manner in respect of the effects on them of treaties concluded by the organization of which they are members, yet without sacrificing the principle.[63]

As initially proposed, draft article 36*bis* specified two ways in which member States could accept rights and obligations deriving from treaties concluded by international organizations.[64] First, consent could be given

---

[60] Reuter (Sixth Report), YILC 1977/II, part one, p. 126, para. 35.
[61] Ibid., p. 126, para. 35.
[62] Ibid.
[63] Reuter (Tenth Report), YILC 1981/II, part one, pp. 67–68, para. 99.
[64] As originally proposed (Reuter (Sixth Report), YILC 1977/II, part one, pp. 128–29), draft article 36*bis* read:
 '1. A treaty concluded by an international organization gives rise directly for States members of an international organization to rights and obligations in respect of other

in advance via the rules of organization, that is, when the constituent instrument envisages that members shall abide by treaties concluded by the organization. Second, circumstances regarding the subject-matter and application of the treaty could serve as evidence both of the intention of the parties to create obligations extending to members, and of the intention of the members to accept such obligations.

This second means for accepting rights and obligations was made stricter over time. The text originally proposed established a presumption of acceptance of rights 'in the absence of any indication of intention to the contrary', and the possibility of implied acceptance of obligations. By the time the first reading of the draft articles was completed, draft article 36*bis* required, additionally, the 'acknowledgement' by all the negotiating parties and the members of the organization that 'the application of the treaty necessarily entails such effects'.[65] The final version of draft article 36*bis* was even stricter, providing that:

> Obligations and rights arise for States members of an international organization from the provisions of a treaty to which that organization is a party when the parties to the treaty intend those provisions to be the means of establishing such obligations and according such rights and have defined their conditions and effects in the treaty or have otherwise agreed thereon, and if:

> parties to that treaty if the constituent instrument of that organization expressly gives such effects to the treaty.
> 2. When, on account of the subject-matter of a treaty concluded by an international organization and the assignment of the areas of competence involved in that subject-matter between the organization and its member States, it appears that such was indeed the intention of the parties to that treaty, the treaty gives rise for a member State to: (i) rights which the member State is presumed to accept, in the absence of any indication of intention to the contrary; (ii) obligations when the member State accepts them, even implicitly.'

[65] Article 36*bis*, adopted on first reading, read as follows: 'Third States which are members of an international organization shall observe the obligations, and may exercise the rights, which arise for them from the provisions of a treaty to which that organization is a party if:

> (a) the relevant rules of the organization applicable at the moment of the conclusion of the treaty provide that the States members of the organization are bound by the treaties concluded by it; or
> (b) the States and organizations participating in the negotiation of the treaty as well as the States members of the Organization acknowledged that the application of the treaty necessarily entails such effects.'

(a) the States members of the organization, by virtue of the constituent instrument of that organization or otherwise, have unanimously agreed to be bound by the said provisions of the treaty; and

(b) the assent of the States members of the organization to be bound by the relevant provisions of the treaty has been duly brought to the knowledge of the negotiating States and negotiating organizations.

Not only the members of an international organization had to 'unanimously agree' to be bound by the relevant rights and obligations, but also to 'duly bring' their assent 'to the knowledge of the negotiating States and negotiating organizations'.

Despite the Special Rapporteur's best efforts, draft article 36bis proved divisive within the Commission and at the 1986 Vienna Conference. In the end, the disagreement between those who thought that the separate legal personality of international organizations implied a complete separation between their obligations and those of their members,[66] and those who thought that the role of member States in the making and implementing of treaties concluded by organizations justified a more flexible regime,[67] could not be solved.

This occurred for a number of reasons. First of all, there was the political concern that draft article 36bis had been devised to cater to the needs of a unique 'supranational organization' – the European Economic Community, as it was then known – and would thus be irrelevant for other international organizations.[68]

Secondly, there were misgivings about the way the provision was conceived and drafted. The first limb of draft article 36bis would have allowed third parties entering into treaty relations with the international organization to rely on the latter's 'internal law'. The source of inspiration for the Commission's proposal had been the provision currently found in Article 216(2) of the Treaty on the Functioning of the European Union, which prescribes that '[a]greements concluded by the Union are binding upon the institutions of the Union and on its Member States'.[69] The question was whether a provision along such lines could be taken to produce effects outside the institutional framework of the organization so that treaty-partners would be entitled, under international law, to require

---

[66] YILC 1981/I, p. 173, para. 31. Also, Ni, YILC 1982/I, p. 33, para. 19.

[67] Riphagen, YILC 1977/I, p. 137, para. 4; Calle y Calle, ibid., pp. 140–41, para. 28; Schwebel, ibid., p. 141, para. 36; Francis, YILC 1978/I, p. 198, para. 25. At the Conference, e.g., Finland, UNCLT 1986/I, p. 176, para. 31.

[68] E.g., Ushakov, YILC 1978/I, p. 191, para. 3.

[69] Art. 216(2) TFEU.

member States to perform and treaty. Though the Commission's intention was to make the rules of the organization relevant only insofar as they can be taken as evidence of assent to the acquisition of treaty rights and obligations by members, draft article 36*bis* would have established a connection between the rules of the organization and general international law for the benefit of third parties.[70] Among other problems, that would have raised the question of who decides whether the rules of the organization may be construed as having the effect of expressing assent.[71] It is revealing that a couple of decades later the European Court of Justice decided, against the spirit of draft article 36*bis*, that the rule in Article 216(2) TFEU 'did not imply that member States were bound towards non-member States and would as a consequence incur responsibility towards them under international law'.[72]

The problem with the second limb of draft article 36*bis* was one of drafting. The ILC had trouble finding an acceptable formulation for the more flexible rule that it was championing. The formulation originally proposed by the Special Rapporteur was met with opposition because it allowed for implicit acceptance of rights and obligations by members during the negotiation of treaties, a solution deemed unacceptable for those advocating a radical separation between the obligations of States and international organizations. The second formulation, adopted on first reading, used stricter but vague language, begging the question of what was to be understood as an 'acknowledgement' that the application of the treaty 'necessarily entails' the effect of creating rights or obligations for member States.[73] The third formulation, adopted on second reading, erred on the side of excessive formalism by requiring that there be 'unanimous agreement' by all the actors concerned and that the assent of member States be brought to the knowledge of the negotiating organizations. A text intended to provide greater flexibility ended up becoming more restrictive than the internal arrangements of those international

---

[70] The challenges arising from attempts to make internal arrangements subject to provisions producing effects in the ambit of general international law are similar to those arising from the implementation of the principle of speciality as discussed in Section 4.3.4.

[71] Ushakov, YILC 1977/I, pp. 138–39, para. 15. Tsuruoka, YILC 1978/I, p. 197, pp. 24, pointed to difficulties arising from the fact that non-members may not have access to tribunals constituted under the IO to interpret the constituent instrument, the CJEU being a prime example.

[72] Case C-327/91, *France v. Commission* [1994] ECR I-3641, para 25 (interpreting what was then Article 300(7) of the Treaty establishing the European Community).

[73] E.g., Ushakov, YILC 1981/I, p. 180, para. 8.

organizations that permit decision-making by majority vote instead of unanimity.[74] In its latest iteration, draft article 36bis had lost its purpose and normative appeal.

Finally, there was the concern that the topic was not yet ripe for codification due to the absence of sufficient practice and precedent to back up the proposed rule. As a member of the Commission noted:

> The decisive factor was not whether such a situation was conceivable in law – as he believed it was – but, rather, whether general practice at present warranted the formulation of a general rule of that type. Opinions were divided, comments and observations expressed by Governments were polarized, and the views of international organizations had not been of great assistance so far.[75]

This critique, which had not received much attention at the Commission, was offered by a few delegations at the 1986 Vienna Conference.[76]

In an excellent study of the history of draft article 36bis, Brölmann suggests that the reason why the provision was unsuccessful lies in the 'inability of general law to enter into the legal sub-system of a subject' and, more specifically, 'the inability of general law to provide rules on the internal practice of international organisations that have a general value'.[77] That is because the law of treaties is 'one-dimensional', 'geared to equal parties' and therefore incapable of accommodating 'layered subjects' such as international organizations when those are seen as 'transparent legal entities'.[78] Although Brölmann's description of the current structure of the law of treaties is accurate, one should be cautious in making inferences about what general international law can or cannot accommodate in the abstract. Had the 1986 Vienna Conference been a

---

[74] E.g., Austria, UNCLT 1986/I, p. 140, paras. 4–7; Switzerland, ibid., p. 142, paras. 19–20; and Council of Europe, ibid., p. 145, para. 54.

[75] Al-Qaysi, YILC 1982/I, p. 54, para. 12. Also, Gaja, 'A "New" Vienna Convention', 265 (arguing that while the result achieved by the Conference may seem 'disappointing', there was 'insufficient practice to establish a reasonable presumption').

[76] Bulgaria, UNCLT 1986/I, p. 173, para. 5; Finland, ibid., p. 176, para. 31; Morocco, ibid., p. 159, para. 10; ILO, ibid., p. 142, para. 23.

[77] Brölmann, 'The 1986 Vienna Convention', p. 139. Chinkin similarly noted that one of the 'disadvantages' of the provision was that 'it was perceived as dealing with "representational" issues that were out of place in the Convention': C. Chinkin, *Third Parties in International Law* (Oxford: Oxford University Press, 1993), p. 94.

[78] C. Brölmann, *The Institutional Veil in Public International Law: International Organizations and the Law of Treaties* (Oxford: Hart, 2005), p. 247.

little less conservative,[79] and the final formulation more satisfactory, draft article 36*bis* (or part of it) could have been successfully adopted. There is nothing preventing general international law from developing so as to provide for rules that make sense of 'layered subjects'.

Brölmann's observation invites reflection on the problems with uncritically extending rules of general international law to international organizations. While Reuter and the ILC persuasively identified a situation in which the proximity between organizations and their members would warrant a regime that is more flexible than the one applying to States, the absence of practice and precedent providing guidance as to how that outcome could be achieved proved fatal to the proposal to depart from the VCLT 1969 text. The 1986 Vienna Conference appears to have grasped the potentially detrimental implications of its agreement to disagree, namely that the decision to reject draft article 36*bis* could be construed as implying that the regime established by Articles 34–38 VCLT 1969, reproduced with minor changes in VCLT 1986, governs the acceptance, by members, of rights and obligations arising from treaties concluded by international organizations.[80] To avoid this inference, a number of delegations urged that a saving clause be added stating that 'any question that may arise in regard to the establishment of obligations and rights for States members of an international organization under a treaty to which that organization is a party' would not be prejudged by the Convention, now found in Article 74(3) VCLT 1986. They preferred to leave a gap in VCLT 1986 than to make the strict regime for the acceptance of rights and obligations laid down in VCLT 1969 apply to members of an international organization by implication.[81]

In the end, it is far from satisfactory that the 1986 Vienna Conference agreed to disagree on a crucial question that had been extensively debated at the ILC. After all, an international conference convened to adopt a codification instrument provides the occasion for adopting solutions arising from conflicting or insufficient practice and precedent and pushing the law forward. It is not clear what one should do with the gap left by

---

[79] In this respect, see Yugoslavia's plea for more progressive thinking: 'article 36*bis* was one of the few articles which implied a decisive step forward in the progressive development of international law. Although it might be argued . . . that practice was not yet sufficiently mature . . ., it would not be the first time that such a step had been taken by a codification conference'. UNCLT 1986/I, p. 176, para. 41.

[80] As warned by the Dutch delegation: UNCLT 1986/I, p. 148, para. 25.

[81] Delegations expressing a preference for a gap included Austria, ibid., p. 140, para. 7; UNIDO, ibid., p. 150, para. 43; Finland, p. 176, para. 33; and ILO, p. 142, para. 23.

Article 74(3) VCLT 1986, and an opportunity to soften the analogy between States and international organizations in a way that reflected the latter's layered character has been missed.

5.2.1.2 Acceptance of Rights and Obligations by Organizations

While much was debated at the Commission as regards the effect of a treaty concluded by international organization on its members, surprisingly little was said about the converse issue: the legal position of an organization in relation to a treaty concluded by its members. Yet, examples abound of treaties concluded by members to assign functions to international organizations, thereby creating rights and obligations for those organizations. The 1969 Vienna Convention on the Law of Treaties itself assigns to the UN Secretary-General the function of depositary.[82] Likewise, human rights conventions adopted under the auspices of the United Nations, including the International Covenant on Civil and Political Rights, ascribe to the Secretary-General a series of roles, including that of providing 'the necessary staff and facilities for the effective performance of the functions' of treaty-monitoring bodies.[83] The question then arises of whether the rules governing the acceptance of such functions (and the corresponding rights and obligations) should not have been made more flexible than those provided by VCLT 1969.

Pondering the issue, Special Rapporteur Reuter observed that the rationale of the *pacta tertiis* rule was to protect the sovereign equality of States, for 'sovereignty [required] that [States] may not be legally committed by the will of a third party'.[84] This led him to suggest that the formalities that VCLT 1969 had put into place as a means of protecting 'the sovereignty and independence of States' would not be justified in the case of international legal subjects which were 'neither sovereign nor equal',[85] and were 'dominated entirely by a different concept' – that of 'performance of a function'.[86] Accordingly, as had been proposed with regard to draft article 36*bis*, Reuter suggested not to

---

[82] Art. 82 VCLT 1969.

[83] Art. 36, 1966 International Covenant on Civil and Political Rights. On this practice and its impact on the budget of the UN, C. Tomuschat, 'International organizations as third parties under the law of international treaties' in E. Cannizzaro (ed.), *The Law of Treaties Beyond the Vienna Convention* (Oxford: Oxford University Press, 2011), pp. 212–22.

[84] Reuter (Sixth Report), YILC 1977/II, part one, p. 120, para. 5.

[85] Ibid., p. 120, para. 6.

[86] Ibid., p. 122, para. 14. See also para. 25.

extend the requirement of acceptance in writing laid down by Article 35 VCLT 1969 to international organizations. This formality should be replaced, instead, with the requirement that the 'third organization' accept the obligation 'in an unambiguous manner and in accordance with [its] rules'.[87] The Commission, however, did not give much consideration to the Special Rapporteur's proposal. Without much debate, it reverted to the original language of VCLT 1969.[88]

The soundness of this strict regime for the acceptance of rights and obligations has been challenged, as Christian Tomuschat pointed out in a recent study, by a 'customary practice' that has emerged in the ambit of the United Nations in which the assignment of certain functions to the organization 'is not seen as the imposition of a duty which requires a formal act on the part of the world organization'.[89] Article 35 VCLT 1986 thus appears to provide an example of a rule that was extended from States to international organizations but overridden by subsequent practice, and for good reason. The fact that States establish international organizations to pursue objectives of international cooperation that may be further implemented via treaties to which the organization is not a party militates for the adoption of rules that do not impose impractical formalities. That the ILC – and later the 1986 Vienna Conference – should have failed to take this into consideration points to the risks of following the analogy between States and international organizations too rigidly.

Even more baffling was the lack of any debate on whether international organizations should be bound by obligations deriving from agreements to which the entirety of its membership is party. It is true that no international organization can formally become a party to a treaty that does not envisage that possibility. But if States act collectively through a body corporate in fields that are covered by existing treaties, it would not be implausible to construe those treaties as establishing rights and obligations for that body corporate and to postulate that, in the light of the fact that all member States are party to the treaty, the body corporate must be deemed to have also accepted those rights and obligations.

This issue was litigated in the *Kadi* case, where there was a challenge against the enforcement by the European Union of sanctions mandated by the UN Security Council against individuals suspected of terrorism.

---

[87] Ibid., p. 127, para. 2.
[88] YILC 1978/I, p. 190, para. 26.
[89] Tomuschat, 'International organizations', p. 220.

While recognising that the UN Charter did not bind the European Community (as it was then known),[90] the Court of First Instance observed that the Community was under an obligation not to 'infringe' or 'impede' the performance of obligations under the Charter, and 'to adopt all the measures necessary to enable its Member States to fulfil those obligations'.[91] The Court stressed that these obligations did not arise 'under general international law', as some member States taking part in the proceedings had argued, but rather 'by virtue of the EC Treaty itself'.[92] But does it make sense to insist on a complete separation between the organizations and members in cases in which all members are bound by the same treaty obligation? It should be noted that such a solution is neither self-evident nor 'logical' nor justified by a systemic analogy between States and international organizations. It is rather a matter of choice, a choice which solves a number of problems but creates others, including the possibility for abuse.

5.2.1.3 Acceptance of Responsibility by Member States

In contrast to the protracted and unsuccessful debates on acceptance of treaty rights and obligations, the discussion at the ILC of the possibility for member States to accept liability for an internationally wrongful act committed by an international organization was fairly straightforward. Article 62 ARIO envisages two situations in which assumption of responsibility may take place: a member or group of members may accept responsibility for the relevant act towards the injured party, or may lead the injured party to rely on its being jointly responsible for that act.[93] Thus, members only incur responsibility for acts of the organization if by their own conduct on the international plane – that is, not merely by participating in decision-making on the institutional plane – they assume such an obligation vis-à-vis the injured party.

The two circumstances envisaged in Article 62 are more flexible than the strict regime for the acquisition of rights and obligations established

---

[90] Case T-315/01, *Kadi v. Council and Commission*, Judgment of 21 September 2005, para. 192.

[91] Ibid., paras. 203–04. This was part of the reasoning that the Court followed to conclude that the regulations implementing UNSC resolutions had to be upheld. On different grounds, the European Court of Justice reversed the Court of First Instance's decision on appeal.

[92] Ibid., para. 207.

[93] These circumstances reflect those already mentioned in the *Institut*'s 1995 Resolution, namely acquiescence and undertakings made by member States (art. 5(b) and (c)(i)).

by VCLT 1969 and VCLT 1986. First, there are no formal requirements for acceptance of responsibility by a member, which means that such an undertaking does not have to be made in writing as required for treaty obligations under Article 35 VCLT 1986.[94] Second, the possibility that a member may 'lead' the injured party to rely on its responsibility allows for a flexible analysis of the circumstances of particular disputes.[95] It seems thus that paragraphs (a) and (b) of Article 62 have succeeded where draft article 36bis failed.

5.2.2 Responsibility for Circumvention of International Obligations

The ARIO contains two provisions seeking to prevent international organizations and their members from taking advantage of each other's separate legal personality to commit internationally wrongfully acts.[96] The first is Article 17, on 'circumvention of an international obligation through decisions and authorizations addressed to members':

1. An international organization incurs international responsibility if it circumvents one of its international obligations by adopting a decision binding member States or international organizations to commit an act that would be internationally wrongful if committed by the former organization.

2. An international organization incurs international responsibility if it circumvents one of its international obligations by authorizing member States or international organizations to commit an act that would be internationally wrongful if committed by the former organization and the act in question is committed because of that authorization.

3. Paragraphs 1 and 2 apply whether or not the act in question is internationally wrongful for the member States or international organizations to which the decision or authorization is addressed.

---

[94] As the commentary explains, '[n]o qualification is given to acceptance' – it may be 'expressly stated or implied and may occur either before or after the time when responsibility arises for the organization': YILC 2011/II, part two, p. 101, para. 6.

[95] But the ILC has sought to clarify that there is 'clearly no presumption that a third party should be able to rely on the responsibility of member States': ibid., para. 10.

[96] See commentary to art. 17, YILC 2011/II, part two, p. 67, para. 1: 'The fact that an international organization is a subject of international law distinct from its members opens up the possibility for the organization to try to influence its members in order to achieve through them a result that the organization could not lawfully achieve directly'. See also commentary to art. 61, ibid., p. 98, para. 1.

The second is Article 61, on 'circumvention of international obligations of a State member of an international organization', whereby the responsibility of members is entailed when they prompt the organization to commit an internationally wrongful act:

1. A State member of an international organization incurs international responsibility if, by taking advantage of the fact that the organization has competence in relation to the subject-matter of one of the State's international obligations, it circumvents that obligation by causing the organization to commit an act that, if committed by the State, would have constituted a breach of the obligation.
2. Paragraph 1 applies whether or not the act in question is internationally wrongful for the international organization.

There are several reasons of principle and policy that militate in favour of rules such as those found in Articles 17 and 61. On the one hand, by preventing members and organizations from making use of their separate legal personality to breach their obligations, such provisions promote legality in international relations. Article 61, in particular, calls for responsible treaty-making and coherence in the creation and performance of international obligations, so that the provision of competences to international organizations does not become the cause of detrimental fragmentation.[97] On the other hand, such provisions counterbalance the principle of independent responsibility, which, applied too rigidly, could lead to problematic results. Given how broad the right for States to create international organizations seems to be, it is necessary to have mechanisms in place that reduce the incentives for abuse.

5.2.2.1 Legal Character and Systemic Function of Provisions on Circumvention

To appraise the role that Articles 17 and 61 may perform in calibrating the analogy between States and international organizations, it is necessary to enquire into their legal status. Are the rules contained in the provisions part of international law as it stands? The commentary to

[97] In the words of the ILC, the fragmentation of international law is characterized by the appearance of 'specialized and (relatively) autonomous rules or rule-complexes, legal institutions and spheres of legal practice' that tend to take place 'with relative ignorance of legislative and institutional activities in the adjoining fields and of the general principles and practices of international law': Conclusions of the Work of the Study Group on the Fragmentation of International Law, YILC 2006/II, part two, p. 178, para. 8.

Article 17, though citing a few statements of support by States and international organizations, does not specify the legal basis for an organization to incur responsibility by compelling or authorising a member to take wrongful action. The Commission seemed to assume that the rule in Article 17 already fell within the scope of the provisions on direction/control and coercion that had been extended to international organizations by analogy in Articles 15 and 16 of the ARIO, respectively.[98] But there are two differences between those provisions. First, while the rules on direction/control and coercion make sense of actions taken on the international plane, the interference covered by Article 17 takes place on the institutional plane. Second, under Article 17 the organization is liable even when the act required or authorised is not wrongful for the member. None of the provisions in the ARS extend responsibility in situations in which the State committing the act is not itself bound by the international obligation breached.

The commentary to Article 61 does not clarify the legal basis for members' responsibility for the circumvention of their international obligations either. But the provision was clearly inspired by a series of judgments by the European Court of Human Rights, the principle to be derived from which – so the ILC implies – would find application outside the European system.[99] In *Waite and Kennedy v. Germany*, for example, the European Court held that it would be incompatible with the purpose and object of the European Convention on Human Rights if the parties were, by attributing competences and immunities to international organizations, 'absolved from their responsibility under the Convention in relation to the field of activity covered by such attribution'.[100] The reasoning of the European Court in the relevant cases does not concern general international law. It rather takes the perspective of the European Convention of Human Rights, the instrument from which the Court derives its jurisdiction. The cases refer to the 'peremptory character' of the Convention and to the '*ordre public*' that it institutes at the European level, which suggests that they are based on the 'special character' that, from the point of view of the European Court, the Convention possesses. There is little suggestion that the Court was expressing the conviction that States cannot make use of international organizations to circumvent

---

[98] Commentary to art. 15, YILC 2011/II, part two, p. 67, para. 3; commentary to art. 16, ibid., p. 68, paras. 4–5; commentary to art. 17, ibid., p. 69, para. 15.

[99] Commentary to art. 61, YILC 2011/II, part two, p. 99, footnote 356.

[100] *Waite and Kennedy v. Germany* (App. no 26083/94) ECHR 1999-I, para. 67.

international obligations in general, even if its reasoning could be taken as the illustration of a more general principle.[101]

The most obvious candidate as normative underpinning for the rules in Articles 17 and 61 is the prohibition on abuse of rights. Whether one characterises the prohibition as a customary rule, a general principle of law or both,[102] the prevailing position in academic commentary, supported by some arbitral and judicial precedent,[103] is that it has become part of the *corpus* of international law.[104] The prohibition has no fixed content and is no easier to apply in international law than in domestic (private) law, but commentators converge on two prongs. A subject of international law abuses a right when it exercises it either to avoid complying with one of its international obligations, or in a way that is incompatible with the purpose ascribed to the right by the international legal order.[105] The prohibition can thus be invoked in support of rules that prevent international organizations and their members from taking advantage of each other's legal personality to evade international obligations. This is particularly clear as regards Article 61, which seeks to limit the extent to which States may misuse their right to constitute (and transfer competences to) international organizations, 'taking advantage of the fact that the organization has competence in relation to the subject-matter' to cause it to commit a wrongful act in their stead.

---

[101] See J. d'Aspremont, 'Abuse of legal personality of international organizations and the responsibility of member States' (2007) IOLR 91, 99–100.

[102] V. Paul, 'The abuse of rights and bona fides in international law' (1977) 28 *Österreichische Zeitschrift für öffentliches Recht und Völkerrecht* 107, 128–29. Given its connection to the principle of good faith, Kolb treats the doctrine as a general principle of law: R. Kolb, *La Bonne Foi en Droit International Public: Contribution à l'Étude des Principes Généraux de Droit* (Paris: Pr Univ de France, 2000), p. 462.

[103] E.g., *Case of the Free Zones of Upper Savoy and the District of Gex (France v. Switzerland)* [1932] PCIJ, Series A/B No. 46, p. 167 (in which the PCIJ decided that French fiscal legislation applied to free zones located in the French territory but that 'a reservation [had to] be made as regards the case of abuse of rights'); and *United States – Import Prohibition of Certain Shrimp and Shrimp Products*, WT/DS58/AB/R, 12 October 1998, para. 158 (in which the Appellate Body stated that 'one application of [the general principle of good faith], the application widely known as the doctrine of *abus de droit*, prohibits the abuse exercise of a state's rights').

[104] Kolb, *La Bonne Foi*, p. 463. See also the extensive literature review pointing towards the acceptance of the principle as *lex lata* at 422ff.

[105] See *Dictionnaire de la terminologie du droit international* (Paris: Sirey, 1960), p. 4 (defining *l'abus de droit* as an 'exercice par un Etat d'un droit d'une manière ou dans des circonstances qui font apparaître que cet exercice a été pour cet Etat un moyen indirect de manquer à une obligation internationale lui incombant ou a été effectué dans un but ne correspondant pas à celui en vue duquel ledit droit est reconnu à cet Etat').

Construing the rules in Articles 17 and 61 as applications of the principle of abuse of rights also sheds light on the role that those provisions play in mitigating normative concerns arising from an analogy between States and international organizations that was taken very far. If international organizations are not only legally autonomous entities operating on the international plane, but also entities to which the principle of independent responsibility applies despite their 'layered' character, the right that States enjoy to limit their liability by acting through a body corporate is very broad indeed. Unlike in domestic legal systems, in which body corporates are the subject of extensive regulation, the rule of incorporation in general international law is incipient and underdeveloped. It is precisely in fields where the legal subjects enjoy great discretion that the prohibition on abuse of rights finds application.[106] By demanding that its addressees refrain from exercising rights in an 'unsociable' manner,[107] it makes sure that wide entitlements are compatible with the goals that justify them – in the case of international organizations, the promotion and operationalisation of international cooperation and global governance.

It is not surprising, therefore, that the *Institut de Droit international* embraced this doctrine in its 1995 Resolution, observing that the rule according to which members did not incur responsibility for acts performed by an international organization was without prejudice to their responsibility under general principles of international law, including the principle prohibiting abuse of rights.[108] In contrast, the ILC did not rely on the doctrine, which is only referred to in the commentary, somewhat dismissively, when the Commission notes that Article 61 'does not refer only to cases in which the member State may be said to be abusing its rights'.[109] Whatever the Commission says, to the extent that Articles 17 and 61 can be construed as a meaningful application of a well-established principle, they have a claim to reflect the *lax lata* and a chance to avoid the fate of provisions that end up discarded as mere progressive development based on policy considerations.[110]

---

[106] M. Byers, 'Abuse of rights: an old principle, a new age' (2002) 47 *McGill Law Journal* 339, 416–19.

[107] See H. Lauterpacht, *The Function of Law in the International Community* (Oxford: Clarendon Press, 1933), p. 286. Also, Kolb, *La Bonne Foi*, pp. 462–70.

[108] Art. 5(b), (1995) 66-I *Annuaire de l'Institut de droit international*, p. 449.

[109] Commentary to art. 61, YILC 2011/II, part two, p. 99, para. 2.

[110] Odette Murray has suggested that what art. 61 attempts to encapsulate are limitations on the right of States to create and operate IOs deriving from the principle of good faith in

5.2.2.2   The Limits of Provisions on Circumvention

The prospects for Articles 17 and 61 to mitigate the principle of independent responsibility depend not only on their legal character but also on whether they are capable of capturing situations of abuse of legal personality found in the practice of international organizations and their members. According to Article 17, the organization will incur liability if it adopts a decision requiring its members to perform an act that would be unlawful for the organization or authorising members to commit such an act, provided that in the latter case the act in question is indeed committed as a result of that authorization. The commentary, however, indicates that the term circumvention 'implies an intention on the part of the international organization to take advantage of the separate legal personality of its members', to be determined having regard to the circumstances of the case.[111] What it would take to establish such an intention is unclear: either a broad approach could be taken with intention to circumvent being inferred from a deliberate act of the organization (in particular when the obligation being breached is only binding on the organization but not on the members) or a narrow approach could be taken requiring actual proof of intent (which might severely limit the range of situations to which Article 17 would apply).

Article 61 presents an even more difficult case, not least because the stakes here – responsibility of members for acts of the organization – are higher. Responsibility for circumvention is entailed when the member 'takes advantage of the fact that the organization has competence in relation to the subject-matter' and '[causes] the organization to commit an act that, if committed by the State, would have constituted a breach of the obligation'. The commentary specifies that there must be a 'significant link between the conduct of the circumventing member State and that of the international organization'.[112] This poses a number of challenges. When can it be said that a State has 'caused' an international

two of its manifestations. The first is *pacta sunt servanda*, limiting the extent of the right to establish IOs when this would put members in violation of their international obligations. The second is abuse of rights, limiting the way in which members may exercise their vote once an organization is established. To her, as is argued here, responsibility for misuse of an IO's separate legal personality arises under well-established 'primary rules' of international law (at 346–48): O. Murray, 'Piercing the corporate veil: the responsibility of member states of an international organization' (2011) IOLR 291.

[111] Commentary to art. 17, YILC 2011/II, part two, p. 68, para. 3.
[112] Commentary to art. 61, ibid., p. 99, para. 7.

organization to commit an act? Must it have overwhelming control over the organization, or does it suffice that it has incited the commission of the act? Would a State's strong and decisive support for an action or omission proposed by another be sufficient to constitute 'circumvention' for that State? Whether the personality of the international organization has been abused by the member State and whether there has been a significant link between the conduct of both entities can only be determined by reference to the particularities of the case, and such a determination may lend itself to abuse.[113]

An emblematic case involving unlawful action via an international organization provides an example both of the promise and of the limitations of Article 61. In 1998, the North Atlantic Treaty Organization launched an aerial bombardment campaign against Serbia, without the authorisation of the UN Security Council, with a view to avoiding an impending humanitarian catastrophe in Kosovo. Serbia instituted proceedings against ten NATO member States before the ICJ to challenge what it viewed as an unlawful use of force.[114] In their preliminary objections to the jurisdiction of the Court, Portugal, France and Italy all argued that NATO was an international organization with separate legal personality in relation to its members.[115] The Court lacked jurisdiction over the dispute, not least because the proceedings had been brought under the compromissory clause in the 1948 Convention on the Prevention and Punishment of the Crime of Genocide, which was clearly inapplicable to the military operation in question.[116] But had the Court

---

[113] The difficulties posed by the notion of 'significant link' are the same presented by the application of the principle prohibiting abuse of rights itself. As Jean-David Roulet points out, 'ce contrôle discrétionnaire accordé au pouvoir judiciaire conduit facilement à des excès', and 'lorsque l'on invoque l'abus de droit, il apparaît extrêmement facile d'ignorer l'existence des dispositions légales sur des prétextes plus ou moins valables': J. D. Roulet, *Le Caractère Artificiel de la Théorie de l'Abus de Droit en Droit International Public* (Neuchâtel: Ed de la Baconnière, 1958), p. 144.

[114] The eight virtually identical judgments given by the Court are reported in [2004] ICJ Rep 279, 279–1450. The proceedings initiated against the USA and Spain were removed from the list on the grounds of manifest lack of jurisdiction.

[115] Preliminary Objections filed by Portugal, 5 July 2000, p. 36, para. 133; Preliminary Objections filed by France, 5 July 2000, pp. 28–29, para. 23; Preliminary Objections filed by Italy, 5 July 2000, p. 19.

[116] The case was however controversially decided on the basis of lack of jurisdiction *ratione personae*, the Court having found that, following the dissolution of the former Yugoslavia, Serbia was a not a member of the UN at the filing of the application and lacked access to the Court. For a discussion, see F. L. Bordin, 'Continuation of membership in the United Nations revisited: lessons from fifteen years of inconsistency in the

been competent on other bases, Serbia could have argued that the members of NATO had 'caused' the organization to act in a way which circumvented their obligations under general international law and Article 2(4) of the UN Charter. Though generally plausible, this line of reasoning would raise some questions. In an international organization where decisions are taken by consensus, does the taking of collective action that circumvents the obligation of members imply that all members 'caused' the organization to act, or is some additional substantive involvement by the member States being sued required? The drafting of Article 61 does not provide guidance as to where to draw the line.

Another problem that stems from the drafting of Article 61 is that it may turn out not to be applicable to situations of abuse that one would expect it to cover. As defined by the ILC, 'circumvention' implies 'the existence of an intention to avoid compliance' and does not extend to 'the unintended result of the member State's conduct'.[117] This means, for example, that it could not be relied upon to invoke the responsibility of EU member States for the Union's failure to implement resolutions of the UN Security Council following the judgment of the European Court of Justice in the *Kadi* case.[118] In *Kadi*, the Court concluded that obligations imposed by an international agreement to which member States are party 'cannot have the effect of prejudicing the constitutional principles of the EC Treaty', and annulled the Regulation that implemented UNSC resolutions ordering the freezing of assets of individuals suspected of supporting or undertaking terrorist activities. On the one hand, transferring to an international organization (the EU) the exclusive competence to implement obligations arising from a treaty to which the organization itself is not a party (the UN Charter) would appear to constitute a clear case of abuse by members of its separate personality, if the organization were to refuse to implement the obligations in question. On the other hand, EU members can hardly be deemed to have 'caused' the Court of Justice of the EU – a judicial body composed of independent and

---

jurisprudence of the ICJ' (2011) 10 *The Law and Practice of International Courts and Tribunals* 315.

[117] Commentary to art. 61, YILC 2011/II, part two, p. 98, para. 1.

[118] Joined Cases C-402/05 P and C-415/05 P, *Kadi and Al Barakaat International Foundation v. Council and Commission* [2008] ECR I-635, para 285. The ECJ confirmed this understanding in *Kadi II*: Joined Cases C-584/10 P, C-593/10 P and C-595/10 P, *Commission and others v. Kadi*, Judgment of 18 July 2013, para. 67.

impartial judges – to annul regulations implementing UNSC resolutions that those members had themselves enacted through their participation in the political organs of the EU. This would only be possible if the notion of 'causing' were stretched as far as to cover the establishment of the Court of Justice itself, an interpretation that would be far from unproblematic.[119]

Ultimately, Article 61 may turn out to be one of those provisions of considerable symbolic value but limited practical relevance, but the principle that it expresses holds promise. Were an international conference convened to adopt a convention on the law of responsibility, it would be interesting to see whether Article 61 would be adopted or whether it would suffer the same fate as draft article 36*bis* in the 1986 Vienna Conference. It would be regrettable if the latter were the case: one should not underestimate the role that Article 61 may play by providing a normative framework under which disputes concerning the extent of the right of States to limit liability by establishing international organizations can be assessed. Articles 17 and 61 ARIO provide a means to calibrate the principle of independent responsibility in the light of actual instances of abuse that courts, tribunals and other forums may be called upon to address as practice in the field evolves.

5.2.3 Enabling Organizations to Perform their International Obligations

If States have the right to establish legally autonomous subjects of international law, it could be argued that they must also have the duty to ensure that those subjects are duly equipped to discharge obligations acquired when they act on the international plane. The ILC faced this question both in the codification of the law of treaties and in the codification of the law of responsibility.

The discussion in the context of the codification of the law of treaties was brief. Regarding the position of members vis-à-vis treaties concluded by their organization, Special Rapporteur Reuter suggested the existence of a 'general principle according to which member States co-operate in all the measures decided on by the organization'. This would impose:

---

[119] A criticism to an earlier version of art. 61, which was discarded on first reading, was that it would establish responsibility for the abuse of legal personality at the level of the creation of the IO: D'Aspremont, 'Abuse of legal personality', 99–100.

duties on them with respect to the agreements of the organization: the passive obligation to respect those agreements and not to hinder their execution and the active obligation to facilitate the execution of the agreements within the limits of their general undertakings.[120]

However, the ILC entertained no provision reflecting this notion. Moreover, neither the Special Rapporteur nor the Commission clarified whether such duties would derive from the general law of treaties – in which case third parties would be entitled to rely on them – or whether they would only arise under the rules of the organization.[121]

In the context of the law of responsibility, the debate revolved around the question of whether members have an obligation to provide organizations with the funds required for them to discharge their obligations of reparation. This is provided for by the constituent instruments of several organizations, as exemplified by Article 17 of the UN Charter.[122] But do similar obligations arise under the general law of responsibility? Special Rapporteur Gaja was not persuaded. Anticipating that States might be hostile to a provision imposing on them the obligation to fund international organizations, Gaja concluded that 'no additional obligation should be envisaged for member States' other than those arising from the rules of the organization.[123] Various members of the Commission disagreed. Alain Pellet proposed a new provision that would have prescribed that '[t]he member States of the responsible international organization shall provide the organization with the means to effectively carry out its obligations' to provide reparation.[124] In Pellet's opinion, it was 'imperative that realistic compromises' be found which, without calling the fundamental principle of independent responsibility into question, would 'guarantee victims a reasonable likelihood of reparation for the injury they had suffered'.[125] To his mind, the obligation to provide organizations with the means to discharge their obligations, rather than

---

[120] Reuter (Second Report), YILC 1973/II, pp. 92–93, para. 105. A similar point was made by Finland at the 1986 Vienna Conference: 'States members of an organization [have] a general obligation under customary international law to observe the organization's treaties, and therefore [can] hardly be seen as real third parties to those treaties': UNCLT 1986/I, 176, para 31.

[121] For the view that this constitutes an internal matter: Aldrich, YILC 1981/I, p. 183, para. 26.

[122] Pursuant to art. 17 UN Charter, '[t]he expenses of the Organization shall be borne by the Members as apportioned by the General Assembly'.

[123] Gaja (Fifth Report), YILC 2007/II, part one, p. 10, para. 30.

[124] YILC 2007/I, p. 144, para. 70.

[125] Pellet, ibid., p. 119, para. 24.

being a provision *de lege ferenda*, would arise under general international law as a 'logical, normal and unavoidable consequence of the fact that the member States of an international organization, by conferring legal personality on the latter, necessarily accepted that it could incur responsibility'.[126]

Pellet's proposal thus constituted an attempt to further calibrate the rule of incorporation in general international law, setting limits on the right of States to establish subjects of international law with separate obligations and responsibility. This broad right should be accompanied with the obligation to ensure that the organization is well equipped to meet the legal consequences of breaches of international law for which it is responsible to the exclusion of its members.[127] That States may limit their individual responsibility by establishing an organization should not mean that they have no collective obligations with regard to the organization's responsibility.

But this proposal to mitigate the principle of independent responsibility proved divisive within the Commission. Several members pointed out that there was no legal basis for an obligation to provide funds,[128] and even members in favour of the proposal thought that it might belong to the realm of progressive development.[129] Nolte disagreed with Pellet's assumption that 'the obligation for member States to provide

---

[126] A/CN.4.SR.3084 (2011), pp. 7–8. For an affirmation of the existence of 'an international contractual obligation' on the part of members to provide IOs with the means to discharge their obligations so as to preserve the autonomy on which their existence as separate international legal persons is premised: C. Ahlborn, 'The Rules of International Organizations', 469–70. Likewise, Blokker has noted that with international legal personality comes 'not only rights but also obligations', among the latter 'that international legal persons must be able to bear the responsibility for their internationally wrongful acts' lest IOs lose their 'ability to operate autonomously': N. Blokker: 'Preparing articles on responsibility of international organizations: does the international law commission take international organizations seriously? A mid-term review' in J. Klabbers and A. Wallendahl, *Research Handbook on the Law of International Organizations* (Cheltenham: Elgar, 2011), p. 327.

[127] Austria shared a similar position: 'the member States that enable an international organization to act on the international plane are accepting the risk that this organization may violate international law ... It is therefore reasonable that the risk has to be borne by the collectivity of the members, while the responsibility to compensate remains entirely with the organization': A/CN.4/636 (2011), p. 25.

[128] Hmoud, YILC 2007/I, p. 138, para. 18; Petric, ibid., p. 146, para. 84; Singh, ibid., p. 159, para. 16, Nolte, ibid., p. 160, para. 53, Melescanu, A/CN.4.SR.3084 (2011), p. 9. Support for the proposal and/or the principle that it embodied was expressed by Candioti, YILC 2007/I, p. 146, para. 80 and Galicki, ibid., p. 146, para. 83.

[129] Vázquez-Bermudez, ibid., p. 160, para. 64.

an international organization with means to fulfil an obligation of reparation was a logical consequence of having conferred legal personality on the organization'.[130] He noted that under municipal law such an obligation hardly accrued from the mere fact that a corporate entity was established,[131] for limitation of responsibility was the very reason why individuals created juridical persons with separate legal personality.

While Pellet's proposal was eventually withdrawn, it catalysed the adoption of Article 40 ARIO. Pursuant to Article 40, which does not have a counterpart in the ARS, the responsible international organization and its members 'shall take the appropriate measures' to ensure that the organization is in a position to discharge its obligation to make reparation. Such measures are those 'that may be required by the rules of the organization', and the commentary clarifies that Article 40 is a provision 'essentially of an expository character'.[132] Therefore, Article 40 falls short of imposing an obligation to fund the organization under general international law.

Yet, Article 40 has some symbolic value, and serves as a reminder – and perhaps as an authority for the view – that '[w]hile the rules of the organization do not necessarily deal with the matter expressly, an obligation for members to finance the organization as part of the general duty to cooperate with the organization may be implied under the relevant rules'.[133] A more difficult question is whether third parties may invoke the obligation of members to 'take all the appropriate measures that may be required by the rules of the organization'. Could the inclusion of this obligation in unequivocal terms in Article 40 be construed as allowing third parties to demand compliance with rules that otherwise would be considered as *res inter alios acta*? If so, then Article 40 might turn out to play a greater role in mitigating the principle of independent responsibility than the Commission intended.

5.3 Concluding Remarks

Because international organizations are layered subjects whose members are international legal persons in their own right, the question arises as to whether they can be properly analogised with States, which, in the eyes of

---

[130] Nolte, A/CN.4/SR.3085 (2011), p. 4.
[131] Ibid.
[132] Commentary to art. 40, YILC 2011/II, part two, para. 82, para. 4.
[133] Ibid., para. 5.

international law, constitute unitary entities. This is a fundamental question because it bears upon the extent of the right that States have to establish new subjects of international law endowed with autonomy to operate on the international plane. Though there do not appear to be limits – except for those set by peremptory norms of general international law – to what States can do collectively through a corporate entity, this does not mean that they have to be regarded as third parties vis-à-vis the obligations and responsibility of the organizations that they create.

Therefore, the ILC's proposal to extend to international organizations the *pacta tertii* rule in the law of treaties and the principle of independent responsibility in the law of responsibility is not justified by a systemic analogy between States and international organizations. The proposition that organizations should be subjected to the same general rules as States when acting on the international plane surely entails that they are bound by their own treaties and responsible for their own acts. It does not entail, nevertheless, that their members can hide behind the institutional veil and shield themselves from the obligations and responsibility of the corporate body. If legal autonomy on the international plane provides a general reason to assimilate States and international organizations, the layered character of international organizations provides a reason to distinguish between them in certain respects.

It seems thus that, in the debates on *pacta tertii* and independent responsibility, other analogies were at play, in particular the analogy with corporate bodies with limited liability under domestic systems. The ILC ended up adopting a sharp distinction between the rights, obligations and responsibility of international organizations and their members on the basis of a rationalisation of existing practice and a strong indication of *opinio juris* as expressed through exchanges with States and international organizations during the two codification projects. To mitigate some normative problems arising from that sharp distinction, the ILC adopted rules on responsibility for circumvention of international obligations and hinted at the need for members to equip international organizations with the means required to perform their international obligations. The picture that emerges is that of an evolving rule of incorporation for international organizations, which on the one hand allows members to limit their individual responsibility, but on the other is finally starting to sketch exceptions that pave the way for future improvement.

PART III

Limits of the Analogy

In Part II, I discussed three main objections that can be made against analogising between States and international organizations. Structural differences between the two categories, and the fact that organizations are created by States, mean that certain customary rules are not relevant for international organizations and that there are limits to the direct role that organizations can play in the making of general international law. That organizations constitute 'layered subjects' provides a systemic objection to extending to them, without adjustments, the *pacta tertii* rule and the principle of independent responsibility, but that objection has been rejected in the *opinio juris* of States and organizations themselves. Finally, the notion of speciality, which is only truly pertinent on the institutional plane, fails to defeat the analogy on the international plane.

It follows that, subject to certain qualifications, the analogy between States and international organizations as legally autonomous entities operating on the international plane provides a general justification to extend rules of general international law from one category to the other. That does not mean, however, that the analogy is a panacea that can or should solve every legal question arising from the activities of intergovernmental institutions, or even most of them. Rather, one must be cautious not to oversell it.

In Part III, two limits of the analogy between States and international organizations are outlined. First, the analogy is only persuasive in the identification of the public international law that applies to organizations on the international plane, playing a more limited role when it comes to the relations between organizations and their members on the institutional plane. This is considered in Chapter 6. Second, the success of rules proposed by analogy depends on their reception by States, organizations and the international legal profession more generally. As discussed in Chapter 7, normative contestation of those rules may lead to the emergence of customary law pointing in a different direction to that suggested by the analogy.

6

Analogy in the Relations between Organizations and Members

The relevant similarity between States and international organizations – legal autonomy on the international plane – explains why rules applying to States ought to apply to organizations when the latter relate to the outside world, that is, maintain 'external relations' that are not governed by their constituent instruments. Those external relations are, of course, just a small part of what international organizations are set up to do. Much of the action takes place on the institutional plane, where the rules of the organization provide for powers, rights and duties for the organization to pursue its mandate, normally involving action that affects its members. What is the role, if any, of the analogy between States and international organizations when one considers not the relations between organizations and the outside world, but the relations between international organizations and their members?

This is a crucial question because it bears upon the reach and practical relevance of rules of general international law such as those articulated by the ILC in its projects on the law of treaties and responsibility. If the rules of general international law do not apply to the relations between international organizations and its members, which comprise the bulk of the activities of intergovernmental institutions, they may be less relevant that one might think. In the case of organizations of universal or quasi-universal membership, such as the United Nations and its specialised agencies, the room for 'external relations' is minimal.

This chapter addresses the question of the role of the analogy between States and international organizations in shedding light on the law that applies to the relations between international organizations and their members. From the outset, a distinction between two categories of relations must be made.[1] The first concerns relations taking place on

[1] The ILC made this distinction when it considered the applicability of the regime of countermeasures to IOs. In his Eighth Report, Gaja invited the Commission to consider the difference between 'on the one hand, non-compliance by a State with its obligations as

the institutional plane, based on bonds of membership and created by constituent instruments and other internal rules. The second comprises relations that take place outside the institutional framework of the organization, and which, though involving entities to which the rules of the organization apply, are ultimately governed by general international law. I argue that while international custom extended by analogy can be applied (alongside the rules of the organization) to relations belonging to the latter category, the analogy reaches its breaking point at the level of internal institutional relations.

6.1   Relations on the International Plane

6.1.1   General International Law as the Applicable Law

Because international organizations and their members act in tandem on the international plane, not all of their relations fall under the institutional framework laid down by the rules of the organization. An indication that a transaction belongs on the international plane is when it takes the form of a bilateral treaty. It is true that all acts that international organizations perform are (or should be) geared towards the fulfilment of functions and purposes defined in constituent instruments and other internal rules. But when an organization and a member express their consent to become a party to a bilateral treaty, they do so not in their 'institutional capacity', but rather as autonomous legal persons operating on the international plane. Thus, the ICJ has described the rights and obligations arising from the headquarters agreement concluded between the World Health Organization and Egypt as a 'contractual legal regime' reached by the parties by 'mutual understandings'.[2] Likewise, the Court noted in *Reparation for Injuries* that it would be 'difficult to see' how the 1946 Convention on the Privileges and Immunities of the United Nations 'could operate except upon the international plane and as between parties possessing international personality'.[3] Those are, indeed, agreements deriving their validity from the international law of treaties as opposed to the rules of the organization.

---

a member of the organization and, on the other, non-compliance with obligations that the member State may have otherwise acquired': A/CN.4/640 (2011), p. 23, para 66. Also, Wood, A/CN.4/SR.3084 (2011), p. 3.

[2] *Interpretation of the Agreement of 25 March 1951 between the WHO and Egypt* (Advisory Opinion) [1980] ICJ Rep 73, p. 92.

[3] *Reparation for Injuries*, p. 179

It was from this premise that the ILC's work on the law of treaties involving international organizations started. While the Commission avoided taking a clear position as to the project's scope of application, the term 'treaty' was broadly defined as 'an international agreement governed by international law and concluded in written form between one or more States and one or more international organizations or between international organizations'.[4] In the commentary, the Commission suggested that agreements between organizations and members would be governed by international law unless a contrary intention was expressed:

> If an agreement is concluded by organizations with recognized capacity to enter into agreements under international law and if it is not by virtue of its purpose and terms of implementation placed under a specific legal system (that of a given State or organization), it may be assumed that the parties to the agreement intended it to be governed by general international law.[5]

Special Rapporteur Reuter pointed out in the debates that the 'internal law' of an international organization could evolve so as to constitute, in theory, 'a highly developed legal system of its own, to which ... a conventional act should be subject in its entirety'. If that came to pass, the relations between the organization and members would be 'removed in their entirety from the sphere of general international law'.[6] But unless this is expressly provided for or otherwise inferred, the ultimate source of the validity of treaties between members and international organizations remains the customary principle *pacta sunt servanda*. Likewise, responsibility for breaches of international obligations owed outside the institutional framework also accrues under general international law. On the international plane, organizations and their members can still be viewed as legally autonomous entities despite the special bonds between them. The analogy between States and international organizations remains plausible, so that rules devised for one category of international legal subjects can be extended to the other.

---

[4] Art. 2(1)(a) VCLT 1986.

[5] Commentary to art. 2, YILC 1982/II, part one, p. 18, para. 4.

[6] Reuter (Third Report), YILC 1974/II, part one, p. 140, para. 6. This was why Reuter had initially proposed to define a 'treaty concluded between States and international organizations or between two or more international organizations' as an agreement governed 'principally' by 'general' international law.

6.1.2   *The Rules of the Organization as* Lex Specialis

That the rules of general international law cover external relations between international organizations and members does not mean, however, that they are always applicable to the same extent as in relations opposing an organization and a third party. Between the organization and a third party, the rules of the organization are *res inter alios acta* which cannot have the effect of displacing the general rules.[7] In contrast, between the organization and its members, constituent instruments and other internal rules may be part of the applicable law as *lex specialis*. To the extent that the rules of the organization constitute a source of rights and obligations both for the organization and its members, they may modify or otherwise affect the general law applying to the engagement in question.

But can the rules of the organization be indeed characterised as *lex specialis*? Christiane Ahlborn has suggested that because an international organization 'is not a contracting party to its constituent instruments under international law', restrictions imposed by those instruments do not apply to relations taking place outside the institutional framework.[8] It is doubtful, however, that the notion of *lex specialis* has to be construed so narrowly. *Lex specialis* is a 'technique of interpretation and conflict resolution' according to which 'wherever two or more norms deal with the same subject matter, priority should be given to the norm that is more specific'.[9] Applying it to relations between an organization and its members means recognising that, even if the character of the rules of the organization is 'constitutional' or 'institutional' as opposed to 'international' or 'contractual', the rules of the organization remain a source of rights and obligations for the entities concerned no matter on what plane they operate. There is no reason why internal rules should not displace the general law in the same way as any other special rule: as the ILC pointed out in its study on fragmentation, '[t]he source of the norm (whether treaty, custom or general principle of law) is not decisive for the

---

[7] 'In the relations between an international organization and a non-member State or organization it seems clear that the rules of the former organization cannot *per se* affect the obligations that arise as a consequence of an internationally wrongful act': commentary to art. 32, YILC 2011/II, part two, p. 78, para. 3.

[8] C. Ahlborn, 'The rules of international organizations and the law of international responsibility' (2012) 8 IOLR 471–72.

[9] Conclusions of the Work of the Study Group on the Fragmentation of International Law, YILC 2006/II, part two, p. 178, para. 5.

determination of the more specific standard'.[10] The fact that an organization and its members, whose relations typically occur under the 'vertical' institutional framework established by the constituent instrument, can also interact on the 'horizontal' international plane presents an unusual opportunity for distinct international legal orders to intersect.[11] That brings an invitation for reconsidering the forms that *lex specialis* may take, and in so doing it is important not to lose sight of the rationale and purpose of the doctrine, namely to provide a structural norm for solving conflicts between rules applying to the same situation.

The proposition that constituent instruments and other internal rules constitute *lex specialis* in the relations between organizations and members is expressed in a few provisions in the ARIO. First, Article 32 prescribes that the responsible organization 'may not rely on its rules as justification for failure to comply with its obligations' of cessation and reparation, but then emphasises that the general rule is 'without prejudice to the applicability of the rules of an international organization to the relations between the organization and its [members]'. This is why the provision was entitled '*relevance* of the rules of the organization', in contrast to its counterpart in the ARS, which is entitled '*irrelevance* of internal law'. Second, Articles 22 and 52 ARIO prescribe that countermeasures may be taken between organizations and members, in reaction to breaches of obligations other than those arising under the rules of the organization, only insofar as 'the countermeasures are not inconsistent with the rules of the organization'. Third, the general clause on *lex specialis* contained in Article 64 ARIO clarifies that special rules that may affect the conditions for the existence of an internationally wrongful act or the content or implementation of the ensuing responsibility 'may be contained in the rules of the organization applicable to the relations between an international organization and its members'.

In contrast, similar provisions are not found in the 1986 Vienna Convention. The most glaring omission is in Article 27, which prescribes that '[a]n international organization party to a treaty may not invoke the rules of the organization as justification for its failure to perform the treaty', without making any special allowances – unlike Article 32 ARIO – for treaties between international organizations and

---

[10] Ibid.

[11] Indeed, that is not the case with States, the subunits of which have very limited scope to participate in international relations in their own name, let alone by concluding treaties with the central government.

members. Article 5, common to VCLT 1969 and VCLT 1986, makes a modest attempt at regulating the question of *lex specialis*. By prescribing that the application of the two Conventions to 'the constituent instrument of an international organization' and to 'any treaty adopted within an international organization' is 'without prejudice to any relevant rules of the organization', it provides a 'broad and variable exception' that may allow the relevant law to develop 'along lines peculiar and appropriate to those instruments and their function in the international community'.[12] But because Article 5 only covers a small range of treaties,[13] it can hardly be construed as a general *lex specialis* clause applying to agreements concluded between organizations and members, unless the notion of 'treaty adopted within an international organization' is stretched far beyond its ordinary meaning.[14]

The reason why the ILC did not enquire into the effect of constituent instruments and other internal rules on treaties concluded by an organization and its members appears to be twofold. First, the Commission treated the matter as one belonging to the law of responsibility. The commentary observes that the rule now contained in Article 27 VCLT 1986 pertains 'more to the regime of international responsibility than to the law of treaties' and as such constitutes 'an incomplete reference to problems which not even the 1969 Vienna Convention had purported to tackle'.[15] Second, the ILC made a deliberate effort not to delve into the boundaries between general international law and the internal law of each organization. As Special Rapporteur Reuter noted in the debates, if

---

[12] S. Rosenne, *Developments in the Law of Treaties 1945–1986* (Cambridge: Cambridge University Press, 1989), p. 257.

[13] Regarding the possibility that IOs be parties to constituent instruments as highly exceptional, the ILC had decided against adopting, on first reading, a provision analogous to art. 5 VCLT 1969: commentary to art. 5, YILC 1982/II, part two, p. 23, para. 1.

[14] The restricted scope of the provision is stressed in the commentary to art. 4, eventually adopted as art 5. VCLT 1969. It explains that the phrase '*adopted* within an international organization' was 'intended to exclude treaties merely drawn up under the auspices of an organization or through use of its facilities and to confine the reservation to treaties the text of which is drawn up and adopted within an organ of the organization' – that is, on the institutional plane: YILC 1966/II, p. 191, para. 3.

[15] Commentary to art. 27, YILC 1982/II, part two, pp. 38–39, para. 4. This was also the opinion of Roberto Ago, then rapporteur on State responsibility: YILC 1977/I, pp. 110–11, para. 14. The commentary adds that, under the law of responsibility, an IO could 'deny a contracting State the benefit of the performance of a treaty if that State has committed a wrongful act against the organization', including '*a breach of the rules of the organization if the State is also a member of the organization*' (para. 4, emphasis original). In this odd passage, the Commission appears to be referring to countermeasures.

an organization 'concluded a treaty with one of its member States and at a later stage made changes in its rules that were binding on all its member States, its constitution might be in conflict with the treaty and with a treaty right or a right derived from a treaty'. To his mind, the Commission 'was not required to resolve problems of that type, since they constituted a special case of conflict, which was covered by the rules of each organization'.[16]

Adding even more ambiguity to the ILC's approach as regards the relevance of constituent instruments and other internal rules is a statement that Reuter made when the Commission debated the rule now found in Article 46 VCLT 1986, on 'provisions of internal law of a State and rules of an international organization regarding competence to conclude treaties'. Reuter suggested that 'in the case of a treaty between an organization and one or more of its members, the question of invalidity was not subject to rules of general international law',[17] as '[c]ases of that kind must be settled by the special law and practice of the organization'.[18] This is however contradicted by the commentary, which implies that the rule in Article 46 is in fact applicable to such treaties. The commentary goes as far as to point out that members 'must be aware of the rules regarding the conclusion of treaties' as they participate in the decision-making of the organization and thus 'assume a share of the responsibility for the conclusion of irregular treaties'.[19]

The contrasting approaches to the role of the rules of the organization as *lex specialis* taken by the ILC in the projects on treaties and responsibility suggest that the precise way in which rights and obligations assumed on the international plane may affect those arising on the institutional plane will depend on the circumstances. In some cases, constituent instruments will seek to clarify the issue, as with Article 103 of the UN Charter, which provides that 'in the event of a conflict

---

[16] Reuter, YILC 1981/I, p. 167, para. 24.

[17] Reuter, YILC 1979/I, pp. 94–95, para. 28.

[18] Ibid. In an essay on the Vienna Conference, Reuter reiterated that the relations between organizations and members 'sont régies par un système juridique individualisé pour chaque organisation': P. Reuter, 'La Conférence de Vienne sur le Droit des Traités entre Etats et Organisations Internationales ou entre Organisations Internationales' in F. Capotorti and others (eds.), *Du Droit International au Droit de l'Intégration* (Baden-Baden: Nomos, 1987), pp. 563–64. He did not further explain, however, how this notion plays out as regards the application of the law of treaties to agreements between members and IOs.

[19] Commentary to art. 46, YILC 1982/II, part two, p. 52, para. 8.

between the obligations under the ... Charter and their obligations under any other international agreement, their obligations under the ... Charter shall prevail'. In other cases, where constituent instruments provide for no rules of conflict, no automatic priority between rules arising from one category or the other should be assumed. That will be a matter for 'contextual appreciation' taking into account other norms of interpretation or conflict resolution, not least the overarching goal envisaged by the 'principle of harmonization', according to which 'when several norms bear on a single issue they should, to the extent possible, be interpreted so as to give rise to a single set of compatible obligations'.[20]

6.1.3   Membership Ties and Obligations of Cooperation

Apart from the role that the rules of the organization play as *lex specialis*, transactions between an organization and members on the international plane may be affected in various ways by normative considerations arising from the 'organic link'[21] that brings them together on the institutional plane. In *Interpretation of the Agreement*, having explained that general international law governed the headquarters agreement concluded between the WHO and Egypt, the International Court noted that '[t]he very fact of Egypt's membership of the Organization entails certain mutual obligations of co-operation and good faith incumbent upon Egypt and upon the Organization.'[22]

The ILC tried to articulate this insight when it considered the applicability of the regime of countermeasures to relations taking place outside the institutional framework. Articles 22(2) and 52 ARIO not only prescribe that countermeasures must not be 'inconsistent with the rules of the organization' – the *lex specialis* point – but also specify that they may only be taken if 'no appropriate means are available for otherwise inducing compliance with the obligations of the responsible international organization concerning cessation of the breach and reparation'. This additional requirement, which finds no counterpart in the law of State responsibility, gives expression to the 'principle of cooperation

---

[20] Conclusions 4 and 6, Conclusions of the Study Group, YILC 2006/II, part two.
[21] The expression is borrowed from Ahlborn, 'The rules of an international organization', p. 450.
[22] *Interpretation of the Agreement*, p. 93.

underlying the relations between an international organization and its members'.[23] The same principle could justify the applicability, between organizations and members, of the rule in Article 51(4) ARIO, according to which countermeasures are to be taken 'in such a way as to limit their effects on the exercise by the responsible international organization of its functions'.[24]

6.2 Relations on the Institutional Plane

6.2.1 The Analogy's Breaking Point

If in the codification and progressive development of the law of treaties the ILC maintained an ambiguous position as to the scope of application of its project, the Commission's ambition for the responsibility project was expressed in much clearer terms. From the outset, the Working Group established to initiate work on the topic acknowledged that 'the great variety of relations existing between international organizations and their member States and the applicability to this issue of many special rules' would 'probably limit the significance of general rules in this respect',[25] but concluded that questions of responsibility arising from those relations should not be excluded from the purview of the project.[26] As a consequence, the definition of 'breach of an international obligation' adopted in Article 10 ARIO includes breaches of obligations 'that may arise for an international organization towards its members under the rules of the organization'. The ARIO thus also purport to cover questions of responsibility arising on the institutional plane. But is this a claim that the ARIO can plausibly make? Can the analogy between States and international organizations provide a justification for extending the rules of State responsibility – or, indeed, any rule of general international law applicable to States – to the sphere of the institutional relations between organizations and members?

The ILC adopted Article 10(2) ARIO against the backdrop of a heated doctrinal debate, which it did not handle particularly well. This debate concerns the character of the 'rules of the organization', that is, whether they are part of public international law or constitute internal law for the

---

[23] Commentary to art. 52, YILC 2011/II, part two, p. 93, para. 2.
[24] Whether that rule can apply between international organizations and third parties is far more doubtful. See the discussion in 7.2.2.
[25] YILC 2002/II, part two, p. 93, para. 467.
[26] Ibid.

organization, comparable to the domestic law of States. It was conceded that this question was 'far from theoretical' for the purposes of the project, as it affected 'the applicability of the principles of international law with regard to responsibility for breaches of certain obligations arising from the rules of the organization'.[27] Having identified the problem, the Commission decided not to solve it, refraining from expressing 'a clear-cut view'.[28] Instead, the commentary suggests, rather cryptically, that 'to the extent that an obligation arising from the rules of the organization has to be regarded as an obligation under international law, the principles expressed in the present article apply'.[29] It then points out that '[b]reaches of obligations under the rules of the organization are not always breaches of obligations under international law'.[30]

The debates within the Commission suggest that the distinction between 'international' and 'internal' obligations under the rules of the organization to which the commentary refers is one between obligations arising from ties of membership (for example, those that arise for members of the United Nations when the UN Security Council adopts a resolution under Chapter VII of the UN Charter) and obligations concerning the functioning of the organs of the organization (for example, the law applicable to international civil servants).[31] The view that ties of membership give rise to international obligations extrapolates from the proposition that treaties (here, constituent instruments) are one of the quintessential sources of obligations for States on the international plane. The rules of the organization are no doubt part of international

---

[27] Commentary to art. 10, YILC 2011/II, part two, p. 64, para. 7.
[28] Ibid.
[29] Ibid.
[30] Ibid.
[31] In the commentary, the Commission refers to the school of thought that draws 'a distinction according to the source and subject matter of the rules of the organization, and exclude, for instance, certain administrative regulations from the domain of international law' (ibid., p. 63, para. 5). The ICJ made a similar distinction in *Kosovo*, when it considered whether the constitutional framework of Kosovo was part of international law for the purpose of replying to the question posed by the UNGA. While it answered this question in the affirmative, the Court's pronouncement on the underlying issue was inconclusive. It stated that '[t]he Constitutional Framework derive[d] its binding force from the binding character of resolution 1244 (1999) and thus from international law', but also that the framework functioned as 'part of a specific legal order, created pursuant to resolution 1244 (1999), which is applicable only in Kosovo and the purpose of which is to regulate ... matters which would ordinarily be the subject of internal, rather than international, law': *Accordance with International Law of the Unilateral Declaration of Independence in Respect of Kosovo* (Advisory Opinion) [2010] ICJ Rep 403, paras. 88–89.

law if by this it is meant that, unlike the constitution of a State,[32] they derive their validity from international law.[33] But as the International Court observed in *Nuclear Weapons (WHO Request)*, while '[f]rom a formal standpoint, the constituent instruments of international organizations are multilateral treaties', they are 'treaties of a particular type', their object being 'to create new subjects of law endowed with a certain autonomy, to which the parties entrust the task of realizing common goals'.[34] The dual character of these treaties, which are 'conventional and at the same time institutional',[35] distinguish them from other multilateral treaties. Once one conceives international organizations as legally autonomous entities operating on the international plane, their internal law must be viewed as functionally analogous to the domestic law of States. As Ahlborn puts it, '[d]uring the life of an international organization [the rules of the organization] operate as a constitution that guarantees the autonomy of an international organization and that of its internal legal order'.[36] That echoes Hans Kelsen's jurisprudential account of the constituent rules of a 'juristic person' as forming a 'partial legal order' which is separate from – albeit in a relationship with – the 'total legal order' under which that juridical person is established.[37]

---

[32] This is without prejudice to the view that, at the philosophical level, domestic law must derive its validity from international law or vice-versa, as Kelsen has argued: H. Kelsen, *Pure Theory of Law* (Berkeley: University of California Press, 1967), pp. 333–34. The point is rather that whereas constituent instruments of IOs are instruments of international law, domestic constitutions are not.

[33] As Pellet pointed out, the rules of the organization are 'anchored in general international law': YILC 2003/I, 27, para 51. Balladore Pallieri has argued, on the grounds that a constituent instrument is 'un acte international, régit par les normes générales du droit international ou par des norms particulières existant à ce sujet dans le droit international', that there is no such a thing as the 'internal law' of IOs. His convoluted analysis conflates the question of the character of the rules of the organization with the question of whether general international law applies to IOs as legal persons: G. Balladore Pallieri, 'Le droit interne des organisations internationales', 1969/II RdC 1, pp. 16–17.

[34] *Legality of the Use of Nuclear Weapons in Armed Conflict* (Advisory Opinion) [1996] ICJ Rep 66, para. 19.

[35] Ibid.

[36] Ahlborn, 'The rules of an international organization', 397–480.

[37] H. Kelsen, *General Theory of Law and State* (Cambridge: Harvard University Press, 1945), pp. 99–100. See also L. Facsaneanu, 'Le droit interne de l'Organisation des Nations Unies' (1957) III *Annuaire Français de Droit International* 319–20; 324–26 (refering to *la théorie de l'institution* developed by German private lawyers which points to the 'aptitude' of all organised – or, more precisely, personified – communities to establish their own autonomous legal system) and G. Hartmann, 'The capacity of international organizations to conclude treaties' in K. Zemanek (ed.), *Agreements of International Organizations and*

The relations taking place on the institutional plane, where the constituent instrument and other internal rules govern, are thus characterised by the 'organic link' existing between the organization and its members, a link whose logic is comparable to that of regimes of constitutional and administrative law within the State.[38] As noted by Judge de Castro in *Appeal Relating to the Jurisdiction of the ICAO Council*:

> each [international] organization has a constitution which provides it with a general rule to which all its members are subject ... It is the fact that the organization is a legal person which prevents the legal relationships between its members being considered as governed by a series of independent bilateral treaties ... Members of the organization are linked together by the constitution, and their relationships are governed by the constitution. Such relationships are those resulting from the status of member of the organization, and not the status of a party to bilateral treaties. This is of the very essence of organizations; it is required by the common interest, and is a necessity for their functioning and effectiveness.[39]

It must be conceded, however, that because international organizations are 'incorporated' by States under general international law, the 'total legal order' can claim at least three roles with regard to the 'partial legal order' of an international organization. First, as discussed below, it constitutes the ultimate source of validity of the institutional framework. Second, just as domestic systems have developed highly developed regimes for the creation and operation of corporate bodies, the international rule of incorporation may evolve over time so as to establish more detailed and demanding requirements for the creation and operation of international organizations. Articles 17 and 61 ARIO, to the extent that they provide for rules that 'pierce the institutional veil', are illustrations of the general law's potential in this regard.[40] Third, the

---

the *Vienna Convention on the Law of Treaties* (Vienna: Springer, 1971), p. 150. In contrast, while persuasively arguing that the 'internal law' of IOs forms autonomous legal orders, Cahier observes that '[l]a personnalité juridique apparaît donc dans ce domaine comme sans importance': P. Cahier, 'Le droit interne des organisations internationales' (1963) 67 RGDIP 563, 574. That makes his argument weaker: the sense in which the rules of the organization can claim to be autonomous from international law is the same sense in which the by-laws of a juristic person can claim to be autonomous from the domestic law of States.

[38] Ahlborn, 'The rules of an international organization', 413.
[39] *Appeal Relating to the Jurisdiction of the ICAO Council (India v Pakistan)* [1972] ICJ Rep 46, p. 130 (sep. op Judge De Castro).
[40] See section 5.2.2.

general law will play a role in the settlement of questions arising from withdrawal from or dissolution of an organization, that is, whenever the 'organic link' ceases to exist.[41] If a member is expelled from the organization or exercises a right of withdrawal, outstanding issues arising from its lapsed membership will be solved outside the institutional context.

General international law cannot, however, claim a direct or immediate role in regulating the relations between an international organization and its members on the institutional plane. This is where the analogy between States and international organizations reaches its breaking point. That is because the two categories of legal subjects can no longer be viewed as legally autonomous entities operating on the international plane but are rather entities in an organic relationship defined by the rights and obligations deriving from a separate legal order. The 'relevant similarity' underpinning the analogy is thus gone. That being the case, the 'partial legal order' that governs on the institutional plane will determine the extent to which rules originating from the 'total legal order' will apply.

6.2.2   The Terms of the Relations between International Legal Orders

If the analogy breaks down at the level of the relations taking place within the institutional framework, it follows that the ARIO's ambition to apply to breaches of the 'internal law' of international organizations cannot be fulfilled without more. Contrary to what the work of the ILC implies, rather than mere *lex specialis* displacing the general law, the rules of the organization serve as the controlling legal system that constitutes and governs the institutional plane. The principle of speciality, which does not affect the analogy between States and international organizations on the international plane,[42] has a completely different import here: from the internal perspective, each international organization is a truly unique entity defined, shaped and constrained by its own rules. As Max Sorensen noted in an early study on the subject, just as there are a series of domestic legal orders, 'there are also different international organisations, each with its own internal law'.[43]

---

[41] See, e.g., Conclusions of the Study Group, YILC 2006/II, part two, p. 180, para. 16.
[42] See section 4.3.4.
[43] M. Sorensen, 'Autonomous legal orders: some considerations relating to a systems analysis of international organisations in the world legal order' (1983) 32 ICLQ 559, 561.

The ILC may thus be criticised for overstepping the bounds of its mission to codify and progressive develop international law.[44] But while general international law is not directly applicable within the institutional framework of an international organization, this does not mean that it may not play a role in the determination of rights, obligations and capacities under constituent instruments and other internal rules. This will happen to the extent that the general law is allowed to penetrate the institutional framework to solve problems which the rules of the organization do not address. The key to understanding the role of the analogy between States and international organizations thus lies in establishing the terms on which relations between legal orders having an international origin occur.[45]

6.2.2.1   A Monistic Presumption?

From the perspective of the international legal system, the terms on which international law relates to municipal law can be described in two principles. First, domestic rules cannot be invoked as a justification not to comply with international obligations, as provided in Article 27 VCLT 1969 and Article 3(2) ARS. Second, as long as compliance is achieved, States are free to choose the means by which they implement their international obligations.[46] While general international law affirms

---

[44] Several international organizations criticised the Commission's approach. In the words of the IMF, '[t]he draft articles should clearly state that relations between an international organization and its members and agents that are covered under the organization's charter are outside their scope'; IMF, A/CN.4/556 (2005), p. 36. Also, European Commission, ibid., pp. 29–30 and UNESCO, A/CN.4/568/Add.1 (2006), p. 18.

[45] As Kelsen explains, the '[t]he relation between the total legal order constituting the State, the so-called law of the State or national legal order, and the juristic person of a corporation is the relation between two legal orders, a total and a partial legal order, between the law of the State and the by-laws of the corporation': *General Theory*, p. 100. For Kelsen, it should be clarified, the same logic applies to the juristic person of the State: 'the State too is a corporation', with 'external obligations and rights ... stipulated by the international, internal ones by the national legal order': *Pure Theory of Law*, p. 290. His work does not deal with international organizations, but the analysis is no doubt apposite. See also G. Arangio-Ruiz, 'International law and interindividual law' in J. Nijman and A. Nollkaemper, *New Perspectives on the Divide between National and International Law* (Oxford: Oxford University Press, 2007), pp. 42–43 (pointing to a '*high degree of similarity* between the relationship of international organs' legal orders to international law and the relationship of national legal systems to international law'). In the ILC, see Koskenniemi, YILC 2005/I, p. 78, para. 34.

[46] The point is clearly stated in A. Cassese, *International Law*, 2nd edn (Oxford: Oxford University Press, 2005), p. 219.

its primacy over domestic law at the level of international responsibility,[47] it seeks neither to determine the content of domestic law[48] nor to affect its validity[49]. States may, in short, adopt whatever constitutional arrangements they wish to regulate the incorporation of international rules into domestic law: the choice between 'monism' and 'dualism' is left to domestic law.[50]

By comparison, the relations between international legal orders are under-conceptualised and the principles that govern them are less clear. It is not disputed that the rules of the organization may regulate the extent to which general international law can be applied on the institutional plane.[51] That much follows from the character of *jus dispositivum* of the overwhelming majority of rules of customary international rules.[52] It would be thus theoretically possible for the constituent instrument of an international organization to exclude the application of general international law altogether from the institutional plane. That said, one way in which the relations between international legal orders differ from those opposing international and municipal law is that international law may affect the validity of the 'internal law' of an international organization. If constituent instruments derive their validity from international law, rules pertaining to the 'internal law' of an organization that stand in violation of peremptory norms of

---

[47] E.g., G. Fitzmaurice, 'The general principles of international law considered from the standpoint of the rule of law (1957) 92 RdC 1, pp. 68–69.

[48] Unless, of course, an international obligation specifically requires the adoption of legislation, as is the case with art. 2, 1969 American Convention on Human Rights and art. 4, 1984 Convention against Torture and Other Cruel, Inhuman or Degrading Treatment or Punishment.

[49] In the words of the PCIJ, '[f]rom the standpoint of International Law and the Court which is its organ, national laws are merely facts which express the will and constitute the activities of States': *Certain German Interests in Polish Upper Silesia* [1926] PCIJ, Series A No. 7, p. 19.

[50] It should be noted that, doctrinally speaking, the debate between monism – the view of international and municipal law constituting one legal system – and dualism – the view of international and municipal law constituting two distinct legal systems – is often misguided and fails to make sense of the practice of national courts: e.g., J. Crawford, *Brownlie's Principles of Public International Law*, 8th edn (Oxford: Oxford University Press, 2012), p. 50.

[51] As D'Aspremont and Dopagne note, as regards the relations between EU law and international law, 'each legal order decides for itself whether or not it incorporates rules laid down in another legal order and, if so, how such an incorporation must be carried out': J. d'Aspremont and F. Dopagne, '*Kadi*: The ECJ's reminder of the elementary divide between legal orders' (2008) 5 IOLR 371, 373.

[52] As recognised, in the context of IOs, by art. 64 ARIO on *lex specialis*.

international law will be void *ipso jure* as prescribed by Articles 53 and 64 VCLT 1969.[53]

But the most important question is neither whether constituent instruments may specify the terms of the relations between international legal orders nor whether general international law may invalidate the rules of the organization. In practice, the crucial issue is the extent to which general international law can be invoked when the rules of the organization are silent on any given matter.[54] In domestic systems, customary international law is typically treated as susceptible of automatic incorporation, so that it can be applied by national courts as a source of domestic law without express authorisation by acts passed by the legislature.[55] In fact, the only alternative to some form of automatic incorporation would be full exclusion, since it would be unfeasible and unproductive for parliaments around the world to legislate on unwritten rules deriving from the practice and *opinio juris* of States. Yet, despite the relative openness to custom that many domestic systems showcase, the actual application of customary rules in domestic law is fraught with difficulties, has a rather exceptional character and raises a number of legitimacy concerns.[56] Is customary international law democratic? Can its application be reconciled with the principle of separation of powers?[57]

This is where one should avoid the temptation to push the analogy between domestic law and constituent instruments of international organizations too far. There are good reasons to regard the internal law of organizations as more permeable to general international law than domestic constitutions. For one, the historical, political and normative

---

[53] See arts. 53 and 64 VCLT 1969. On the invalidity of decisions of IOs that are in breach of peremptory norms, see A. Orakhelashvili, *Peremptory Norms in International Law* (Oxford: Oxford University Press, 2006), pp. 465–69.

[54] A separate question, which is beyond the scope of this study, is how treaties are incorporated into the internal law of IOs.

[55] For example, this is the established position, whether via constitutional provisions or court decisions, in the United Kingdom, the United States, Germany, Italy and Russia: Crawford, *Brownlie's Principles*, pp. 67–71; 80–82; 88–93.

[56] On the paucity of examples of meaningful application of custom by UK courts, see R. O'Keefe, 'The doctrine of incorporation revisited' (2008) 79 BYIL 7, 23–44. Also: P. Sales and J. Clemens, 'International law in domestic courts: the developing framework' (2008) 124 *Law Quarterly Review* 388, 415–16 (comparing reliance on custom by domestic courts unfavourably with reliance on treaties, given the lack of 'legitimacy of the law-making process in relation to the formation of CIL').

[57] D. Feldman, 'Monism, dualism and constitutional legitimacy' (1999) 20 *Australian Year Book of International Law* 105, 106–07. Also, Sales and Clemens, 'International law', 389–94.

context in which the question of relations involving international legal orders is posed differs from that characterising the relations between international law and domestic law. International organizations are a direct creation of the international legal system. Most of the political values underpinning strong dualist positions that assert the autonomy of domestic law in relation to international law do not have the same import when one regards institutions comprising States. There is, moreover, a practical reason for constituent instruments to embrace international law. The internal law of international organizations seldom contains rules exhaustively determining how the obligations and responsibility of the organization and its members vis-à-vis each other are to be ascertained. Organizations such as the European Union, which comprises a robust internal legal system overseen by courts with compulsory jurisdiction, remain the exception. The practical relevance of rules of general international law for international organizations was in fact one of the reasons why the ILC sought to extend the scope of application of the ARIO to matters arising on the institutional plane:

> even if one [considers] that the rules of the organization [are] special rules that prevailed over general international law, it must be acknowledged that they [do] not cover all questions relating to responsibility of the organization. It [is] therefore important to determine whether the international law of responsibility [provides] a backdrop that filled any gaps in the existing special rules.[58]

Of course, general international law can only be relevant for relations on the institutional plane if it is capable, in the light of its structure and content, of providing solutions to problems that constituent instruments and other internal rules do not address. The traditional dualistic position is that international law and domestic law must be viewed as separate legal systems because they have different sources, comprise different subjects and regulate different subject-matters.[59] That is surely not the case with international legal orders. Most rules that apply in the relations between States on the international plane can, in theory, play a role in relations involving members and the organization on the institutional plane.

---

[58] Gaja, YILC 2005/I, p. 64, para. 55.
[59] H. Triepel, 'Les rapport entre le droit interne et le droit international' (1923) 1 RdC 77, 80–91.

A systemic justification for a more nuanced approach to relations between international legal orders can be found in the ILC's Conclusions on Difficulties arising from the Diversification and Expansion of International Law adopted in 2006. The Conclusions, based on the work of a Study Group on the Fragmentation of International Law, deal with the position of so-called special or self-contained regimes vis-à-vis general international law.[60] These are defined as groups of 'rules and principles concerned with a particular subject matter', applicable as *lex specialis* and often having 'their own institutions to administer the relevant rules'.[61] The Commission did not specifically address the legal systems of personified entities with legal autonomy to operate on the international plane, which is puzzling given that international organizations may have the strongest claim to form self-contained regimes.[62] Nevertheless, its analysis provides a useful starting point for articulating principles applicable to relations between international legal orders.

According to the ILC's Conclusions, while a special regime 'prevails over general law' as *lex specialis*,[63] general law applies to fill the gaps left by the special rules[64] and to take over from the special rules whenever the special regime 'fails'.[65] That general international law will be applicable to issues arising from the dissolution of an international organization or from a member's withdrawal has been noted above. But why should one presume, as the Commission does, that general law may fill gaps in highly specialised regimes, let alone those constituting subjects of international law? The report prepared by the Study Group on Fragmentation begins by noting that 'the claim (almost never heard) that self-contained regimes are completely cocooned outside international law resembles the views by late-nineteenth century lawyers about the (dualist) relation

---

[60] See Conclusions of the Working Group, paras. 11–12.
[61] Ibid., para. 11.
[62] Rather, the focus of the ILC was on specialised treaty regimes, especially the European system of human rights and the WTO. While the WTO is of course an IO, it is peculiar in that it mostly serves as a forum for the adoption of trade-related regulation by States and as a mechanism for dispute settlement. Thus, the ILC study did not specifically look into the role of general law in the relations between the WTO and its members on the institutional plane.
[63] Conclusions of the Working Group, p. 178, para. 14.
[64] Ibid., p. 179, para. 15.
[65] Ibid., p. 180, para. 16.

between national and international law'.[66] It then argues that '[w]hatever the validity of this view under national law, it is very hard to see how it could be applied to relations between international legal "regimes" and general international law',[67] and concluded that:

> It is in the nature of 'general law to apply generally' – namely in as much as it has not been specifically excluded. It cannot plausibly be claimed that these parts of the law ... have validity only as they have been 'incorporated' into the relevant regimes. There never has been any act of incorporation. But more relevantly, it is hard to see how regime-builders might have agreed not to incorporate (that is, opt out from) such general principles.[68]

This echoes Joost Pauwelyn's suggestion that 'in their treaty relations states can "contract out" of one, more or, in theory, all *rules* of international law (other than those of *jus cogens*), but they cannot contract out of the *system* of international law'.[69]

Those are propositions worth considering. While the legal systems established by treaties constituting international legal subjects are arguably even more 'autonomous' from general international law than highly specialised treaty regimes, they are also creations of the international legal system. The institutional plane on which the relations between organizations and members take place is a derivation of the international plane where the general law applies. While the analogy between States and international organizations does not always work there, that does not mean that it will always be implausible. To press the point, one just has to think of those internal rules that, in the context of the ARIO, the ILC thought would give rise to 'international' obligations. When a member fails to comply with a binding decision taken by a political organ of the organization, general rules regarding attribution of conduct, existence of

---

[66] Koskenniemi (Rapporteur), 'Report of the Study Group of the ILC: Fragmentation of International Law', A/CN.4/L.682 (2006) 93, para. 176.

[67] Ibid., pp. 93–94, para. 177.

[68] Ibid., pp. 96–97, para. 185.

[69] J. Pauwelyn, *Conflict of Norms in Public International Law: How WTO Law Relates to other Rules of International Law* (Cambridge: Cambridge University Press, 2003), p. 37. He adds: "'contracting out' of general international law by treaty must take place explicitly in the sense that silence means 'contracting in'" (at 215). Similarly, Simma and Pulkowski have argued that 'general international law provides a systemic fabric from which no special regime is completely decoupled', and that 'by framing a prescription in legal terms, states have opted to subordinate a particular issue to the logic of international law as a whole': B. Simma and D. Pulkowski, 'Of planets and the universe: self-contained regimes in international law' (2006) 17 EJIL 483, 529.

the breach, circumstances precluding wrongfulness such as *force majeure* and the duty to provide reparation may be readily applied between organizations and members if this is not precluded by the rules of the organization.[70]

This is why the monistic presumption that the ILC adopted in its work on fragmentation is also relevant for the relations between general international law and the internal law of international organizations. Martti Koskenniemi, Chairman of the fragmentation group, noted that the question of relations between international legal orders 'was clearly closely linked to the interaction between *lex specialis* and *lex generalis*' and argued that it should not be implied that the 'internal law' of an organization 'constituted a self-contained or entirely separate regime'.[71] It is telling that even the Court of Justice of the EU has been as consistent in affirming the autonomy of the legal order of the European Union[72] as in describing its relationship with international law in monistic terms. On the grounds that the EU 'must respect international law in the exercise of its powers', the ECJ has affirmed that rules of customary international law 'are binding upon the Community institutions and form part of the Community legal order'.[73]

6.2.2.2   Limits of the Monistic Presumption

While there are good reasons to adopt a monistic presumption for the application of general international law on the international plane, the internal law of international organizations presents certain specificities when compared to the specialised treaty regimes on which the ILC focused its study on fragmentation. Applying the general law to special regimes normally involves construing the special rules in a way that

---

[70] In *Walz v. Clickair SA*, for example, the CJEU referred to the concept of injury enshrined in art. 31(2) ARS as 'common to all the international law sub-systems' and expressing 'the ordinary meaning to be given to the concept of damage in international law': Case C-63/09, *Walz v. Clickair SA* [2010] ECR I-4239, para. 27.

[71] Koskenniemi, YILC 2005/I, pp. 78–79, para. 34. He added that '[m]ost of the major international organizations had special rules to deal with a breach of an internal rule, and it was clear that such rules ought to take precedence over the general rules that the Commission was drafting, but that certainly did not mean that general law was set aside'.

[72] As per the *Van Gend en Loos* case and the classic affirmation that 'the Community constitutes a new legal order of international law': Case C-25/62, *Van Gend en Loos v. The Netherlands* [1963] ECR 1, 12.

[73] Case C-162/96, *Racke GmbH & Co v. Haptzollant Mainz* [1998] ECR I-3655, para. 46. Also, Case C-286/90, *Anklagemyndigheden v. Poulsen and Diva Navigation* [1992] ECR I-6019, para 9.

meets the requirements of the 'principle of harmonization', according to which 'when several norms bear on a single issue they should, to the extent possible, be interpreted so as to give rise to a single set of compatible obligations'.[74] The goal is to guarantee that the special regime interferes to the least extent possible with other rights and obligations that the parties owe to each other or third parties. But when a special regime has the effect of creating a personified entity, the application of general international law to the relations between the organization and their members may give rise to a significant concern: that the rights, obligations and capacities that the organization enjoys on the international plane are unduly invoked to expand the competences that the organization possesses at the institutional level.

Finn Seyersted's argument on the 'inherent powers' of international organizations illustrates the problem. More than anyone, Seyersted championed the view of international organizations as legal subjects enjoying rights, obligations and capacities analogous to those of States.[75] He emphasised the distinction between general international law and the internal law of organizations, and convincingly argued that rights, obligations and capacities to operate on the international plane could only derive from international law. On this basis, he decried the 'implied powers doctrine' as fallacious and suggested that it ought to be discarded.[76] For Seyersted, international organizations did not need to rely on the powers expressly or implicitly provided in their constituent instruments to perform international acts. Rather, he appears to suggest that international organizations are only unable to take action when their constituent instruments so prohibit.[77]

It seems that at this point Seyersted's doctrine of inherent powers turns into an argument on how constituent instruments must be construed.[78] But what Seyersted may have failed to appreciate is that even if

---

[74] Conclusions of the Study Group, YILC 2006/II, p.178, para. 4.

[75] F. Seyersted, *Common Law of International Organizations* (Leiden: Nijhoff, 2008), p. 396.

[76] E.g., ibid., pp. 32–33.

[77] See his account of constitutional limitations in F. Seyersted, 'International personality of intergovernmental organizations: do their capacities really depend upon their constitutions?' (1964) 4 *Indian Journal of International Law* 1, 23–25.

[78] It should be noted that this may not have been Seyersted's intention, given his insistence on the distinction between 'the inherent external legal capacity to act on a voluntary basis as an equal partner and inherent internal jurisdiction over organs and their members as such – on the one hand – and extended power to exercise functional jurisdiction over or in . . . member States or private individuals . . . on the other hand': *Common Law*, p. 69. Yet, perhaps because his main concern was to respond to the idea that the source of the

the implied powers doctrine fails to explain the rights, obligations and capacities that international organizations enjoy under general international law, it may be fairly convincing as a doctrine of constitutional interpretation for international organizations. As developed by international courts and tribunals, it has the merit of combining a principle of effective interpretation with a principle of legality.[79] On the one hand, if international organizations are to perform their functions and fulfil their purposes, it is necessary that their skeletal constituent instruments be construed purposefully with the aid of teleological considerations. On the other hand, just as is the case with any other institution exercising authority under a public law framework, an international organization must be able to show that its acts are based on pre-defined competences. This is not to say that the proposition that international organizations have rights, obligations and capacities under general international law may not be a relevant factor for the interpretation of constituent instruments. But complex questions of constitutional interpretation cannot be dealt with uncritically via the implementation of the monistic presumption or perfunctory analogies with States.

The ILC's debate on the permissibility of countermeasures against breaches of rules of the organization provides an example on point. Following a debate as to whether the regime of countermeasures in the ARS should be extended to international organizations at all,[80] the Commission initially adopted a provision allowing for countermeasures between organizations and members to the extent that they 'are not inconsistent with the rules of the organization' and 'no appropriate means are available for otherwise inducing compliance' of the responsible entity.[81] Subject to the requirement that no other 'appropriate means' be available, the provision meant that countermeasures could have a place in relations taking place on the institutional plane. On second reading, however, the Commission changed its position. A new paragraph was added to Articles 22 and 52 ARIO to the effect that countermeasures may not be taken by organizations or their members 'in response to a breach of an international obligation under the rules of the organization unless such countermeasures are provided for by those

---

rights, obligations and capacities of IOs is their internal law alone, he failed to give to the constitutional question a more nuanced treatment.

[79] See Section 4.3.1.
[80] As discussed in Section 7.2.2.
[81] See arts. 21 and 51 as adopted on first reading: YILC 2009/II, part two, pp. 47 and 67.

rules'. The Commission justified this default prohibition on counter-measures on the institutional plane by referring to the 'obligation of close cooperation that generally exist between an international organiza-tion and its members' and the 'special ties' between them.[82] To the extent that the internal law of an international organization establishes 'special ties' for members and their organizations, it may preclude recourse to countermeasures. That was the position that the Court of Justice of the EU took in *Commission v. Luxembourg and Belgium*:

> the Treaty [establishing the ECC] is not limited to creating reciprocal obligations between the different natural and legal persons to whom it is applicable, but establishes a new legal order which governs the powers, rights and obligations of the said persons, as well as the necessary procedures for taking cognizance of and penalizing any breach of it. Therefore, except where otherwise expressly provided, the basic concept of the Treaty requires that the Member States shall not take the law into their own hands, except where otherwise expressly provided, the basis concept of the Treaty.[83]

But can such a categorical prohibition equally arise at the level of general international law? In the absence of practice or precedent supporting it, that is doubtful.[84] But, even if *de lege ferenda*, the provisions proposed by the ILC are not necessarily out of place. A provision in the ARIO that endorsed the availability of countermeasures for breaches of obligations on the institutional plane might have taken the analogy between States and international organizations too far, paving the way for arguments of questionable systemic value. In fact, the position taken on first reading in the ARIO had been used as authority for the proposition that members of the United Nations could take lawful countermeasures against the UN Security Council under international law by disobeying resolutions

---

[82] Commentary to art. 22, YILC 2011/II, part two, p. 72, para. 6; commentary to art. 52, ibid., p. 94, para 8.

[83] Joined Cases C-90/63 and 91/63, *Commission v. Luxembourg and Belgium* [1964] ECR 625, 631.

[84] Indeed, Special Rapporteur Gaja was hesitant to state a general rule on the issue: while the inadmissibility of countermeasures within the institutional framework may be 'how the rules of several international organizations have to be understood', the ARIO did not 'purport to offer criteria for interpreting the rules of the organization in general or the rules of a particular organization': Gaja (Eighth Report), A/CN.4/640 (2011), p. 23, para. 67. In the debates, a member had suggested that the issue be reserved by means of a saving clause: Wood, A/CN.4/SR.3084 (2011), p. 5.

adopted under Chapter VII of the UN Charter.[85] According to a commentator, the provisions in the UN Charter do not 'explicitly prohibit countermeasures, and since they provide no appropriate means for otherwise inducing compliance of the UN with its obligation of cessation and reparation, the availability of countermeasures by [member States] against the UN must be affirmed'.[86] It is not difficult to discern the reason why the Commission would wish to distance itself from this argument. Rules devised for a decentralised community comprising legally autonomous entities are not always suited for application in institutional settings characterised by stronger ties of solidarity as is the case with the United Nations. This provides a reason to limit recourse to unilateral action to grounds that are provided by, or otherwise compatible with, the constituent instrument and other internal rules, rather than uncritically filling the gap with the means of 'private justice' envisaged by the international law of States. If any inspiration is to be drawn from the general law in this context, it should instead come from the well-accepted methods for peaceful settlement listed in Article 33 UN Charter.[87] In the words of a member of the Commission:

> international organizations [are] typically governed by special regimes and [have] renounced, at least implicitly, taking the law into their own hands. In setting up international organizations, States [create] the mutual expectation that the application of the rules of the organization [will] ultimately lead to the settlement of any dispute that might arise . . . That [is] true not only for organizations such as the European Community, which [has] a system of judicial remedies, but also for the United Nations and its specialized agencies. The Charter of the United Nations [has], after all, established the organized international community of States and [has] created a legal framework and procedures that [risk] being undermined if secondary rules which, while making sense in the context of the responsibility of reciprocally sovereign States, [are] formally imposed on relations between an international organization and its members.[88]

---

[85] A. Tzanakopoulos, *Disobeying the Security Council: Countermeasures against Wrongful Sanctions* (Oxford: Oxford University Press, 2011), pp. 154–90.

[86] Ibid., p. 157. This line of reasoning was compatible with the text of arts. 22 and 52 as adopted on first reading.

[87] Art. 33, UN Charter: 'The parties to any dispute, the continuance of which is likely to endanger the maintenance of international peace and security, shall, first of all, seek a solution by negotiation, enquiry, mediation, conciliation, arbitration, judicial settlement, resort to regional agencies or arrangements, or other peaceful means of their own choice.'

[88] Nolte, YILC 2009/I, p. 11, para. 51.

6.3   Concluding Remarks

It is beyond the scope of this study to provide a full account of the terms of the relations between international legal orders. The point to be emphasised here is that the analogy between States and international organizations is only persuasive when the entities concerned can be viewed as legally autonomous entities operating on the international plane. In contrast, at the institutional level, where the rules of the organization constitute the governing legal system, the extent to which the general law is relevant is a matter of constitutional interpretation, even if there are good reasons to adopt a monistic presumption favouring its incorporation. In a sense, that the relations on the institutional plane mark the breaking point of the analogy reinforces the view that States and international organizations are analogous on the international plane. As is the case with States, when international organizations are viewed as legal subjects under general international law, their legal systems have to be regarded as distinct, and relatively autonomous, from general international law.

7

Normative Contestation of the Analogy

The analogy between States and international organizations provides a general justification for making propositions about the rights, obligations and capacities of international organizations on the international plane in situations of uncertainty. But that analogy's role in the development of the law of international organizations should not be overestimated. Because analogies are particularised exercises in which the relevant similarity between the 'source situation' and the 'target situation' has to be assessed in the light of the circumstances of each and every situation of uncertainty, any general analogy such as the one covered in this study allows room for contestation. It must be conceded that solutions provided by systemic reasoning have a somewhat provisional character, which means that they can be overtaken by other tendencies as they are received, debated and applied by the participants in the legal system. Contestation may lead to certain analogical solutions being accepted in practice and others being rejected.

This chapter looks into how normative contestation – here broadly defined as reasoned opposition by entities and persons influencing the legal discourse[1] – may pose a limit to the influence of the analogy between States and international organizations. Grounds for normative contestation can be distinguished from the objections to the analogy discussed in Part II in that, rather than generating prescriptions of doctrine or principle against viewing States and international organizations as comparable entities operating on the international plane, they encapsulate differing and more loosely expressed worldviews about what

---

[1] This includes, first and foremost, States and international organizations themselves, but also members of the 'epistemic community' formed by members of the international legal profession, on which see, e.g., O. Schachter, 'The invisible college of international lawyers' (1977) 72 *Northwestern University Law Review* 217 and A. Bianchi, 'Epistemic communities' in J. D'Aspremont and S. Singh, *Concepts for International Law* (forthcoming Edward Elgar, 2018).

international organizations are or ought to be. One such worldview is the normative anxiety, implicit in some uses of the distinction between 'original/primary' subjects and 'derivative/secondary' subjects of international law,[2] that international organizations have to be either protected or put in their place. Those to whom the analogy described in this study is unappealing because 'international organizations are not States!' may proactively advocate for other visions of what the public international law of international organizations should look like, and thus be a force for change and innovation.

This chapter surveys examples of normative contestation of the analogy between States and international organizations when controversial rules of general international law were at stake. For convenience, the distinction between 'primary rules' and 'secondary rules' of international law that the ILC has proposed to delimit the scope of its project on State responsibility will be used.[3] While 'primary rules' comprise substantive rules of conduct, 'secondary rules' comprise the 'underlying structures of interaction and rule-making at the international level'.[4] Normative contestation relating to 'primary rules' is likely to be greater than contestation relating to 'secondary rules' for two reasons. First, the ILC's work on treaties and responsibility provided a public platform in which similarities and differences between States and organizations as regards certain 'secondary rules' could be discussed and, to a degree, settled. Second, extending to organizations the substantive rights and obligations of States is bound to give rise to greater controversy than extending the more abstract structural frameworks under which those rights and obligations are acquired and discharged.[5] It is at the level of rules of conduct that perceived differences between States and international organizations are likely to be fiercely debated and alternative visions proposed. That said, as the discussion below shows, secondary rules have also given rise to normative contestation, which precludes reading too much into a

---

[2] See section 4.2.
[3] YILC 2001/II, part two, p. 31, para. 2. The phrase is sometimes used to describe other 'structural' rules of international law such as the law of treaties.
[4] J. Crawford, *The International Law Commission's Articles on State Responsibility* (Cambridge: Cambridge University Press, 2002), p. 15.
[5] Controversy surrounding substantive rules of international law was indeed the reason why the ILC adopted the distinction between primary and secondary rules in the law of State responsibility: Crawford, *The International Law Commission's Articles*, p. 15.

distinction that has more to do with the structure and role of certain rules than with the conditions for their existence or validity.[6]

7.1 Contestation in the Application of 'Primary Rules' to International Organizations

7.1.1 Law of Immunities

While the law of treaties and responsibility of international organizations has followed in the footsteps of the rules that apply to States, the law applying to their immunities has been following its own path.[7] The customary law of State immunity was only codified recently with the adoption of the 2004 UN Convention on Jurisdictional Immunities of States and their Property, not yet in force. In contrast, from an early stage, the approach elected to regulate the immunities of international organizations has been the adoption of organization-specific treaty rules.

Despite the variety of existing organizations, there is remarkable uniformity in the way in which their immunity has been handled. First, constituent instruments typically comprise a provision to the effect that, as exemplified by Article 105 of the UN Charter, the organization 'shall enjoy in the territory of each of its Members such privileges and immunities as are necessary for the fulfilment of its purposes', and its officials 'shall similarly enjoy such privileges and immunities as are necessary for the independent exercise of their functions'.[8] Second, supplementary agreements are often concluded to regulate the

---

[6] Some writers have suggested that while secondary rules of customary international law may apply to IOs, that is not true for primary rules: e.g., J. Klabbers, 'Sources of international organizations' law: reflections on accountability' in J. d'Aspremont and S. Besson, *The Oxford Handbook on the Sources of International Law* (Oxford: Oxford University Press, 2017), pp. 998–1000. Because of their generality and structural character, secondary rules may be more relevant for all IOs than many regimes of primary rules, but it is doubtful that labelling a rule as 'primary' or 'secondary' can tell much about whether it can be extended to an IO by analogy or not.

[7] An international law immunity is a procedural bar that prevents a State or other entity to exercise a jurisdiction that it would otherwise possess. It typically applies to debar the courts of the State of the forum from adjudicating on matters pertaining to foreign States and their officials. See generally J. Crawford (ed.), *Brownlie's Principles of Public International Law*, 8th edn (Oxford: Oxford University Press, 2012), pp. 488–91.

[8] Art. 105, UN Charter. Slight variations can be found in the constituent instruments of the Food and Agriculture Organization (art. XV), of the International Monetary Fund and of the entities forming the World Bank group. The constituent instruments of NATO and the African Union do not comprise a provision on immunities.

organization's immunities further. The 1946 Convention on the Privileges and Immunities of the United Nations provides an example of the typical approach, which is to grant:

(i) 'immunity from every form of legal process' to the organization itself, subject to the possibility of waiver;

(ii) immunity *ratione personae* – coextensive to that accorded by international law to diplomatic agents – to a select group of high-ranking officials of the organization (in the case of the UN, the Secretary-General and Assistant Secretaries-General);

(iii) inviolability (that is, protection from any form of arrest or detention) and immunity *ratione materiae* 'in respect of words spoken or written and all acts done by them in their capacity as representatives' to other officials of the organization, and to representatives sent by member States to sit in political organs of the organization or participate in conferences which the organization convenes.[9]

Third, headquarters agreements provide for additional rules concerning privileges and immunities applicable to the relations between the organization and its host State.

These treaty regimes depart from several tenets of the customary law that binds States. For one, international organizations are generally accorded 'absolute immunity' while States are only entitled to 'relative immunity'. The customary law of State immunity has evolved from a regime of absolute immunity from the jurisdiction of foreign courts to a doctrine of relative immunity that allows for exceptions for commercial transactions, torts committed by foreign officials in the territory of the State of the forum, certain employment disputes, among others.[10] The asymmetry between the degree of immunity between the two categories of international legal subjects has been traditionally justified by the need

---

[9] While the regime of immunity *ratione personae* attaches to particular offices and covers acts taken both in an official and a private capacity for as long as the agent remains in office, the regime of immunity *ratione materiae* attaches to all acts performed in an official capacity. See in general C. Wickremasinghe, 'Immunities enjoyed by officials of States and international organizations' in M. Evans (ed.), *International Law*, 4th edn (Oxford: Oxford University Press, 2014), p. 255.

[10] That is so to the extent that even though constituent instruments typically mention the 'purposes' of international organizations, which could be taken as a criterion for relative immunity, supplementary treaties unequivocally provide for 'immunity from every form of legal process'. See the discussion in A. Orakhelashvili, 'Responsibility and immunities: similarities and differences between international organizations and States' (2014) 11 IOLR 114, 158–62.

to ensure the autonomy of the organizations in relation to its member States. In the words of Wilfred Jenks:

> The basic function of international immunities is to bridle the sovereignty of States in their treatment of international organisations. This bridling of sovereignty is as much in the interest of States as in that of international organisations. While it debars each State from illicit interference, it also protects it from such interference by other States. It represents, indeed, an indispensable guarantee to each member State that the organization will not become, by means of pressure and constraint which are not fully apparent and over which there is therefore no possibility of control, an instrument of the policy of other States directed against its own policy and interests, but will serve legally the common interest as determined by the recognised constitutional processes of the organisation.[11]

In contrast, the treaty rules on the immunities of officials of international organizations are fairly similar to those accruing for State officials. Immunity attaches to acts performed in an official capacity, with only a select class of high-ranking officials being accorded immunity *ratione personae*. But there are a number of differences when it comes to the particulars. For example, officials of international organizations are accorded inviolability, which most State officials do not enjoy. Moreover, representatives of member States in the organization – a category that does not find an easy analogue in diplomatic law – do not benefit from the immunity *ratione personae* that diplomatic agents enjoy in the receiving State under the 1961 Vienna Convention on Diplomatic Relations and customary international law. This means that a diplomat serving at her country's permanent mission to the United Nations in New York City enjoys a less favourable immunity regime than her colleagues serving at their country's embassy in Washington D.C.

It is not surprising that treaty regimes have been the preferred approach to deal with the immunities of international organizations and their officials. The use of the treaty form allows for the development of immunity regimes that cater to each organization's needs and promotes greater legal certainty in the relations between organizations and member States than would be the case if the matter was left to custom. It does not follow, however, that questions concerning the customary rules that apply to the immunity of international organizations can be completely avoided. When an international organization interacts with third parties or takes action causing harm to nationals of third States,

---

[11] W. Jenks, *International Immunities* (London: Stevens, 1961), p. 167.

constituent instruments, conventions on privileges and immunities and headquarter agreements are not in principle applicable. And even when a dispute arises between a member State and the organization, customary international law may be of relevance in construing unclear or ambiguous treaty provisions.[12]

But are international organizations entitled to invoke immunity before domestic courts as a matter of customary international law? This is a controversial question that has elicited opposing answers not only in academic commentary but also in the judgments of domestic courts. Even textbooks on international organizations disagree, with Schermers and Blokkers and Amerisanghe stating that international organizations may claim immunity under customary international law, and Sands and Klein saying that, with the exception of the United Nations, they may not. [13] The case law of domestic courts is similarly convoluted. At one end of the spectrum, the Dutch Supreme Court upheld the immunity of the Iran-US Claims Tribunal on the basis of 'unwritten international law'.[14] At the other, the Italian Supreme Court of Cassation rejected the proposition that the European University Institute, as an international organization, could invoke immunity under custom.[15] As Ryngaert has shown, domestic courts are sometimes reluctant to recognise a customary right to plead immunity.[16]

In a recent study, upon considering existing State practice and *opinio juris*, Michael Wood came to the conclusion that 'it cannot be said that there is a "general practice accepted as law" establishing a customary rule

---

[12] Art. 31(3)(c) VCLT 1986.

[13] Contrast Schermers and Blokker, *International Institutional Law*, p. 493 and Amerasinghe, *Principles of the Institutional Law*, pp. 345–47 with Sands and Klein, *Bowett's Law of International Institutions*, p. 493. Klabbers takes a less unequivocal position: *An Introduction*, p. 149.

[14] *Spaans v. Iran-United States Claims Tribunal*, Dutch Supreme Court, Case No. 12627, 20 December 1985, translation in (1987) 18 *Netherlands Yearbook of International Law* 357.

[15] *Pistelli v. European University Institute*, Supreme Court of Cassation, Case No. 20995, 28 October 2005, Guida al diritto 40 (3/2006), available in ILDC 297.

[16] C. Ryngaert, 'The immunity of international organizations before domestic courts: recent trends' (2010) 7 IOLR, 121, 124–25. Also: A. Reinisch, *International Organizations before National Courts* (Cambridge: Cambridge University Press, 2000), pp. 145–57, and M. Orzan, 'International organizations and immunity from legal process: an uncertain evolution' in R. Virzo and I. Ingravallo (eds.), *Evolutions in the Law of International Organizations* (Leiden: Nijhoff, 2015), pp. 367–72.

of immunity' for international organizations.[17] It is difficult to find fault with the particulars of Wood's analysis: if the question posed is whether a rule of custom has emerged through the accumulation of State practice and *opinio juris*, the most convincing answer seems to be in the negative. But is this really the right question to ask? The lack of uniformity in practice and precedent creates a situation of uncertainty that has to be solved in the way that fits best within the international legal system.[18] Should this gap be filled by recourse to the *Lotus* principle, so that in the absence of an express customary prohibition on the exercise of jurisdiction by domestic courts over international organizations States are at liberty to do so? Or should the customary law of immunities that apply to States be instead extended to international organizations by analogy?

Commentators and domestic judgments denying the existence of a customary rule of immunity for international organizations reject the analogy on the grounds that the maxim *par in parem non habet imperium* – which underpins the law of State immunity – only applies to sovereign equals.[19] In *Pistelli v. EUI*, the Italian Supreme Court of Cassation noted that it was 'not clear that the principle *par in parem non habet iurisdictionem* ... [had] been extended by customary law to all international organisations with specific legal personality under international law' and concluded that because it was 'impossible to place States and international organisations on the same level, the privileges and immunities the latter enjoy can only arise from specific agreements'.[20] Likewise, Robert Jennings has suggested that 'recourse even by analogy to the legal position of sovereigns [is] wholly unnecessary and illogical'.[21] Those positions are informed by the view that States, the original subjects of international law, are sovereign while international organizations, the derivative subjects, are not.

---

[17] M. Wood, 'Do international organizations enjoy immunity under customary international law?' (2013) 10 IOLR 287, 317. Coming to the same conclusion: Orzan, 'International organizations', pp. 371–72 and Reinisch, *International Organizations before National Courts*, p. 157.

[18] See section 1.2.2.

[19] See P. Webb, 'Should the "2004 UN State Immunity Convention" serve as a model/ starting point for a future UN convention on the immunity of international organizations?' (2013) 10 IOLR 319, 324–26.

[20] *Pistelli v. European University Institute*, para. 9 (as reported in ILDC).

[21] R. Jennings, 'Foreword' in P. Bekker, *The Legal Position of Intergovernmental Organizations: A Functional Necessity Analysis of Their Legal Status and Immunities* (Dordrecht: Nijhoff, 1994), at vii.

While denying the label of 'sovereign' to international organizations is appropriate, that does not mean that the customary rules on immunity that apply to States cannot be extended to international organizations on the grounds that both categories comprise legally autonomous entities operating on the international plane. The line of reasoning adopted by the Italian court falls short for two main reasons. First, it does not do justice to the rationale of the rules of State immunity: achieving an orderly system for the bringing of international claims that prioritises international forums over domestic courts. If States were to exercise jurisdiction over one another through claims brought before domestic courts, that would result in an unpredictable mechanism for the unilateral enforcement of international obligations that might threaten their coexistence as self-governing entities. While international organizations are not 'sovereign', they are self-governing institutions operating outside the jurisdiction of their members and third parties. Their coexistence with other self-governing entities would be threatened if a third party were given a free pass to subject them to its jurisdiction.

Second, any exercise of jurisdiction over an organization ultimately entails an indirect exercise of jurisdiction over its member States. Even though the organization and its members constitute separate legal persons, allowing third parties to exercise jurisdiction over the organization would in practice imply that there is an exception to immunity when States act collectively through international organizations. As Jenks put it:

> Where no agreement concerning immunities has been negotiated with a third State the organisation will not be able to rely in relation to that State on any general provision of its own Constitution providing for appropriate immunities as an international obligation of that State. It does not follow that the organisation has no legal rights in such a situation. The rights which it is entitled to claim may be less extensive than those which it is entitled to claim in relation to its own members, but the organisation cannot reasonably be regarded in relation to third States as a group of private persons with no legal status of any kind; at the lowest it is a group of States acting collectively ... A third State has, of course, no obligation to allow such an entity to operate on its territory, but if it allows it to do so it must, it is suggested, respect the immunities appropriate to such an entity.[22]

---

[22] Jenks, *International Immunities*, p. 33.

The question that arises next is what adjustments the law of State immunity requires when it is extended to international organizations. Commentators and domestic courts sometimes fall for the slippery-slope of functionalist approaches, contending that 'the international privileges and immunities recognized by customary law are those that each individual organization requires in order to discharge its responsibilities independently and without interference'.[23] That leads them to deny the applicability, to an international organization, of the exceptions to immunity that have been carved out for States. The need to protect the independence of the organization or to allow the organization to perform its functions can be a powerful argument in the interpretation of constituent instruments and treaties between organizations and members.[24] It cannot, however, justify the imposition of functional immunities on third parties. If the rules that apply to States are extended by analogy because, like States, international organizations are autonomous entities operating on the international plane, it makes no sense for the rules of general international law applying to those organizations to be more protective than the rules of State immunity.[25]

This sentiment is captured in the judgment by the US Court of Appeals for the Third Circuit in the *OSS Nokalva v. European Space Agency* case. Nokalva, a provider of software services to the ESA, brought proceedings complaining about the Agency's distribution of software to third-parties without due compensation. The Court was required to apply the US Organizations Immunity Act, which granted to certain international organizations (including the ESA) 'the same immunity from suit and every form of judicial process as is enjoyed by foreign governments'. In doing so, it construed the statute as incorporating the commercial transactions exception found in the customary law of State immunity and US domestic law, noting that:

> If a foreign government, such as Germany, had contracted with [Novalka], it would not be immune from suit because the [Foreign State Immunity Act] provides that a foreign government involved in a commercial arrangement such as that in this case may be sued ... We find no

---

[23] E.g., Amerasinghe, *Principles of the Institutional Law*, p. 346.

[24] A functionalist view may well work in a case in which a dispute on immunity arises between an organization and a member State given that the constituent instrument will apply as *lex specialis*. See the discussion in Section 6.1.2.

[25] E. Gaillard and I. Pingel-Lenuzza, 'International organisations and immunity from jurisdiction: to restrict or to bypass' (2002) 51 ICLQ 1, 4–5.

compelling reason why a group of states acting through an international organization is entitled to broader immunity than its member States enjoy when acting alone. Indeed, such a policy may create an incentive for foreign governments to evade legal obligations by acting through international organizations.[26]

Given the diversity between international organizations and their limited mandates, certain exceptions to State immunity may be in practice inapplicable to most organizations. At the same time, it is not difficult to see why extending exceptions to State immunity to international organizations could be problematic. As non-territorial entities operating in territory under the jurisdiction of its members or even third States, international organizations are more exposed to the application of foreign domestic law than States.[27] But in a day and age where the law of immunities is the subject of increasing criticism, in particular when it gets in the way of the enforcement of the rights of individuals, it is unconvincing to propose a rule of absolute immunity for international organizations under general international law. If one resorts to analogical reasoning to fill the gap in a situation of uncertainty, the exceptions ought to be extended together with the rules.

In short, the analogy between States and international organizations remains persuasive when it comes to the immunities that international organizations and their agents can claim under general international law. But the normative contestation with which it has been met, in particular in the judgments of domestic courts, exemplifies the role that perceptions of differences in status between the categories of subjects of international law may play in the further development of the law. If the position that international organizations are not entitled to claim immunity in custom because they are not sovereign were to take hold in the practice of domestic courts, a customary rule would probably emerge to rebut the analogy. The law of immunities of international organizations thus presents a case of a subfield in flux, and it is difficult to predict where the interaction between the analogy's systemic pull and the ensuing normative contestation will lead.

---

[26] *OSS Nokalva, Inc. v. European Space Agency*, 617 F.3d 756 (3rd Cir. 2010). For a discussion of other cases applying to IOs exceptions to State immunity, Reinisch, *International Organizations before National Courts*, pp. 196–97.

[27] That constitutes yet another incentive for concluding treaties envisaging generous immunities.

7.1.2 Law of Armed Conflict

Under contemporary international law, States are prohibited from using force unilaterally except in self-defence.[28] Military action, whenever necessary, is to be deployed by or with the authorisation of the UN Security Council, following the procedures laid down in Chapter VII of the Charter of the United Nations. In the *Nicaragua* case, the International Court ruled that the prohibition on the unilateral threat or use of force in international relations is also found in customary international law.[29] But can the regime on the use of force that applies to States be extended to international organizations? Those were questions that arose incidentally for the ILC in the projects on treaties and responsibility of international organizations.

Article 52 VCLT 1969 provides that '[a] treaty is void if its conclusion has been procured by the threat or use of force in violation of the principles of international law embodied in the Charter of the United Nations'. In discussing whether to extend it to international organizations, the Commission noted that, while examples of international organizations coercing or being coerced into concluding treaties could not be found, such examples could certainly be imagined.[30] Given that international organizations are not party to the UN Charter,[31] the Commission debated whether the 'principles of international law embodied in the Charter' would apply to them. It concluded that the phrase a 'group of states' employed in the definition of aggression adopted by the UN General Assembly[32] also covered international organizations, and that as a result there was 'sufficient authority for recognizing that an international organization may in theory be regarded as making unlawful use of armed force'.[33] This conclusion was corroborated by Chapter VIII of the UN Charter, under which 'regional agencies' are required to seek an authorisation from the Security Council before they conduct any operations involving the use of force.[34]

---

[28] Articles 2(4) and 51 UN Charter.
[29] *Military and Para-Military Activities in and against Nicaragua (Nicaragua v USA)* (Merits) [1986] ICJ Rep 135, paras. 183–92.
[30] Commentary to art. 52, YILC 1982/II, part two, p. 55, para. 4.
[31] Ushakov, YILC 1979/I, p. 131, para. 30.
[32] UNGA Res. 3314 XXIX (1974), art. 1(b).
[33] Commentary to art. 52, YILC 1982/II, part two, p. 56, para. 6.
[34] Ibid, p. 56, para. 7. Article 53 of the UN Charter prescribes that '[t]he Security Council shall, where appropriate, utilize such regional arrangements or agencies for enforcement action under its authority. But no enforcement action shall be taken under regional arrangements or by regional agencies without the authorization of the Security Council.'

As the ultimate adoption of Article 52 VCLT 1986 suggests, the Commission and the 1986 Vienna Conference had no difficulty in accepting that international organizations are bound by the prohibition on the unilateral use of force.[35] The analogy with States proved persuasive: States cannot do collectively what they pledged not to do individually. A similar position has come to be accepted as regards the application of rules of international humanitarian law to international organizations. In the past, the United Nations – which is not a party to treaties laying down rules of humanitarian international law – maintained an ambiguous stance on the matter,[36] animated by the idea that 'a horizontal relationship between the United Nations and another party to the armed conflict is antithetical to a world order organized pursuant to the principles expressed in the UN Charter and supervised by the United Nations'.[37] That stance was clarified in 1999, when the Secretary-General issued a 'Bulletin on the Observance by the United Nations forces of international humanitarian law' for the purpose of 'setting out fundamental principles and rules' of the *jus in bello* applicable to the UN.[38] It is thus clear that the UN, acting through the Secretariat, has undertaken to comply with the customary rules by which it is widely held to be bound.[39]

---

[35] Certain members of the Commission, however, criticized this for being 'based on highly theoretical considerations which they felt need not be stressed': commentary to art. 52, YILC 1982/II, part two, p. 56, para. 8.

[36] Until the end of the 1990s, the organization consistently committed to abide by the "principles and spirit" of IHL, and several times provided reparation for victims of breaches of IHL perpetrated by members of the UN Forces, but the extent to which it considered itself bound by the rules of IHL was indicated on a case-by-case basis: see U. Palwankar, 'Applicability of international humanitarian law to United Nations peacekeeping forces' (1993) 23 *International Review of the Red Cross* 227.

[37] R. Glick, 'Lip service to the laws of war: humanitarian law and United Nations armed forces' (1995–96) 17 *Michigan Journal of International Law* 53, p. 59.

[38] The Bulletin, which contains nine sections covering some of the most fundamental principles of the treaty regimes constituting the law of armed conflict, sometimes goes beyond existing customary law: D. Shraga, 'UN peacekeeping operations: applicability of international humanitarian law and responsibility for operations-related damage' (2000) 94 AJIL 406, 408. But see M. Zwanenburg, *Accountability of Peace Support Operations* (Leiden: Nijhoff, 2005), p. 84 (pondering that 'it seems that not all the customary rules of international law are included, but rather a summary of what were considered the most important rules in the context of peace support operations').

[39] Institut de Droit International, *Resolution on Conditions of Application of Humanitarian Rules of Armed Conflict to Hostilities in Which United Nations Forces May Be Engaged*, art. 2 (1971): 'The humanitarian rules of the law of armed conflict apply to the United Nations as of right, and they must be complied with in all circumstances by United

In contrast, the debate on whether international organizations enjoy the right to self-defence has been more polarising. It came up in the Commission's discussion of Article 21 ARS, according to which '[t]he wrongfulness of an act of a State is precluded if the act constitutes a lawful measure of self-defence taken in conformity with the Charter of the United Nations'. Special Rapporteur Gaja initially suggested extending the rule in Article 21 ARS to international organizations. To him, 'it was far from inconceivable that an international organization may find itself in the same situation as a State',[40] and references to self-defence in the mandates of peacekeeping and peace-enforcement forces confirmed that 'self-defence constitutes a circumstance precluding wrongfulness' for organizations.[41] Nevertheless, that proposal gave rise to controversy. Members of the Commission accepted that international organizations could be the victim of an armed attack, especially when they are tasked with the interim administration of a territory, as in the case of the UN missions in East Timor and Kosovo,[42] or when they deploy troops in fulfilling their mandate.[43] The majority view was that in those situations the international organization concerned should be able to claim self-defence. An issue upon which the Commission did not agree, however, was whether an international organization has the right to react to an armed attack targeting their headquarters, and, if so, what the character of that right would be. In the debates, a few members suggested that self-defence was an exclusive right of States,[44] while others thought that the right could not be the same for States and international organizations.[45]

In the light of this disagreement, the Special Rapporteur recommended reserving the issue by means of a saving clause.[46] Yet, the sense that the

---

Nations Forces which are engaged in hostilities'). Also: Glick, 'Lip service', 106; and Hirsch, *The Responsibility of International Organizations*, pp. 32–37.

[40] Gaja (Fourth Report), YILC 2006/II, part one, p. 107, para. 15.

[41] Ibid., para. 17.

[42] Escarameia, YILC 2009/I, p. 8, para. 30; Nolte, ibid., p. 10, para. 48; Dugard, ibid., p. 19, para. 36. The UN Transitional Administration in East Timor was established by UNSC Res. 1272 (1999), while the UN Interim Administration Mission in Kosovo was established by UNSC Res. 1244 (1999).

[43] Escarameia, YILC 2006/I, p. 65, para. 4; Brownlie, ibid., p. 70, para. 20; Commissário Afonso, ibid., p. 25, para. 14.

[44] Rao, YILC 2006/I, p. 74, para. 11; Melescanu, YILC 2009/I, p. 18, para. 23; Kamto, ibid., pp. 24–25, para. 12; Hmoud, ibid., p. 76, para. 19.

[45] Brownlie, YILC 2006/I, 70, para 20; Commissário Afonso, YILC 2009/I, p. 20, para. 25.

[46] Gaja (Seventh Report), YILC 2009/II, part one, p. 85, para 59. Gaja also referred to 'the many critical comments expressed by States and international organizations in this regard'.

ARIO would stray too far from the ARS if it implied that the right to self-defence could not be – at least to a certain extent – invoked by international organizations was so strong that the Commission ultimately decided to replicate Article 21 ARS with a few changes. Article 21 ARIO thus prescribes that '[t]he wrongfulness of an act of an international organization is precluded if and to the extent that the act constitutes a lawful measure of self-defence under international law'. The text thus reflects a compromise. On the one hand, 'the concept of self-defence which has ... been elaborated with regard to States should be used also with regard to international organizations' for reasons of 'coherency'.[47] On the other hand, the phrase 'if and to the extent' accommodates the view that the right may be 'limited in scope' and is not to be 'equated with that of States'.[48] In the end, the Commission did not take a position as to the 'the conditions under which an international organization may resort to self-defence', which 'pertain to the primary rules' and lie, as a result, outside the scope of the ARIO.[49]

While the right to self-defence is the flipside of the prohibition on force, the debates suggest that members of the Commission, States and international organizations are more inclined to accept that international organizations are bound by the prohibition on the use force and by the rules of humanitarian international law than that they have a right to use force. This provides a neat example of normative contestation when analogical reasoning results in extending to international organizations a right deriving from a primary rule that applies to States. Should the 'secondary' or 'derivative' subjects of international law also have an exceptional right to use force in international relations? Or is self-defence so exceptional that it should be reserved for States only? Those are questions that will permeate future debates on the law on the use of force as regards international organizations.

7.2 Contestation in the Application of 'Secondary Rules' to International Organizations

In the ILC's discussions on the law of treaties and responsibility, perceptions as to the status of international organizations were behind a number of proposals that altered – or would have altered – certain

---

[47] Commentary to art. 21, ILC Report 2011, A/66/10, 113, para 2.
[48] Vázquez-Bermúdez (reporting for the Drafting Committee), A/CN.4/SR.3014 (2009) 7.
[49] Commentary to art. 21, YILC 2011/II, part two, p. 71, para. 4.

'secondary rules' that apply to organizations under the general law. Normative contestation was particularly noticeable when rules devised for States were themselves perceived as problematic or undesirable. This was the case with the regime of reservations in the law of treaties, and with rules on the defence of necessity, invocation of responsibility and the taking of countermeasures in the law of responsibility.

Not all of the proposals to abandon an analogy between States and international organizations considered in this section were adopted by the ILC, much less the most radical of those. Still, the underlying debates are worth revisiting because they shed light on how differences in status as arguments for differentiation were invoked, discussed and accepted or rejected.

7.2.1   Reservations to Treaties

The rules on reservations to treaties under VCLT 1969 are among the most challenging and controversial in the contemporary law of treaties.[50] The *Reservations to the Genocide Convention* advisory opinion given by the International Court in 1950 catalysed the change from a regime in which reservations could not be made unless expressly permitted or unanimously accepted to a regime that allows for reservations that do not conflict with the treaty's object and purpose.[51] The current regime embodies a tension between the normative goals of ensuring wide participation in multilateral treaties and preserving the integrity of the text of the agreement.[52] Against the backdrop of this tension, disagreement as to the possibility of analogising between States and international organizations led to a number of alternative proposals at the ILC, which could have constituted significant departures from the letter and spirit of the 1969 Vienna Convention.

Special Rapporteur Reuter initially proposed to replicate the rules on reservations found in VCLT 1969. According to him, there was 'no reason to put international organizations in a situation different from

---

[50] Art. 2(1)(d) defines reservation as 'a unilateral statement, however phrased or named, made by a State, when signing, ratifying, accepting, approving or acceding to a treaty, whereby it purports to exclude or to modify the legal effect of certain provisions of the treaty in their application to that State'.

[51] *Reservations to the Convention on Genocide* (Advisory Opinion) [1951] ICJ Rep 15.

[52] On the controversy, A. Pellet, 'Article 19 – Convention of 1969' in O. Corten and P. Klein, *The Vienna Conventions on the Law of Treaties: A Commentary*, v. 1 (Oxford: Oxford University Press, 2011), pp. 418–21.

that of States in the matter of reservations', for it was 'the quality of being a "party" to a treaty which [governed] the whole system of reservations'.[53] He rejected the idea that organizations should not be entitled to make reservations because they were not sovereign, pointing out that reservations could not be 'qualified at the ethical level'.[54] Several members of the Commission disagreed, nonetheless. It was suggested that while States remained free to make reservations to the extent envisaged in VCLT 1969, international organizations should be subject to a stricter regime, either because of the character of the treaties that they conclude,[55] or because of the normative imperative to restrict the right to make reservations in general.[56] Those taking the view that States and international organizations should be assimilated retorted that equality in treaty relations had to be maintained.[57] Differences between the two categories of legal subjects should justify the adoption of the most flexible regime available, not the most restrictive.[58]

Reuter then made a series of alternative proposals. At first, he suggested fully departing from VCLT 1969 and applying the unanimity rule to international organizations: only expressly authorised or unanimously accepted reservations should be permissible.[59] Later, he suggested extending the VCLT 1969 regime to treaties between international organizations only, and adopting a more restrictive regime for certain treaties in which both international organizations and States participate.[60] This was the position that prevailed on first reading, when the drafting committee adopted a provision to the effect that:

---

[53] Reuter (Fourth Report), YILC 1975/II, p. 36, para. 2.

[54] Ibid. 36, para. 3.

[55] That is, treaties of a technical character as opposed to 'law-making treaties'; see Ago, YILC 1977/I, p. 77, para. 27; Ushakov, ibid., p. 78, para. 35; Quentin-Baxter, YILC 1978/I, p. 84, para. 35. Ushakov wanted the Commission to adopt different regimes for treaties between IOs, treaties between States with marginal participation of IOs, and treaties between IOs with marginal participation of States: YILC 1977/I, p. 168, paras. 11–15.

[56] Ago, YILC 1977/I, pp. 90–91, para. 31 (noting that '[t]he system of reservations was necessary but at the same time regrettable, since it deprived treaties of their general character', and that it was doubtful 'whether the confusion ... should be aggravated by according international organizations excessive power to make reservations').

[57] Vallat, YILC 1977/I, p. 90, para. 26.

[58] Riphagen, ibid., p. 87, para. 9. Also, Riphagen, YICL 1981/I, p. 37, para. 27.

[59] See Reuter's proposal in YILC 1975/I, p. 246 (which, nevertheless, safeguarded the application of the more flexible VCLT 1969 regime to 'a treaty concluded between States on the conclusion of a general conference, in which one or more international organizations participate on the same footing as those States').

[60] Reuter, YILC 1977/I, p. 95, para. 23.

When the participation of an international organization is essential to the object and purpose of a treaty between States and one or more international organizations or between international organizations and one or more States, that organization, when signing, formally confirming, accepting, approving or acceding to that treaty, may formulate a reservation if the reservation is expressly authorized by the treaty or if it is otherwise agreed that the reservation is authorized.[61]

The rationale behind this proposal was that, as a result of their special position as subjects of international law, the character of the participation of international organizations in treaties might vary. Whenever organizations were allowed to participate in a treaty on the same footing as States, the VCLT 1969 regime could be extended to them without restrictions. But in cases in which they joined a treaty that assigned specific functions to them, so that their participation should be regarded as essential for the fulfilment of the treaty's object and purpose, no reservations should be admissible except for those authorised by the treaty.[62] In a similar vein, the Commission adopted on first reading a 'draft article 19*ter*', without a counterpart in VLCT 1969, limiting the right of international organizations to object to reservations made by States. Objections could only be made if this possibility was 'expressly granted … by the treaty or … a necessary consequence of the tasks assigned to the international organization' and the organization's participation was 'not essential to the object and purpose of the treaty'.[63]

On second reading, however, both the Special Rapporteur and the Commission had a change of heart. Pointing to examples from international practice,[64] Reuter reverted to his initial idea that in a project concerned with the 'regime of treaty instruments, rather than the general status of international organizations, it is indeed equality that should come first, since the whole regime of treaty commitments itself is based on the freedom and equality of parties'.[65] He also came to criticise draft article 19*ter* and the restriction there imposed on the right of international organizations to object to reservations. To his mind, the right

---

[61] Draft art. 19*bis*, YILC 1981/II, part two, p. 65.
[62] In this respect, Reuter pointed out that it could 'even be asserted that, where an international organization participated in a treaty because of its functions, it lost its right to formulate reservations': YILC 1977/I, p. 95, para. 20.
[63] YILC 1981/II, part two, p. 65.
[64] Reuter (Tenth Report), YILC 1981/II, part one, p. 57, paras. 57–58.
[65] Ibid., p. 58, para. 59. In support of the proposal, Vallat, YILC 1981, p. 32, para. 47 and Calle & Calle, ibid. 32, p. 43.

to object is 'linked to the status of signatory, contractor or party to a treaty in a natural and indissoluble manner' because 'an objection constitutes a response to an allegedly unlawful act, namely the formulation of [an impermissible] reservation'.[66]

As a result, the text eventually sent to the 1986 Vienna Conference replicated that of Articles 19–23 VCLT 1969.[67] In the commentary, the Commission concluded that '[t]he principle of freedom to formulate reservations that had been established for States is also valid for international organizations', this being 'in accordance with the wishes of such organizations and, it would seem, with a number of pointers from the realm of practice'.[68] But it did so with one exception. Article 19(a) VCLT 1969 prescribes that a States expressing its consent to be bound by a treaty may formulate a reservation unless 'the reservation is prohibited by the treaty'. The draft sent to the Conference added to this rule the proviso that a reservation would be equally prohibited if it could be 'otherwise established that the negotiating States and negotiating organizations were agreed that the reservation is prohibited'. The Commission offered no justification for this addition, which had not even been mentioned in the commentary. This led delegations at the Vienna Conference to question the Special Rapporteur, who served as an Expert Consultant for the Conference, about the reasons for the proposed change. Reuter described the addition as establishing 'a slight limitation to [the] freedom to make reservations', both on States and international organizations, in the light of the 'somewhat delicate character' and 'particular nature' of treaties involving international organizations.[69] Delegations were not convinced that departing from the text of VCLT 1969 was appropriate, and, as a consequence, the last-minute 'slight limitation' introduced by the Commission did not make it into Article 19 VCLT 1986.[70]

The long, protracted and meandering debate on reservations to treaties at the ILC shows that normative contestation may result not only from anxiety about the status of international organizations but also from anxiety about the substantive rules being extended from one category to the other. In the end, both the Commission and the States meeting at

---

[66] Reuter (Tenth Report), YILC 1981/II, part one, p. 61, para. 73.
[67] Díaz González (reporting for the Drafting Committee), YILC 1981/I, p. 262, para. 21.
[68] General commentary to section 2, YILC 1982/II, part two, p. 34, para. 14.
[69] Reuter (Expert Consultant), UNCLT 1986/I, p. 97, para. 31.
[70] See the amendment proposed by Austria, UNCLT 1986/II, p. 70, para. 70.

the Vienna Conference shared the intuition that neither of those anxieties justified adopting special rules for international organizations.

7.2.2 Countermeasures

When the ILC considered the issue of implementation of the responsibility of an international organization, Special Rapporteur Gaja recommended that the rules on countermeasures laid down by the ARS be replicated in the ARIO. Countermeasures create a license for a State to take unilateral action with a view to restoring legality whenever another State commits an internationally wrongful act. They provide the default mechanism for the unilateral enforcement of international obligations in the decentralised international legal system.[71] This was why the ILC decided, in formulating the ARS, that it was preferable to provide for countermeasures under strict procedural conditions than to exclude them from the purview of the law of State responsibility.

The debate on whether that regime of 'private justice' should be extended to international organizations echoed the debate on reservations to treaties some three decades earlier. Some members were of the opinion that international organizations should not be allowed to take or be the subject of countermeasures, given their special character as subjects of international law.[72] Others were opposed to countermeasures as such, noting that they constituted an 'archaic and primitive practice' that the ILC should not extend to international organizations 'in the interest of the progressive development of international law'.[73] A third

---

[71] See e.g., D. Alland, 'The definition of countermeasures' in J. Crawford, A. Pellet and S. Oleson, *The Law of International Responsibility* (Oxford: Oxford University Press 2009), p. 1129. As Crawford notes, '[t]he concept of countermeasures is recognised both by governments and international courts and tribunals as a legitimate form of peaceful self-help under general international law, a necessary feature of the framework of "private justice" in a decentralized system': J. Crawford, *State Responsibility: General Part* (Cambridge: Cambridge University Press, 2013), p. 684.

[72] E.g., Escarameia, YILC 2008/I, p. 28, para. 5 (noting that '[u]nlike States, international organizations were legally created entities, which had specific mandates spelled out in their constituent instruments. It was very objectionable whether such powers would include, even implicitly, the power to apply countermeasures, a possibility that was in any case criticized in respect of States themselves'). Also expressing reservations to the analogy in this context: Brownlie, YILC 2006/I, p. 70, para. 21.

[73] Economides pointed out that 'countermeasures constituted an archaic and primitive practice that worked to the advantage of the strong, who took justice into their own hands by adopting unilateral measures': YILC 2006/I, p. 81, para. 5. Similarly, McRae observed that 'one might take the view that countermeasures were the relic of a primitive

group took the opposite stance, noting that, once the regime of counter-measures had been – for better or worse – recognised for States, there would be no reason not to extend it to international organizations. Organizations should be equally empowered to invoke and implement the responsibility of an entity that breaches international obligations owed to them.[74]

The debate reached such a stalemate that it was necessary for the Commission to convene a Working Group to decide whether or not countermeasures should be covered by the ARIO.[75] In the end, this Working Group came to an affirmative conclusion.[76] A factor carrying some weight was that States had not indicated in comments to the Commission that they believed that international organizations should be denied the right to take countermeasures.[77] In other words, the normative contestation here originated from academia rather than from the realm of politics. The regime laid down by Articles 49–54 ARS was thus extended by analogy to the implementation of the responsibility of an international organization by third parties and vice-versa.[78]

The supposedly 'special character' of international organizations has resulted, however, in the addition of an additional limitation to the right to take countermeasures against international organizations, which finds no equivalent in the ARS. According to Article 51(4) ARIO, countermeasures are to be taken 'in such a way as to limit their effects on the exercise by the responsible international organiza-tion of its functions'. The commentary explains this additional limita-tion as follows:

system based solely on the use of force, the expansion of which through a process of progressive development of international law was to be discouraged rather than pro-moted'; YILC 2008/I, p. 29, para. 3.

[74] Matheson, YILC 2006/I, p. 72, para. 30; Dugard, YILC 2008/I, p. 35, para. 29; Hmoud, YILC 2008/I, p. 39, para. 52.

[75] Gaja, summarising the debate noted that '[t]he Commission was so divided as to whether there should be a chapter on countermeasures and, if so, to what extent international organizations should be considered entitled to adopt them, that the best course would be to form a working group, which could attempt to find a consensus': YILC 2008/I, p. 55, para. 63.

[76] Candioti (reporting for the Working Group), YILC 2008/I, p. 135, paras. 150–57.

[77] Gaja, YILC 2008/I, p. 31, para. 33.

[78] The ARIO do not expressly deal with the invocation and implementation by an inter-national organization of the responsibility of a State. The commentary notes that this gap is to filled by an analogical application of the ARS. See commentary to art. 1, YILC 2011/II, part two, p. 41, para. 10.

> One matter of concern that arises with regard to countermeasures affecting international organizations is the fact that countermeasures may hamper the functioning of the responsible international organization and therefore endanger the attainment of the objectives for which that organization was established. While this concern could not justify the total exclusion of countermeasures against international organizations, it may lead to asserting some restrictions. Paragraph 4 addresses the question in general terms.[79]

A case can be made in favour of this additional limit in the case of countermeasures taken in the relations between organizations and their members, which are further regulated by Articles 22 and 52 ARIO.[80] But Article 51(4) is meant to apply to all countermeasures, even those that third parties may take against international organizations. Why the performance of the organization's functions should be of any concern to non-members is unclear, especially in the absence of practice or precedent pointing in that direction. The idea underlying the proposal appears to be that international organizations are entities performing 'public functions' that should not be disrupted, and that in this respect they would be different from States.[81] Nevertheless, the 'public character' of the functions that different international organizations perform may be in the eye of the beholder. As Klabbers observed, 'non-universal entities are structurally incapable of devoting themselves solely to public tasks: their public tasks, however respectable, are inevitably bound up with the protection of the interests of their citizens'.[82]

In short, though normative contestation did not stop the regime of countermeasures between States from being extended to international organizations, it did result in a provision seeking to limit action taken against organizations. Whether Article 51(4) will stand the test of international practice remains to be seen.

---

[79] Commentary to art. 51, YILC 2011/II, part two, p. 93, para. 7.

[80] As discussed in Section 6.2.2.2.

[81] Paragraph 4 originates from the debates that took place within the Working Group established to deal with the issue of countermeasures, which had 'agreed that the draft articles should specify the need for countermeasures to be taken in such a manner as to respect the specificity of the targeted organization, in other words, the effect of countermeasures on the larger purposes of the organization, its capacity to perform its functions, and so forth': Candioti (reporting for the Working Group), YILC 2008/I, p. 135.

[82] Klabbers, 'Unity, diversity, accountability', 20.

7.2.3 Necessity

Necessity is possibly the most controversial of the circumstances precluding wrongfulness codified in the ARS.[83] Before the International Court declared it 'as recognized by customary international law', there was a heated debate about whether the defence was well established.[84] The discussion on whether necessity could preclude the wrongfulness of an internationally wrongful act of an international organization resulted in one the most visible departures from the ARS based on a perceived different in status between States and international organizations.

In the law of State responsibility, necessity precludes the wrongfulness of a breach of an international obligation if the conduct in question is 'the only way for the State to safeguard an essential interest against a grave and imminent peril'. According to Special Rapporteur Gaja:

> While a State may be considered as entitled to protect an essential interest that is either its own or of the international community, the scope of interests for which an international organization may invoke necessity cannot be as wide. One cannot assimilate, for instance, the State's interest in surviving with that of an international organization in not being extinguished. Nor are international organizations in the same position as States with regard to the protection of essential interests of the international community.[85]

The Commission ended up accepting the position taken by the Special Rapporteur. As a result, Article 25 ARIO contains an important limitation on the right of international organizations to invoke necessity: they may not rely on the defence to safeguard their own interests, but only those of their members or the international community as a whole. While debate on this issue was not extensive, a few members were sceptical that this departure from Article 25 ARS was persuasive. As Paula Escarameia pointed out, a comparison between States and international organizations could in fact lead to the opposite conclusion: it is often the case that interests protected by certain organizations are 'more important' and 'have far wider implications in terms of international affairs' than the

---

[83] Far an exhaustive study: F. Paddeu, *Justification and Excuse in International Law* (Cambridge: Cambridge University Press, 2018), pp. 334–429.
[84] Compare *Gabčíkovo-Nagymaros Project (Hungary/Slovakia)* [1997] ICJ Rep 7, paras. 40–41 with *Rainbow Warrior (New Zealand v. France)* (1990) 20 RIAA 217, 254. This question is not yet completely settled: Paddeu, *ustification and Excuse*, p. 414.
[85] Gaja (Fourth Report), YILC 2006/II, part one, p. 112, para. 41.

interests of States.[86] Another member noted that the interests of both categories of legal subjects would be at least 'comparable', especially when an organization is 'charged with the governance of a territory and the protection of the lives and welfare of its population'.[87]

Revealing the normative concerns at stake, the commentary to Article 25 ARIO justifies the departure from the ARS on policy grounds:

> the scarcity of practice and the considerable risk that invocability of necessity entails for compliance with international obligations suggest that, as a matter of policy, necessity should not be invocable by international organizations as widely as by States.[88]

Thus, the ground for contestation animating the departure from the analogy was a policy argument in favour of restricting the right to rely on necessity as a circumstance precluding wrongfulness. If the ILC's position is well received in the practice of States and the case of international courts and tribunals, it will provide a neat example of a departure from the analogy as a result of normative contestation.[89]

7.2.4   Invocation of Responsibility by an 'Interested Organization'

Article 49 ARIO was modelled upon Article 48 ARS and deals with the question of invocation of responsibility by a State or international organization other than the injured State or international organization. Article 48(1)(b) ARS recognises the legal interest of all States to invoke responsibility in cases where the obligation breached is owed to the international community as a whole. In contrast, Article 49(3) ARIO contains an additional requirement, namely that an international organization may only invoke responsibility 'if safeguarding the interest of the international community as a whole underlying the obligation breached is within [its] functions.

---

[86] Escarameia, YILC 2006/I, p. 66, para. 8.

[87] Matheson, ibid., p. 72, para. 33. Likewise, Michael Wood argued that 'there was no reason to subject an international organization's right to invoke necessity to conditions different from those that applied to States' and suggested that the provision be aligned with art. 25 ARS: A/CN.4/SR.3084 (2011), p. 5.

[88] Commentary to art. 25, YILC 2011/II, part two, p. 75, para. 4. The commentary further describes the approach as a 'compromise' between 'the view of those who favour placing international organizations on the same level as States and the opinion of those who would totally rule out the invocability of necessity by international organization'.

[89] E.g., Economides, YILC 2006/I, p. 81, para. 3.

This additional requirement, which comes across as a throwback to the principle of speciality,[90] was inserted to reflect the opinion that a number of States had voiced in the Sixth Committee of the UN General Assembly.[91] As Germany noted in a comment on the draft, 'it appears to be too far-reaching to grant [such] an entitlement to all international organizations, regardless of the functions entrusted to them by their members', for, 'unlike States, international organizations do not have general legal competence but only functional competencies limited to the performance of their respective mandates and purposes'.[92] The debate thus echoes that concerning proposals to change the regimes of reservations and countermeasures, the difference being that normative contestation here came from the political front. Referring to the functions of international organizations in its draft was a way for the Commission to impress upon States that differences between the two categories of subjects were being taken seriously, and thereby make the end product of its work more palatable from a political point of view.

What the legal consequences of the limitation found in Article 49(3) ARIO are is less clear. Can a third party challenge an organization's standing by relying on the fact that the organization does not have the function of safeguarding an interest of the international community? This solution would stand at odds with the system established by the ARIO, and one may question whether having the limitation in place is a price worth paying to assuage States of a political concern that ultimately does not stand scrutiny.

7.3 Concluding Remarks

The more the analogy between States and international organizations results in increasingly specific prescriptions, the greater the incentives

---

[90] See Section 4.3.

[91] Gaja (Sixth Report), YILC 2008/II, part one, p. 24, para. 36. The Commission did not doubt that IOs should have that legal interest. Confronted with a suggestion to limit the provision further by making it applicable only to IOs of a universal character, the Special Rapporteur argued that 'since a State could individually invoke responsibility for the same breach, it seems more coherent to accept that even a small number of States could establish an international organization that includes among its functions the protection of the general interest underlying the obligations and that the same organization could do what the States are entitled to do individually': Gaja (Seventh Report), YILC 2009/II, part one, p. 93, para. 109.

[92] Germany, A/CN.4/636 (2011), p. 30.

for normative contestation by States, organizations and members of the international legal profession become. This is particularly noticeable when one looks at discussions surrounding polemical 'primary rules' (such as the right to self-defence) and polemical 'secondary rules' (such as necessity and countermeasures). Revisiting the rules that apply to States for the purpose of the analogical exercise invites reflection not only on the plausibility of the analogy but also on the appropriateness of the original rules themselves. The examples discussed in this chapter show that departures from the analogy have been proposed and justified on the basis not only of perceived differences between States and international organizations as original/primary and derivative/secondary subjects but also on normative anxieties relating to the potential effects of widening the scope of certain rules of international law that have been contested also for States.

On the one hand, the cases here considered show that normative contestation does not necessarily lead to desirable results: it may rather lead to the drawing of arbitrary distinctions between States and international organizations. One should resist uncritical notions of what 'sovereignty' entails, and bear in mind that the fact that a rule of international law – whether 'primary' or 'secondary' – raises concerns is not in itself a reason not to extend it to international organization. This is why the ILC's work on reservations and (for the most part) countermeasures ended where it started. Taking those detours and engaging with various grounds for normative contestation persuaded the Commission of the wisdom of embracing the analogy. Be that as it may, those detours suggest that political acceptance or contestation of the analogy is bound to have a central role in how the law of international organizations will coalesce. The field of immunities presents the clearest illustration: if judgments by domestic courts denying immunity under custom to international organizations and their agents accumulate and converge over time, that will give rise to a customary rule that expressly departs from the position adopted for States.

While there is a risk that certain departures may not be principled, normative contestation may serve a constructive purpose. By emphasising a relevant similarity between the situations being compared, analogical reasoning sometimes disregards relevant differences. Whenever analogy is used not incrementally but rather as a general method (the possibility explored in the present study) it runs the risk of becoming a blunt instrument. What has been missing from the debates surveyed in this chapter, alas, is contestation grounded on a sophisticated conception of what international organizations are or should be, capable of generating practical solutions that remain coherent with the foundations of the international legal system. But normative contestation that elevates the current system and promotes progressive values and visions should be embraced rather than feared.

～

Conclusion

Drawing the Threads Together

In carrying out the projects that culminated in the adoption of the 1986 Vienna Convention on the Law of Treaties between States and International Organizations and the 2011 Articles on the Responsibility of International Organizations for Internationally Wrongful Acts, the International Law Commission extended to international organizations rules that had been originally envisaged for States. The Commission either viewed the two categories of international legal subjects as falling under common principles, or saw 'little' or 'no reason' to distinguish between them. While this insight was never properly articulated nor embraced by the Commission, it provides the clearest illustration that the development of the public international law of international organizations has been marked by an analogy between States and international organizations.

In this study, I have investigated how analogical reasoning can help us approach the question of the application of general international law to international organizations as we wait for practice and precedent in this area to develop. Because analogical reasoning is an application of the requirement that like cases be treated alike, it justifies extending the rules in a legal system to novel situations with which they share a relevant similarity. Reasoning by analogy is not to be conflated with arguments about the existence of customary rules as traditionally understood, that is, it is not a substitute for general practice accompanied by a sense of legal obligation. But it provides, in its own context and on its own terms, a justification for making propositions about the content of the law in situations of uncertainty. This is why neither the ILC projects on treaties and responsibility nor other attempts to extend rules from States to international organizations should be dismissed, without more, as *de lege ferenda* or 'progressive development' of the law.

The justifying power of analogical reasoning depends on a judgement as to the 'relevant similarity' between the situation covered by the rule and the situation to which the rule is being extended. Thus, the authoritativeness of the analogy between States and international organizations depends on the plausibility of the comparison between the two categories of international legal subjects. For that comparison to even become possible, one must take a position on a question which the ILC and several commentators have long evaded: the status of international organizations under international law. If international organizations are conceptualised as a category of legal subjects under customary international law, it is possible to compare them with the category of entities possessing statehood. If instead they are viewed as corporate entities existing only for and among the parties to their constituent instruments as a matter of the law of treaties, it follows that each organization is unique in the eyes of general international law and that no comparison between them and States *qua* categories of legal subjects is possible. While taking a position on the status of inter-national organization under international law is no easy task – one would be hard-pressed to make categorical claims about what the accepted structural norms that define membership in the international community are – I argued that the conception that offers the best rationalisation of existing principle and practice is that of international organizations as legal subjects under general international law. The 'subject conception' makes sense of interactions between organizations and third parties, is represented in contemporary commentary on international organizations and the more recent work of the ILC, and finds support in the jurisprudence of the International Court of Justice. It appears that the legal profession is coming to terms with the fact that the emergence of international organizations has brought about a genuine structural change in the international legal system and is more open to accepting that an 'international rule of incorporation' is starting to take shape.

Once international organizations are conceptualised as international legal subjects, the analogy becomes persuasive if it can be shown that as a category they share a 'relevant similarity' with States that justifies extending to them rules of general international law. Because intergov-ernmental institutions are set up in a way that places them outside the jurisdiction of any individual State, they are legally autonomous from their members, just as States are legally autonomous from each other. Moreover, like States, international organizations do not only operate on an institutional plane, but also on the international plane where general international law applies. As a result, rules that establish rights, obligations and capacities for the legally autonomous subject *par excellence* – the State – can be plausibly extended to international organizations by analogy. The rationale explaining – and providing the normative justification for – this view is that States are free to act collectively through international organizations but may not contract out of the international legal system in doing so.

Of course, even if international organizations are viewed as a category of legal subjects operating on the international plane, differences that they bear in relation to States can have the effect of rebutting the analogy on a case-by-case basis. For one, there are certain structural differences between the categories requiring adjustments to the rules originally devised for States. Moreover, there are two lines of argument in international legal discourse that oppose the analogy. First, there is the 'principle of speciality', according to which international organizations are a diverse group of entities with limited competences to be contrasted with States, the bearers of the 'totality of international rights and obligations'. Second, it can be argued that international organizations are 'layered subjects' of international law: created and composed by States, they should not be viewed as unitary entities in the same way as States are.

Arguments on speciality were rehashed at the ILC, the Sixth Committee of the UN General Assembly and the 1986 Vienna Conference on the Law of Treaties over and over again. That international organizations are 'derivative subjects' of international law to be contrasted with States led the Commission to adopt a circumspect approach to the role of their practice in the formation of rules of customary international law and *jus cogens*. Yet, other arguments on speciality were for the most part defeated, and for good reason. Speciality accurately describes differences between States and international organizations and differences between international organizations themselves when one takes the standpoint of the internal architecture of each particular organization. But it fails to generate prescriptions affecting the comparison between the two categories of legal subjects on the international plane. Integrating constitutional limitations on the powers of international organizations into general international law would require legal regimes that apply on the international plane to enforce rules originating from the institutional plane. If this were the case, third parties would be allowed to rely on those rules. The problems posed by that solution became clear in the debates leading to the codification of the law of treaties and responsibility. Making the rules of the organization relevant, without more, for the external relations of international organizations would defeat the goals of stability and accountability that the law of treaties and the law of responsibility seek to promote.

The question of whether international organizations should be treated as unitary entities as opposed to 'layered subjects' is fundamental because it bears upon the position of international organizations and their members vis-à-vis each other's treaty obligations and responsibility for wrongful acts. Whether international organizations are seen as 'transparent' or 'opaque' from the standpoint of general international law determines the outer bounds of the right that States have to establish new subjects of international law. I argued that viewing an international organization as a legally autonomous entity operating on the international plane does not entail that its obligations and responsibility must be kept separate from those of its members. It can be plausibly maintained that when States take collective action through a corporate body, they should act as guarantor of obligations acquired by that body and incur responsibility – whether joint and severally or on a subsidiary basis – for its wrongful acts. This view would promote coherence in the international legal system, as States would not be entitled to circumvent their obligations and responsibility by establishing corporate entities. And yet, an analogy between States and international organizations with regard to the *pacta tertii* rule and the principle of independent responsibility was pursued at the ILC and the 1986 Vienna Conference because that was clearly the solution that States and international organizations themselves favoured in the exchanges that those codification projects facilitated. For better or for worse, keeping international organizations and their members separate is a policy solution justified by the desirability of facilitating collective action and protecting organizations from undue interference by members and, as such, it carried the day. That said, provisions such as Articles 17, 40 and 61 ARIO ensure that some of the normative anxieties arising from taking the analogy too far are not left unaddressed. Those provisions place limits on the use of the organization's separate personality and point to the need for enabling international organizations to fulfil their obligations.

In short, save as it concerns basic structural differences, international law-making and the 'layered subjects objection', the analogy between States and international organizations is for the most part plausible. But the analogy only works on the international plane, when the argument is made at the level of the external relations that international organizations maintain with their members or third parties. Whenever one considers the relations between organizations and members taking place within the institutional framework established by constituent instruments and other internal rules, neither the organization nor its members can be regarded as 'legally autonomous entities operating on the international plane' any longer. Instead, in that ambit they are entities linked by organic bonds that operate under the 'internal' legal system of the organization. This is thus the point where the analogy breaks down and the boundaries of general international law have to be delineated. This is also the context in which the principle of speciality finds its true application, as each international organization is unique in the extent and character of their goals and competences on the institutional plane. While there may be good reasons to adopt a monistic presumption for the applicability of general international law on the institutional plane, the general law can only be incorporated insofar as it is compatible with – and usefully complements – the rules of the organizations.

Another limit to the analogy between States and international organizations is posed by the context of normative contestation in which prescriptions deriving from the analogy are made, tested, adopted and opposed in a legal order whose backbone remains customary. Different worldviews as to what international organizations are or ought to be provide a filter for the reception and consolidation of analogical solutions in the practice of the relevant stakeholders. There is a risk that some forms of normative contestation – overplaying visions of international organizations as 'derivative' subjects of international law – may create more problems than they solve, as seen, for example, in the debates on the law of immunities and some questionable restrictions adopted by the ILC to the rules on the defence of necessity, invocation of responsibility and countermeasures. But normative contestation also adds dynamism to law-making processes and may be the source of some desirable future developments in the law of international organizations.

Analogy, the ILC and the Future of the Law of International Organizations

It is fitting to conclude a study on the analogy between States and international organizations with a few reflections on the significance of the two endeavours in which that idea was most prominently given concrete form: VCLT 1986 and the ARIO. If the analysis sketched here is plausible, the bulk of the work of the ILC on treaties and responsibility can be better understood and, to an extent, defended. This does not mean, however, that the ILC can escape criticism. To the present author, some of the innovations proposed by the Commission miss the mark, and the Commission's ambivalence as to the distinction between the international plane and the institutional plane is misleading and objectionable. The fact that the 1986 Vienna Conference was unable to agree on a rule on acceptance by member States of rights and obligations provided in treaties concluded by international organizations is a frustrating example of the analogy being taken too far and left unmitigated. And then there was the Commission's failure to provide a richer methodological justification for the approach that it took in its codification projects. Behind the analogical method lies an intricate series of arguments that raise many questions that the projects on treaty and responsibility did not address. It is regrettable that the Commission not only failed to explore how the systemic reasoning that justifies its intuition may enhance the authoritativeness of its projects, but also engaged in self-sabotage by evasively stating that the ARIO lean towards 'progressive development'.

But the important normative question to ponder is what is gained and what is lost when analogy is resorted to, especially in the context of the codification and progressive development of international law. Is it normatively desirable that international organizations be assimilated to States? Are instruments such as VCLT 1986 and the ARIO relevant and helpful? A main objection to the type of work done by the ILC is that topics that have not attracted sufficient practice and precedent are simply not suitable for codification. Should the ILC have waited for more practice to emerge before embarking on the codification of the law of treaties and responsibility of international organizations?

By carrying out those projects, the ILC has brought to the fore legal questions that States and organizations often fail to prioritise – a state of affairs which is only made worse by the sparse participation of international organizations in dispute settlement mechanisms. Putting a legal framework in place, the Commission has created an incentive for general international law to be applied to international organizations. Moreover, as the Netherlands noted with regard to the ARIO, there is a value in filling the gaps through the 'open and multilateral process' of codification and progressive development under the United Nations. The alternative was to have the same done, in an 'ad hoc and improvised manner', by members of the legal profession turning to VCLT 1969 and the ARS for guidance whenever an issue involving the rights, obligations and capacities of international organizations under the general law arose.[1] And if there is one criticism to the ILC that comes across as unfair when one surveys the history of VCLT 1986 and the ARIO is that the Commission did not try to take the 'special characteristics' of international organizations into account. One often sees the Commission and its Special Rapporteurs striving to find principled bases for distinguishing between States and international organizations – doing their best to leave their mark and show that they were not trading on past glories – but finding themselves ultimately unable to uphold distinctions that did not prove persuasive.

I suggest that any effort to develop the law of international organizations by analogy with the law of States is justifiable insofar as it is seen as a starting point rather than a finishing line. Generally speaking, the 1986 Vienna Convention and the 2011 Articles provide ingenious snapshots of the most plausible version of the content of the general law of treaties and responsibility of international organizations at present. They fill, on a provisional basis, the formidable gap that was created with the emergence of that still relatively new category of entities on the international plane. If it so happens that practice and precedent come to contradict rules formulated on the basis of analogy, the Commission's effort will still have been worthwhile as a step in a larger process. In many respects, it should be noted, innovation through developments in international practice would be desirable. For example, the radical separation between the obligations and responsibility of organizations and members – a case in which the analogy was taken too far – may lead to objectionable results. Over time, and through normative contestation, general international law should establish further limits to the right of States to set up and act through international organizations, fashioning a rule of incorporation that is more detailed and better calibrated. Principled contestation should be embraced, not resisted.

In conclusion, those first steps that the ILC has taken towards the elucidation of the general rules that apply to the treaties and responsibility of international organizations constitute a valuable contribution to reducing uncertainty and consolidating the image of international

[1] Netherlands, A/CN.4/636/Add.1 (2011), p. 6. As Catherine Brölmann noted as regards VCLT 1986, 'the codification of the law of treaties for organizations became a conscientious exploration of the legal nature of organisations and of the limits of the law of treaties system', providing a 'valuable record of theoretical and doctrinal development': *The Institutional Veil*, pp. 261–62.

organizations as entities fully integrated into the international legal system. They show how legal reasoning can be employed by institutions and the legal profession to advance the law in a radically decentralised legal system: rooted in custom and devoid of courts with compulsory jurisdiction, international law is a fertile ground for reasoning by principle and reasoning by analogy to play their gap-filling role. It is hoped that endeavours such as the 1986 Vienna Convention and the 2011 Articles on the Responsibility of International Organizations will lay the foundations for further development, leading to the emergence of more sophisticated rules for these remarkable institutions that, comprising the full spectrum that ranges from public law agencies to private law companies, have forever transformed international cooperation.

Abi-Saab, G. 'La Commission du Droit International, la codification et le processus de formation de droit international' in United Nations, *Making Better International Law: Proceedings of the United Nations Colloquium on Progressive Development and Codification of International Law* (1998)

Ahlborn, C. 'The rules of international organizations and the law of international responsibility' (2012) 8 *IOLR* 397

Akande, D. 'International organizations' in M. Evans (ed.), *International Law*, 4th edn (Oxford: Oxford University Press, 2014)

Alexy, R. *A Theory of Legal Argumentation* (Oxford: Oxford University Press, 1989)

Alland, D. 'The definition of countermeasures' in J. Crawford, A. Pellet and S. Oleson (eds.), *The Law of International Responsibility* (Oxford: Oxford University Press 2009)

Alvarez, J. 'Book review: international organisations and their exercise of sovereign powers' (2007) 101 *AJIL* 674

International Organizations as Law-Makers (Oxford: Oxford University Press, 2005)

Amerasinghe, C. F. *Principles of the Institutional Law of International Organizations*, 2nd edn (Cambridge: Cambridge University Press, 2005)

'International legal personality revisited' (1995) 47 *Austrian Journal of Public and International Law* 123

'Liability to third parties of member states of international organizations: practice, principle and judicial precedent' (1991) 85 *AJIL* 259

Arangio-Ruiz, G. 'International law and interindividual law' in J. Nijman and A. Nollkaemper (eds.), *New Perspectives on the Divide between National and International Law* (Oxford: Oxford University Press, 2007)

Bankowski, Z. 'Analogical reasoning and legal institutions' in P. Nerhot (ed.), *Legal Knowledge and Analogy: Fragments of Legal Epistemology, Hermeneutics and Linguistics* (Dordrecht: Kluwer, 1991)

Beaulac, S. 'An inquiry into the international rule of law' (2007), EUI Max Weber Programme Series, Working Paper No. 2007/14 <http://cadmus.eui.eu/handle/1814/6957> accessed 11 Feb 2017

Benvenisti, E. 'The law of global governance' (2014) 368 RdC 47

Berman, F. 'The ILC within the UN's legal framework: its relationship with the Sixth Committee' (2007) 49 GYIL 107

Besson, S. 'Theorizing the sources of international law' in S. Besson and J. Tasioulas (eds.), The Philosophy of International Law (Oxford: Oxford University Press, 2010)

Bianchi, A. 'Epistemic communities' in J. D'Aspremont and S. Singh, (eds.), Concepts for International Law (forthcoming with Edward Elgar, 2018)

Bingham, T. The Rule of Law (Penguin Books, 2011)

Blix, H. M. 'Contemporary aspects of recognition' (1970) 120 RdC 587

Blokker, N. 'International organizations and customary international law: is the international law commission taking international organizations seriously?' (2017) 14 IOLR 1

'Member State responsibility for wrongdoings of international organizations: beacon of hope or delusion?' (2015) 12 IOLR 319

'Preparing articles on responsibility of international organizations: does the International Law Commission take international organizations seriously? A mid-term review' in J. Klabbers and A. Wallendahl (eds.), Research Handbook on the Law of International Organizations (Cheltenham: Edward Elgar, 2011)

Bodansky, D. 'Non liquet and the incompleteness of international law' in B. Charzournes and P. Sands (eds.), International law, the International Court of Justice and Nuclear Weapons (Cambridge: Cambridge University Press, 1999)

Bogdandy, A., Damm, P. and Goldmann, M., 'Developing the publicness of public international law: towards a legal framework for global governance activities' in A. von Bogdandy and others (eds.), The Exercise of Public Authority by International Institutions (Heidelberg: Springer, 2010)

Bordin, F .L. 'Reflections of customary international law: the authority of codification conventions and ILC draft articles in international law' (2014) 63 ICLQ 535

'Continuation of membership in the United Nations revisited: lessons from fifteen years of inconsistency in the jurisprudence of the ICJ' (2011) 10 The Law and Practice of International Courts and Tribunals 315

Bothe, M. 'The WHO request' in B. Charzournes and P. Sands (eds.), International law, the International Court of Justice and Nuclear Weapons (Cambridge: Cambridge University Press, 1999)

Brewer, S. 'Exemplary reasoning: semantics, pragmatics, and the rational force of legal argument by analogy' (1996) 109 HLR 923

Brölmann, C. The Institutional Veil in Public International Law: International Organizations and the Law of Treaties (Oxford: Hart, 2005)

'The 1986 Vienna Convention on the Law of Treaties: the history of draft article 36bis' in J. Klabbers (ed.), Essays on the Law of Treaties (The Hague: Nijhoff, 1996)

'Member states and international legal responsibility: developments of the institutional veil' (2015) 12 *IOLR* 358

Brownlie, I. 'The responsibility of states for the acts of international organisations' in M. Ragazzi (ed.), *International Responsibility Today: Essays in Memory of Oscar Schachter* (Leiden: Nijhoff, 2005)

Burton, J. W. *World Society* (Cambridge: Cambridge University Press, 1972)

Byers, M. 'Abuse of rights: an old principle, a new age' (2002) 47 *McGill Law Journal* 339

Cahier, P. 'Le droit interne des organisations internationales' (1963) 67 *RGDIP* 563

Canaris, K. W. *Systemdenken und Systembegriff in der Jurisprudenz: Entwickelt am Beispiel des deutschen Privatrechts* (Berlin: Duncker und Humblot, 1983)

Cançado Trindade, A. A. *The Access of Individuals to International Justice* (Oxford: Oxford University Press, 2012)

Cassese, A. *International Law*, 2nd edn (Oxford: Oxford University Press, 2005)

Charney, J. 'Universal international law' (1993) 87 *AJIL* 529

Chinkin, C. *Third Parties in International Law* (Oxford: Oxford University Press, 1993)

Crawford, J. (ed.). *Brownlie's Principles of Public International Law*, 8th edn (Oxford: Oxford University Press, 2012)

Crawford, J. 'Chance, order, change: the course of international law' (2013) 365 *RdC* 13

State Responsibility: General Part (Cambridge: Cambridge University Press, 2013)

'Sovereignty as a legal value' in J. Crawford and M. Koskenniemi (eds.), *Cambridge Companion of International Law* (Cambridge: Cambridge, 2012)

The Creation of States in International Law, 2nd edn (Oxford: Oxford University Press, 2006)

The International Law Commission's Articles on State Responsibility (Cambridge: Cambridge University Press, 2002)

d'Aspremont, J. 'Abuse of legal personality of international organizations and the responsibility of member States' (2007) *IOLR* 91

d'Aspremont, J. and Dopagne, F. '*Kadi*: The ECJ's reminder of the elementary divide between legal orders' (2008) 5 *IOLR* 371

Daillier, P., Forteau, M. and Pellet, A. *Droit International Public*, 8th edn (Paris: LGDJ, 2009)

Dannenbaum, T. 'Dual attribution in the context of military operations' (2015) 12 *IOLR* 401

Daugirdas, K. 'How and why international law binds international organizations' (2016) 57 *Harvard International Law Journal* 325

David, E. 'Article 34' in O. Corten and P. Klein, (eds.), *The Vienna Conventions on the Law of Treaties. A Commentary*, v. II (Oxford: Oxford University Press, 2011)

Dictionnaire de la terminologie du droit international (Paris: Sirey, 1960)

Dugard, J. 'The secession of states and their recognition in the wake of Kosovo' (2013) 375 *RdC* 9

'How effective is the International Law Commission in the development of international law? A critique of the ILC on the occasion of its fiftieth anniversary' (1998) 23 *South African Journal of International Law* 33

Dupuy, R. J. 'Coutume sage et coutume sauvage' in S. Bastid, (ed.), *Mélanges Offerts à Charles Rousseau: La Communauté Internationale* (Paris: Pedone, 1974)

Dworkin, R. *Law's Empire* (Cambridge: Harvard University Press, 1986)

Engisch, K. *Einführung in das juristische Denken*, 2nd edn (Stuttgart: Kohlhammer, 1959)

Facsaneanu, L. 'Le droit interne de l'Organisation des Nations Unies' (1957) III *Annuaire Français de Droit International* 319

Feldman, D. 'Monism, dualism and constitutional legitimacy' (1999) 20 *Australian Year Book of International Law* 105

Fennessy, J. G. 'The 1975 Vienna Convention on the Representation of States in their Relations with International Organizations of a Universal Character' (1976) 70 *AJIL* 62

Finnis, J. *Natural Law and Natural Rights*, 2nd edn (Oxford: Oxford University Press, 2011)

Fitzmaurice, G. 'The general principles of international law considered from the standpoint of the rule of law' (1957) 92 *RdC* 1

Forni, F. 'Diplomatic protection in EU law: what's new under the sun?' (2014) 9 *The Hague Journal of Diplomacy* 150

Franck, T. *The Power of Legitimacy among Nations* (New York: Oxford University Press, 1990)

Fry, J. 'Assumption of Responsibility' in A. Nollkaemper and I. Plakokefalor (eds.), *Principles of Shared Responsibility in International Law: An Appraisal of the State of the Art* (Cambridge: Cambridge University Press, 2014)

Fuller, L. *The Morality of Law* (New Haven: Yale University Press, 1964)

Gaillard, E. and Pingel-Lenuzza, I. 'International organisations and immunity from jurisdiction: to restrict or to bypass' (2002) 51 *ICLQ* 1

Gaja, G. 'A "new" Vienna Convention on Treaties between States and International Organizations or between International Organizations: a critical commentary' (1988) *BYIL* 253

Geslin, A. 'Réflexions sur la repartition de la responsabilité entre l'organisation internationale et ses etats membres' (2005) 109 *RGDIP* 539

Glenn, H. P. *Legal Traditions of the World*, 4th edn (Oxford: Oxford University Press, 2010)

Glick, R. 'Lip service to the laws of war: humanitarian law and United Nations armed forces' (1995–96) 17 *Michigan Journal of International Law* 53

Goldsmith, J. and Levinson, D. 'Law for States: international law, constitutional law, public law' (2009) 122 *HLR* 1791

Hafner, G. 'Is the topic of responsibility of international organizations ripe for codification? Some critical remarks' in U. Fastenrath and others (eds.), *From Bilateralism to Community Interest* (Oxford: Oxford University Press, 2011)

Hahn, H .J. 'Euratom: The Conception of an International Personality' (1958) 71 *HLR* 1001

Hart, H. L. A. *The Concept of Law*, 2nd edn (Oxford: Clarendon Press, 1997)

Hartmann, G. 'The capacity of international organizations to conclude treaties' in K. Zemanek (ed.), *Agreements of International Organizations and the Vienna Convention on the Law of Treaties* (Vienna: Springer, 1971)

Hernández, G. *The International Court of Justice and the Judicial Function* (Oxford: Oxford University Press, 2014)

Hirsch, M. *The Responsibility of International Organizations towards Third Parties: Some Principles* (Dordrecht: Nijhoff, 1995)

Hoffmeister, F. 'Litigating against the European Union and its member States: who responds under the ILC's draft articles on international responsibility of international organizations?' (2010) 21 *EJIL* 723

Holmes, O. W. 'The path of law' (1987) 10 *HLR* 457

Jenks, C. W. 'International legal personality of international organizations' (1945) 22 *BYIL* 267

International Immunities (London: Stevens, 1961)

Jennings, R. 'Foreword' in P. Bekker, *The Legal Position of Intergovernmental Organizations: A Functional Necessity Analysis of Their Legal Status and Immunities* (Dordrecht: Nijhoff, 1994)

Kammerhofer, G. 'Gaps, the "Nuclear Weapons" advisory opinion and the structure of international legal argument between theory and practice' (2009) 80 *BYIL* 333

'Uncertainty in the formal sources of international law: customary international law and some of its problems' (2004) 15 *EJIL* 523

Kelsen, H. *Principles of International Law* (New York: Holt, 1967)

Pure Theory of Law (Berkeley: University of California Press, 1967)

General Theory of Law and State (Cambridge: Harvard University Press, 1945)

'Recognition in international law: theoretical observations' (1941) 35 *AJIL* 605

Kennedy, D. *A Critique of Adjudication: {fin de siècle}* (Cambridge: Harvard University Press, 1997)

Kingsbury, B. 'Sovereignty and inequality' (1998) 9 *EJIL* 599

'The International Legal Order' in P. Cane and M. Tushnet (eds.), *Oxford Handbook of Legal Studies* (Oxford: Oxford University Press, 2003)

Kingsbury, B. and Donaldson, M. 'From bilateralism to publicness in international law' in U. Fastenrath and others (eds.), *From Bilateralism to Community Interest* (Oxford: Oxford University Press, 2011)

Kingsbury, B., Krisch, N. and Stewart, R. 'The emergence of global administrative law' (2005) 68 *Law and Contemporary Problems* 15

Klabbers, J. 'Sources of international organizations' law: reflections on accountability' in J. d'Aspremont and S. Besson (eds.), *The Oxford Handbook on the Sources of International Law* (Oxford: Oxford University Press, 2017)

An Introduction to International Organizations Law, 3rd edn (Cambridge: Cambridge University Press, 2015)

'The transformation of international organizations law' (2015) *EJIL* 9

'Unity, diversity, accountability: the ambivalent concept of international organisation' (2013) 14 *Melbourne Journal of International Law* 1

'Global governance before the ICJ: re-reading the WHA opinion' (2009) *Max-Planck Yearbook of United Nations Law*

'On Seyersted and his *Common Law of International Organizations*' (2008) 5 *IOLR* 381

'The paradox of international institutional law' (2008) 5 *IOLR* 151

'The life and times of the law of international organizations' (2001) 70 *Nordic Journal of International Law* 287

'Presumptive personality: the European Union in international law' in M. Koskenniemi (ed.), *International Law Aspects of the European Union* (The Hague: Kluwer, 1998)

Klein, P. *La Responsabilité des Organisations Internationales dans les Ordres Juridiques Internes et en Droit des Gens* (Brussels: Bruylant, 1998)

Kohen, M. and Heathcote, S. 'Article 42' in O. Corten and P. Klein (eds.), *The Vienna Conventions on the Law of Treaties: A Commentary*, v. II (Oxford: Oxford University Press, 2011)

Kolb, R. *La Bonne Foi en Droit International Public: Contribution à l'Étude des Principes Généraux de Droit* (Paris: Pr Univ de France, 2000)

Koskenniemi, M. *From Apology to Utopia: The Structure of International Legal Argument* (Cambridge: Cambridge University Press, 2005)

Ladeur, K. H. 'The analogy between logic and dialogic of law' in P. Nerhot (ed.), *Legal Knowledge and Analogy: Fragments of Legal Epistemology, Hermeneutics and Linguistics* (Dordrecht: Kluwer, 1991)

Larenz, K. and Canaris, C. W. *Methodenlehre der Rechtswissenschaft*, 3rd edn (Berlin: Springer, 1996)

Lauterpacht, E. 'Judicial review of acts of international organizations' in L. B. Chazournes and P. Sands (eds.), *International Law, the International Court of Justice and Nuclear Weapons* (Cambridge: Cambridge University Press, 1999)

Lauterpacht, H. 'Some observations on the prohibition of "*non liquet*" and the completeness of the law' in E. Lauterpacht (ed.), *International Law* (Cambridge: Cambridge University Press 1970–2004)

The Development of International Law by the International Court (London: Stevens, 1958)

Private Law Sources and Analogies of International Law (Archon Books, 1937)

The Function of Law in the International Community (Oxford: Clarendon Press, 1933)

Lefkowitz, D. '(Dis)solving the chronological paradox in customary international law: a Hartian approach' (2008) 21 *Canadian Journal of Law and Jurisprudence* 129

MacCormick, N. *Legal Reasoning and Legal Theory* (Oxford: Clarendon Press, 1978)

Rhetoric and the Rule of Law: A Theory of Legal Reasoning (Oxford: Oxford University Press, 2005)

Massineo, F. 'Attribution of conduct' in A. Nollkaemper and I. Plakokefalor (eds.), *Principles of Shared Responsibility in International Law: An Appraisal of the State of the Art* (Cambridge: Cambridge University Press, 2014)

McCorquodale, R. 'Defining the international rule of law: defying gravity?' (2016) 65 *ICLQ* 277

Mendelson, M. 'The definition of "international organization" in the international law commission's current project on the responsibility of international organizations' in M. Ragazzi (ed.), *International Responsibility Today* (Leiden: Martinus Nijhoff, 2005)

Morgenstern, F. *Legal Problems of International Organizations* (Cambridge: Grotius, 1986)

Mosler, H. 'Réflexions sur la personnalité juridique en droit international public' in Baugniet, (ed.), *Mélanges Offerts à Henri Rolin* (Paris: Pedone, 1964)

Murphy, S. 'Codification, progressive development, or scholarly analysis? The art of packaging the ILC's work product' in M. Ragazzi (ed.), *The Responsibility of International Organizations: Essays in Memory of Sir Ian Brownlie* (Leiden: Nijhoff, 2013)

Murray, O. 'Piercing the corporate veil: the responsibility of member states of an international organization' (2011) *IOLR* 291

Neff, S. 'In search of clarity: *non liquet* and international law' in K. Homi and M. Bohlander (eds.), *International Law and Power: Perspectives on Legal Order and Justice* (Leiden: Nijhoff, 2009)

Nollkaemper, A. 'Dual attribution: liability of the Netherlands for conduct of Dutchbat in Srebrenica' (2011) 9 *Journal of International Criminal Law* 1143

O'Keefe, R. 'The doctrine of incorporation revisited' (2008) 79 *BYIL* 7

Odermatt, J. 'The development of customary international law by international organizations' (2017) 66 *ICLQ* 491

Oppenheim, L. 'Le caractère essential de la Société des Nations' (1919) 26 *RGDIP* 234

Orakhelashvili, A. 'Responsibility and immunities: similarities and differences between international organizations and States' (2014) 11 *IOLR* 114

Peremptory Norms in International Law (Oxford: Oxford University Press, 2006)

Orzan, M. 'International organizations and immunity from legal process: an uncertain evolution' in R. Virzo and I. Ingravallo (eds.), *Evolutions in the Law of International Organizations* (Leiden: Nijhoff, 2015)

Paasivirta, E. 'Responsibility of a member state of an international organization: where will it end? (2010) 7 *IOLR* 49

Paasivirta, E. and Kuijper, P. J. 'Does one size fit all?: the European Community and the responsibility of international organizations' (2007) 36 *Netherlands Yearbook of International Law* 169

Paddeu, F. *Justification and Excuse in International Law* (Cambridge: Cambridge University Press, 2018)

Palwankar, U. 'Applicability of international humanitarian law to United Nations peace-keeping forces' (1993) 23 *International Review of the Red Cross* 227

Parlett, K. *The Individual in the International Legal System* (Cambridge: Cambridge University Press, 2011)

Paul, V. 'The abuse of rights and bona fides in international law' (1977) 28 *Österreichische Zeitschrift für öffentliches Recht und Völkerrecht* 107

Paulus, A. 'The international legal system as a constitution' in J. Dunoff, and J. Trachtman, (eds.), *Ruling the World? Constitutionalism, International Law, and Global Governance* (Cambridge: Cambridge University Press, 2009)

Pauwelyn, J. *Conflict of Norms in Public International Law: How WTO Law Relates to Other Rules of International Law* (Cambridge: Cambridge University Press, 2003)

Pellet, A. 'International organizations are definitely not States: cursory remarks on the ILC Articles on the Responsibility of International Organizations' in M. Ragazzi (ed.), *The Responsibility of International Organizations* (Leiden: Nijhoff, 2013)

'Article 19 – Convention of 1969' in O. Corten and P. Klein, (eds.), *The Vienna Conventions on the Law of Treaties: A Commentary*, v. 1 (Oxford: Oxford University Press, 2011)

'Responding to new needs through codification and progressive development' in V. Gowlland-Debbas (ed.) *Multilateral Treaty-Making: The Current Status of Challenges to and Reforms Needed in the International Legislative Process* (The Hague: Nijhoff, 1998)

Portmann, R. *Legal Personality in International Law* (Cambridge: Cambridge University Press, 2010)

Posner, R. *How Judges Think* (Cambridge: Harvard University Press, 2008)

Pronto, A. 'Reflections on the scope of application of the articles on the responsibility of international organizations' in M. Ragazzi (ed.), *Responsibility of International Organizations* (Leiden: Nijhoff, 2013)

Proulx, V. J. 'An uneasy transition? Linkages between the law of State responsibility and the law governing the responsibility of international organizations'
in M. Ragazzi (ed.), *Responsibility of International Organizations* (Leiden:
Nijhoff, 2013)

Rama-Montaldo, M. 'International legal personality and implied powers of international organizations' (1970) 44 *BYIL* 111

Rawls, J. *A Theory of Justice* (Oxford: Oxford University Press, 1999)

Raz, J. 'Legal reasons, sources and gaps' in J. Raz, (ed.) *The Authority of Law*
(Oxford: Clarendon Press, 1979)

  'The rule of law and its virtue' in J. Raz, *The Authority of Law* (Oxford:
  Clarendon Press, 1979)

Reinisch, A. 'Sources of international organizations' law: why custom and general
principles are crucial' in S. Besson and J. D'Aspremont (eds.), *The Oxford
Handbook of the Sources of International Law* (Oxford: Oxford University
Press, 2017)

  International Organizations before National Courts (Cambridge: Cambridge
  University Press, 2000)

Reuter, P. 'La Conférence de Vienne sur le Droit des Traités entre Etats et
Organisations Internationales ou entre Organisations Internationales' in F.
Capotorti and others (eds.), *Du Droit International au Droit de l'Intégration*
(Baden-Baden: Nomos, 1987)

Roberts, A. 'Clash of paradigms: actors and analogies shaping the investment
treaty system' (107) *AJIL* 45

Rosenne, S. *Developments in the Law of Treaties 1945–1986* (Cambridge: Cambridge
University Press, 1989)

Roulet, D. J. Le *Caractère Artificiel de la Théorie de l'Abus de Droit en Droit
International Public* (Neuchâtel : Ed de la Baconnière, 1958)

Ryngaert, C. 'The immunity of international organizations before domestic courts:
recent trends' (2010) 7 *IOLR*, 121

Sales, P. and Clemens, J. 'International law in domestic courts: the developing
framework' (2008) 124 *Law Quarterly Review* 388

Sarooshi, D. 'The role of domestic public law analogies in the law of international
organizations' (2008) 5 *IOLR* 237

Schachter, O. 'The invisible college of international lawyers' (1977) 72 *Northwestern University Law Review* 217

Schermers, H. 'The legal bases of international organization action' in R. J. Dupuy
(ed.), *A Handbook on International Organizations*, 2nd edn (Dordrecht:
Nijhoff, 1998)

Schermers, H. and Blokker, N. *International Institutional Law: Unity within Diversity*, 5th edn (Leiden: Nijhoff, 2011)

Schmalenbach, K. 'International organizations or institutions, general aspects'
(2006) *Max-Planck Encyclopedia of Public International Law*

Scobbie, I. 'International organizations and international relations' in R. J. Dupuy (ed.), *A Handbook on International Organizations*, 2nd edn (Dordrecht: Nijhoff, 1998)

Seidl-Hoheverden, I. *Corporations in and under International Law* (Cambridge: Grotius, 1987)

Seyersted, F. *Common Law of International Organizations* (Leiden: Nijhoff, 2008)
International personality of intergovernmental organizations: do their capacities really depend upon their constitutions?' (1964) 4 *Indian Journal of International Law* 1

Shadikhodjaev, S. and Pak, N. 'Cessation and reparation in the GATT/WTO legal system: a view from the law of State responsibility' (2007) 41 *Journal of World Trade* 1237

Shraga, D. 'UN peacekeeping operations: applicability of international humanitarian law and responsibility for operations-related damage' (2000) 94 *AJIL* 406

Simma, B. and Pulkowski, D. 'Of planets and the universe: self-contained regimes in international law' (2006) 17 *EJIL* 483

Sinclair, G. F. 'Towards a postcolonial genealogy of international organizations law' (2018) 31 *Leiden Journal of International Law*

Sinclair, I. *The International Law Commission* (Cambridge: Grotius Publications, 1987)

Siorat, L. *Le Problème des Lacunes en Droit International: Contribution à l'Étude des Sources du Droit et de la Fonction Judiciaire* (Paris: Librairie Générale de Droit et de Jurisprudence, 1958)

Slaughter, A. M. *A New World Order* (Princeton: Princeton University Press, 2008)

Sorensen, M. 'Autonomous legal orders: some considerations relating to a systems analysis of international organisations in the world legal order' (1983) 32 *ICLQ* 559

Spiermann, O. '*Lotus* and the double structure of international legal argument' in B. Charzournes and P. Sands (eds.), *International law, the International Court of Justice and Nuclear Weapons* (Cambridge: Cambridge University Press, 1999)

Stone, J. '*Non-liquet* and the function of law in the international community' (1959) 35 *BYIL* 124

Talmon, S. 'Determining customary international law: the ICJ's methodology between induction, deduction and assertion' (2015) 26 *EJIL* 417
'Responsibility of international organizations: does the European Community require special treatment?' in M. Ragazzi (ed.), *International Responsibility Today* (Leiden: Nijhoff, 2005)
'The Security Council as world legislature' (2005) 99 *AJIL* 175
'The Constitutive versus the declaratory theory of recognition: *tertium non datur?* (2004) 75 *BYIL* 101

Tamanaha, B. *On the Rule of Law: History, Politics, Theory* (Cambridge: Cambridge University Press, 2004)

Thirlway H. 'Concepts, principles, rules and analogies: international and municipal legal reasoning' (2002) 294 *RdC* 265

Tomka, P. 'Custom and the International Court of Justice' (2013) 12 *The Law and Practice of International Courts and Tribunals* 195

Tomuschat, C. 'International organizations as third parties under the law of international treaties' in Cannizzaro (ed.), *The Law of Treaties Beyond the Vienna Convention* (Oxford: Oxford University Press, 2011)

Triepel, H. 'Les rapport entre le droit interne et le droit international' (1923) 1 *RdC* 77

Tzanakopoulos, A. *Disobeying the Security Council: Countermeasures against Wrongful Sanctions* (Oxford: Oxford University Press, 2011)

Vattel, E. *The Law of Nations* (Indianapolis: Liberty Fund, 2009)

Verdirame, G. *The UN and Human Rights: Who Guards the Guardians?* (Cambridge: Cambridge University Press, 2011)

  '"The divided west": international lawyers in Europe and America' (2007) 18 *EJIL* 553

Villa, V. 'Legal analogy between interpretive arguments and productive arguments' in P. Nerhot (ed.), *Legal Knowledge and Analogy: Fragments of Legal Epistemology, Hermeneutics and Linguistics* (Dordrecht: Kluwer, 1991)

Villalpando, S. 'Codification light: a new trend in the codification of international law at the United Nations' (2013) VIII *Brazilian Yearbook of International Law* 117

Virally, M. 'Definition and classification of international organizations: a legal approach' in G. Abi-Saab (ed.), *The Concept of International Organization* (Paris: Unesco, 1981)

Waldron, J. 'Are sovereigns entitled to the benefit of the international rule of law?' (2011) 22 *EJIL* 315

  'The concept and the rule of law' (2008–2009) 43 *Georgia Law Review* 1

A. Watts and R. Jennings (eds.), *Oppenheim's International Law*, 9th edn (Harlow: Longman, 1992)

Watts, A. 'The international rule of law' (1993) 36 *GYIL* 15

Webb, P. 'Should the "2004 UN State Immunity Convention" serve as a model/ starting point for a future UN convention on the immunity of international organizations?' (2013) 10 *IOLR* 319

White, N. *The Law of International Organisations* (Manchester: Manchester University Press, 2005)

Wilde, R. 'Enhancing accountability at the international level: the tension between international organisation and member state responsibility and the underlying issues at stake' (2006) 12 *ILSA Journal of International and Comparative Law* 395

Williams, J. F. 'The legal character of the bank for international settlements' (1930) 24 *AJIL* 665

Wolff, C., *The Law of Nations Treated According to a Scientific Method* (Oxford: Clarendon Press, 1934)

Wood M., 'Do international organizations enjoy immunity under customary international law?' (2013) 10 *IOLR* 287

'"Weighing" the Articles on Responsibility of International Organizations'

Wouters, J. and Odermatt, J. 'Are all international organizations created equal?' (2012) 9 *IOLR* 7

Zaccaria, G. 'Analogy as legal reasoning: the hermeneutic foundation of the analogical procedure' in P. Nerhot (ed.), *Legal Knowledge and Analogy: Fragments of Legal Epistemology, Hermeneutics and Linguistics* (Dordrecht: Kluwer, 1991)

Zemanek, K. 'The United Nations Conference on the Law of Treaties between States and International Organizations or between International Organizations: the unrecorded history of its "general agreement"' in K. H. Böckstiegel (ed.), *Völkerrecht, Recht der internationalen Organisationen, Weltwirtschaftsrecht: Festschrift für Ignaz Seidl-Hohenveldern* (Cologne: Heymann, 1988)

Zwanenburg, M. *Accountability of Peace Support Operations* (Leiden: Nijhoff, 2005)

INDEX

abduction, 19–20. *See also* analogy
abuse of rights, 175–78
acceptance of responsibility, 162–72
acceptance of treaty obligations, 162–72
acceptance of treaty rights, 162–72
African Union, 214–15
agents, 96–99
Ago, Roberto, 81, 192
Agreement Establishing the World
    Trade Organization (1994), 63,
    111–12
American realist school, 17–18
analogical reasoning. *See* analogy
analogies, 18–27, 238–45
    challenging, 24–27
    in codification and progressive
      development, 35–48
    domestic law, 1–3, 28, 54
    ILC and, 242–45
    in international law, 35–48
    in international legal reasoning, 13
    morality of, 26
    normative pedigree, 25–26, 38–39
    private law, 2
    structure, 18–27
    systemic, 1–8
    as well-drawn, 24–27
analogy between States and
    international organizations
    breaking point of, 195–210
    limits of, 185
    normative contestation of, 212–37,
      242
    objections to, 87
    overview of, 1–11, 238–45
AOI. *See* Arab Organization for
    Industrialization

Appeal Relating to the Jurisdiction of the
    ICAO Council (ICJ), 195–210
Application of the Convention on
    the Prevention and Punishment
    of the Crime of Genocide
    (ICJ), 26–27
Arab Organization for Industrialization
    (AOI), 155–61
ARIO. *See* Articles on the
    Responsibility of International
    Organizations for Internationally
    Wrongful Acts
armed conflict, law of, 222–25
Arrest Warrant case, 18–27
ARS. *See* Articles on the Responsibility
    of States for Internationally
    Wrongful Acts
Articles on the Responsibility of
    International Organizations for
    Internationally Wrongful Acts
    (ARIO), 3–4, 8, 39–47, 59
    ARS departed from by, 233–34
    Article 5, 152
    Article 6, 99, 152
    Article 7, 153–54
    Article 8, 138–39
    Article 10, 195–210
    Article 15, 173–74
    Article 16, 173–74
    Article 17, 172–83, 198
    Article 21, 223–25
    Article 22, 190–95, 206–10, 230–32
    Article 25, 139, 233–34
    Article 32, 190–94
    Article 40, 180–84
    Article 46, 102–4, 143–44
    Article 49, 139, 141–42, 234–35

CAMBRIDGE STUDIES IN INTERNATIONAL AND COMPARATIVE LAW

Books in the Series